CRICUT

Sarah Crafts

Table of Contents

CRICUT FOR BEGINNERS 1

Introduction 3

Chapter 1: - Why Do You Need It? 5

Chapter 2: - What Is a Cricut Machine? 6

Chapter 3: - The Different Cricut Models 8

Chapter 4: - Cricut Tools and Accessories 15

Chapter 5: - How to Use a Cricut Material 21

Chapter 6: - Frequent Cricut Problems-How to Solve Them 25

Chapter 7: - Maintenance of the Cricut Machine 29

Chapter 8: - Comparison between Cricut Machines 33

Chapter 9: - Common Mistakes and How to Avoid and Solve Them 36

Chapter 10: -41+ Tips and Tricks 41

Conclusion 46

CRICUT MAKER **47**

Introduction 49

Chapter 1: What Is the Cricut Machine 51

Chapter 2: How to Use a Cricut Machine 65

Chapter 3: Design Space Software Secrets and the Design Space App 75

Chapter 4: Maintenance of the Cricut Machine 99

Chapter 5: Tips for Solving Cricut Design Space Problems 108

Chapter 6: Best Software to Use 110

Conclusion 115

CRICUT PROJECT IDEAS **117**

Introduction 119

Chapter 1: What is a Cricut Machine? 120

CHAPTER 2: SETTING UP YOUR CRICUT MACHINE ON DESIGN SPACE 131

CHAPTER 3: CRICUT PROJECTS WITH SYNTHETIC LEATHER 138

CHAPTER 4: GREAT CRICUT EXPLORE PROJECTS 147

CHAPTER 5: CHRISTMAS CRICUT PROJECTS 162

CHAPTER 6: VALENTINE CRICUT PROJECT IDEAS 168

CHAPTER 7: SPRING PROJECT IDEAS 175

CHAPTER 8: HALLOWEEN CRICUT PROJECT IDEAS 182

CHAPTER 9: DRAWING PROJECTS 191

CHAPTER 10: PROJECTS TO CREATE WITH PAPER 201

CHAPTER 11: PROJECTS TO CREATE WITH VINYL 209

CHAPTER 12: PROJECTS TO CREATE WITH FABRIC 218

CHAPTER 13: CRICUT PROJECTS TO CREATE WITH GLASS 226

CHAPTER 14: TIPS AND TECHNIQUES FOR THE DESIGN CANVAS PLATFORM 232

CHAPTER 15: FAQ 236

CONCLUSION 239

CRICUT DESIGN SPACE **241**

INTRODUCTION 243

CHAPTER 1: WHAT MACHINE SHOULD I BUY 245

CHAPTER 2: STARTING A NEW PROJECT 271

CHAPTER 3: INTERMEDIATE AND ADVANCED LEVEL PROJECTS 293

CHAPTER 4: TIPS AND TRICKS FOR BEGINNERS 314

CHAPTER 5: SELLING AND MAKE MONEY 326

CHAPTER 6: FAQ 330

CONCLUSION 334

CRICUT EXPLORE AIR 2 .... **336**

INTRODUCTION 338

HOW TO SET UP YOUR CRICUT MACHINE FOR WINDOWS/MAC AND iOS/ANDROID 341

HOW TO CUT HEAVYWEIGHT AND LIGHTWEIGHT MATERIALS 345

How to Design with the Cricut Machine 347

Maintenance of the Cricut Machine 355

FAQ About the Cricut Explore Air 360

Cricut Explore Air 2 Tips 362

Cricut Explore Air Project Ideas 364

How to Make Stickers with Cricut 366

How to Make DIY Paper Succulent with Your Cricut 368

How to Make Personalized Paper Bookmarks Using Your Cricut Machine 370

How to Make a Frosty Wreath 372

Vinyl 375

Working with the Design Space App 380

Making Money with Cricut: 50+ Business Ideas You Can Make with Your Cricut
.... 388

FAQ 395

Conclusion 403

CRICUT BUSINESS **405**

Introduction 407

Chapter 1: - Cricut Business Plan 409

Chapter 2: - Where to Find Materials for Project Ideas 413

Chapter 3: - Where Can I Find Business? 420

Chapter 4: - Facebook and Instagram 425

Chapter 5: - Etsy 429

Chapter 5: - Business Ideas You Can Make with Your Cricut 433

Chapter 6:- Cricut Project with Vinyl 439

Chapter 7: - Other Cricut Project 445

Conclusion 453

CRICUT FOR BEGINNERS

*The Exact Guide That Will Turn a Cricut Beginner into a Cricut Pro |
BONUS 41+ Essential Cricut Tips, Tricks and Hacks*

Introduction

The world of craft is filled with many design problems to solve, Cricut Machines come into aid to solve many of those problems.

A Cricut is a cutting system that helps you to cut and make beautiful and amazing crafts with materials that you didn't even know existed, that's the short answer. You can also sketch, emboss, and produce folding lines to realize 3D designs, birthday cards, boxes, etc. depending on the layout you have.

The Cricut device has several usages in addition to being a cutter machine for a scrapbooking design. It is possible to make use of the designs to produce items like welcoming memory cards, wall surface decorations, therefore a lot more. You need to think artistically. There are no borders, as well as they're all a figment of your creative imagination if there are actually.

There is a myriad of projects you can complete by using the Cricut Machine: you will discover the wonderful world of arts and crafts and you will make your project ideas become reality.

If you don't have much experience with these types of devices, don't worry. We've got you covered. You will find that the guidelines presented in this book are both easy to understand and simple to implement. You won't have to contend with complicated technical instructions written by some electronics nerd. You will find the information contained in this book in simple and plain English. This is what makes using the Cricut Machine so easy. Plus, you will find that it's much more fun when you don't have to deal with complex explanations.

Each of the chapters has been written to guide you through the process of deciding which machine to get through your first couple of projects. Best of all, you can take this information to make the best possible choice for you. After all, the sky's the limit when you use your imagination!

This book has been written with the average user in mind. All you need is the willingness to let your imagination fly. When you do so, you can make wonderful ideas become reality. Besides, there are thousands of project ideas you can use to make your creations come to life.

If that isn't enough to get you excited, then you ought to know that setting up the Cricut Machine is easy and doesn't require any special technical knowledge. All you need is a computer and the companion software that goes with it. This software is freely available when you purchase the Cricut Machine. You can use it on both your computer and a mobile device such as a tablet.

So, let's start with the wonderful creations you have in mind. Feel free to let your imagination wander. Ultimately, when you let your ideas take hold, you'll be able to render anything virtual to something possible.

Surely, you haven't seen anything like this before. Come on, let's get on with it! The sooner you start, the faster you can make your wildest ideas come to life.

So, go ahead, try Cricut, and begin your crafting journey!

Chapter 1: - Why Do You Need It?

If you picked up this book, you most likely know that a Cricut machine can help make all sorts of useful shapes for your artwork or hobby. But what exactly does this machine do and how does it work?

If you decided to purchase one of these neat tools, you were probably drawn by the possibility of being able to streamline the cutting of different shapes on a variety of materials.

7 Signs That Cricut Will Help You To Enjoy Your Life With Your Family

1. Memories and special moments are recorded.

2. You can make various kinds of crafts and decorate gifts for others.

3. Stamp out pictures from photos and layouts from magazines with an easy way, either applies to single photographs or multiple pages. (This feature is called "Collage").

4. You can make unique cards, scrapbooking, etc., with holiday theme projects you can do at home.

5. The Cricut is a great assistance for the people who are making birthday invitations, etc.

6. You can create your own greeting cards and make handmade paper crafts

7. You can also make customized labels to have different shapes and decorated with your favorite colors

Believe it or not, you don't need to be a professional expert to use the Cricut. It is a very user-friendly device that will help you create beautiful cards, scrapbooking and other things in no time at all.

Perhaps you're wondering if all these things are possible to do with Cricut, and if so, what type of machine will you need and how much will the work cost. Keep reading to find out the answers to these questions (and so much more!).

Chapter 2: - What Is a Cricut Machine?

A Cricut is a machine that cuts and embosses images and designs onto paper, cardstock, vinyl, fabric or heat transfer sheets.

This is useful if you don't have enough time, skill, or precision to do your own manual cutting. You can use it to make ornaments, shirts, or all kinds of useful stickers with laser precision and accuracy (Sund, 2010).

Cricut is a brand that features multiple products. They carry embossers and heat presses, but more importantly, they feature die-cutting machines that ended up becoming a household name. A Cricut machine is a die-cutting apparatus that you can use at home for your creative projects, artwork, and crafts. However, there is a twist with these machines that makes them unique and highly convenient. They are smart machines that can cut all sorts of shapes out of paper, vinyl, thin plates of cardboard, all sorts of MDF (medium-density fibreboard), wood, and other materials.

Moreover, the latest versions of Cricut machines can also draw with pens, and they can score your paper or cardboard for easy and precise folding (think next-level—intricate yet effortless origami artwork, for example).

The Cricut name alone refers to the brand, but the popularity of their die-cutting machines made its use synonymous with these specific cutters. While the limits to the utilization of Cricut cutters solely depend on your imagination, the mechanics behind how they operate are a different issue. The proper use of Cricut machines requires an understanding of how they work, as well as how they should be used to get the best value for your investment.

How Do Cricut Die-Cutting Machines Work?

Cricut machine cutters operate simply and conveniently. First, you need to create a design, which needs to be in an image form, on your computer. After this, you need to send your shape to the cutting machine via a Bluetooth connection or a USB cable.

After the machine receives the right shape to be cut, it then operates its computer which navigates a cutting blade. The principle is similar to how a printer works with its ink nozzle, but here, the machine's computer guides the plate to cut an exact copy of the shape that you created on your computer.

Aside from cutting, the newest Cricut models can emboss, engrave, score, and write using the same principle. This means that working with a Cricut machine covers three main operations:

- Creating your design

- Sending it to the machine and telling it what to do (cut, write, engrave, etc.)

- Doing the hard work while you sit back and sip on your coffee

Your Cricut machine will come with a couple of add-ons, like different cutter models, cords, instructions, a cutting mat, and more. You will also receive a USB cable and a power adapter, and even one or two dozen projects that you can start making as soon as you plug in your machine. Depending on the model you choose, you can get a special writing pen and scoring wheels as well.

As you can see, the Cricut die-cutting machine isn't a simple cutter. For example, let's say you want to make your own wedding invitations. A Cricut lets you design the layout and text, size, and shape right on your computer. After that, all you need to do is get the correct type of paper ready, insert it into the machine, and let it cut out the card shapes, draw on the text, and score your wedding invitations for folding if needed. Neat, right?

No longer will you need to make an order, then wait to see if your invitations turned out well nor will you have to send the cards back if the writing is wrong. The machine also results in much lower expenses, and arguably, much more convenience since you are creating just the type of card you envisioned.

The trick with using Cricut machines is that you'll have to learn how to work with each model's specific brand software, which is free to download. This book will help you do that as well, so relax and enjoy the read!

Aside from the brand's software, you can also use other apps that are compatible with the machine, but this book will focus on creating designs and images from scratch on the brand's app.

Chapter 3: - The Different Cricut Models

The Everyone who has being in the crafting business for a while, are aware of the Miraculous working of Cricut Machines. The machines are superb; they make a variety of cuts up to the best Iron-on works. One unique thing about these various machines is that each of them has unique functions that will suit your different imagined designs and crafts. So, the model you will choose depends on what exactly you would want to make. Let me talk you through the best Cricut Machines of the year, 2020. First and foremost, I will start by showing you the top five on the list and others:

1.   Cricut Maker: Presently, this is the number one among all the Cricut Machines. It contains numerous features that cannot be found in other Cricut Machines. It comes with hundreds of digital sewing patterns and suitable features such as a USB port and a Docking slot. It is not done yet; this machine also allows you access through your computer or smartphone. The Cricut Maker can do much more than we expect either as a beginner or a long time Crafter. It is easy to operate but so versatile that you are fascinated as you keep on gathering experience. Though this machine is the costliest among all, the benefit outweighs the cost.

Functions:

- It cuts 250+ materials

- It has 10x cutting capacity more than others

- It performs over digital sewing patterns

- This Machine has the capacity to cut wood

- It works with 12+ tools for pro-level engraving, debossing, scoring, and others.

2.   Cricut Explore Air 2: This machine is referred to as the Best Valued Machine among all. It is because of its great color and ability to cut over 100 materials. The Bluetooth technology attached to it allows for a wireless cutting of materials; this is just one among its amazing features. A smart set Dial function comes with this machine that many users love, which sets the right pressure and depth for the cutting material. It is this feature that makes it the best Cricut machine for vinyl. Are you looking for a Cricut machine with great value at an affordable price? Then go for Explore Air 2 because it has been tested and trusted by Crafters, especially myself. Its features are not up to the features of the Maker. One can still be assured that it does the majority of the work performed by Maker. It is this attribute that makes it popular among many crafters.

Functions:

- It cuts over 100+ materials

- It has 2x fast cut and writing capacity

- It cuts vinyl easily

3.   Cricut Joy: This Machine is the latest in the market of Cricut. Furthermore, it is the most compact Cricut cutting machine so far. Cricut Joy is greatly smaller than the two previously mentioned Machines. It is easily moved from one place to another, with only 5.5 inches and only 3.9Ibs (1.75kg). Like its predecessors, Cricut Joy permits you to customize your designs using broad types of line weights and pen types. The draw, write, and doodle functions can design any patterns, letters, numbers, shapes, objects, and many more. Portability is the machine's chief goal; if you really want portable work, go for this machine. It is a compact and straightforward cutting machine for fun DIY projects.

Functions:

- Cuts over 50+ materials

- Cuts up to 20-feet long and 4-in wide

- It can produce a continuous cut without a cutting mat.

4.   Cricut EasyPress 2: Cricut produces not just a cutting machine, but it also produces some of the most performing iron-on machines. Among them is the Cricut EasyPress 2. One of the features attached to this machine is an insulated safety base coupled with an auto-shutoff. It comes with specific temperature control of up to 400°F.

Functions:

- Permits for specific temperature control

- Provides excellent results in not less than 60 seconds

- It's best suitable for shirt making

5.   Cricut EasyPress Mini: Cricut EasyPress Mini, as the name implies, is the lower version of EasyPress 2, which comes with limited features. They both are best suited for T-SHIRT making but just that this particular one has low capacity production.

Functions:

- It functions well for a smaller heat transfer project

9

- It provides better results in less than 120 seconds

- It is best suitable for T-Shirt making

6.   Cricut Brightpad: Cricut Brightpad is the best Machine for weeding. The weeding feature makes it possible for you to complete all your crafting projects with little or no stress. It can be used on any table or desk simply because it is light, thin, and greatly portable. Accompanied by the Machine are a wall power adapter, a USB power cord, and a warranty.

Functions:

- Used for all forms of weeding

- Used for a variety of tracing

- Used for different kinds of quilting

7.   Cricut Explore Air: It is the best suited Cricut Machine for all beginners. It is very easy to use; it cuts and draws simultaneously, hence the reason it was recommended for beginners. This machine comes with all the features you need. Additionally, its price is highly affordable.

Functions:

- Cuts all kinds of shapes with excellent precision in sizes extending from 1/4 to 111/2-inch-wide by 231/2 inches tall.

- It can cut a card and then write a personalized message at the very spot you want them

- It can cut a box and score the fold lines in one step

8.   Cricut Explore Air One: It is the most primary electronic cutting machine. It is most suitable for personal crafting projects because it is not as powerful as the higher Cricut machines. Among the features is that it allows you to design from any location by applying its free cloud-based apps for Windows, Androids, Mac, and IOS. On the other way round, you can upload your own designs for free and cut. It is not the dream machine for professional crafters, and presently, it is longer available in the Cricut market.

Functions:

- It cuts all manner of materials except wood as among the Cricut materials

- It can write, design, and draw various shapes

9. Cricut Cuttlebug: Are you looking for an excellent but affordable die-cutting and highly decorating Machine, go for the Cricut Cuttlebug. Is it the right option for you? It comes with an A2 embossing folder, two metal dies, and an embossing mat.

Functions:

- Cricut Cuttlebug die-cutting and embossing machine comes with a versatile and portable choice for cutting and embossing a wider variety of materials

- It cuts and embosses a broader assortment of materials such as foils, tissue paper, ribbon, acetate ribbon, and slim leather

- Cuts and embosses cardstock

- Produces professional-looking outcomes with profound, smooth embossing and clean, hard cuts

- Works with other top embossing binders and cutting dies.

Top 5 Cricut Machine Projects

Now, we come to the truly fun part of working with a Cricut machine. When being creative with a Cricut, your only limitations stem from the type of materials the machine can handle and its installed features. Other than that, the shapes you'll create and the purpose they'll serve are left to your imagination.

Various types of these cutters will be covered in the next chapter, as they have slightly different features and potentials. For now, though, we will go over some of the amazing things you can create with a Cricut.

Scrapbooking and decorations. If you want to make an amazing vision board, a scrapbook, or an inspirational poster, a Cricut is a neat tool to have since finished products like these can cost quite a bit. A Cricut lets you print and cut shapes, words, letters, or even entire sentences and quotes. With this in mind, you can use it for a cleverly designed organization panel or a vision board, to cut out meaningful quotes and add them to your journal, scrapbook, or hang on a wall, and so much more.

Cards and envelopes. Whether it's a gift card, a letter, or an event invitation, the average Cricut has built-in operations that can either streamline the cutting and folding of shapes or incorporate beautiful prints and embossment for a finer look. Having this possibility in your own home can make your life a lot easier. From not having to run and buy envelopes, to being able to make personalized invitations for your child's birthday or even creating luxury greeting cards and business cards—the possibilities are endless with a Cricut machine. Plus, printing and sending family pictures to make holiday cards will save you major bucks. Ordering personalized products such as these can cost hundreds of dollars, but printing and cutting with your machine costs next to nothing. All you need to do is grab your chosen type of paper, and you're good to go.

Home and accessories. Cricuts can cut through smaller pieces of fabric, and you can use them to make easy baby onesies, leggings, and shirts. All you need to do is either create or download a pattern, let the machine do its work, and then sew in the pieces of fabric knowing that they'll be just the right design and fit. The same principle can be used when making or repurposing linens, mats, or wall decals. Imagine being able to repurpose a worn-out T-shirt into a small pillowcase or a fine towel. Cool, right? Cricut machines also give you the possibility to make your own window decals, organization labels, banners, and buntings.

Interior design. Aside from being able to cut unique decorations, a Cricut is also ideal for making your own painting stencils, picture frames, and quote artwork. You can also use it to make a matching pillow, sofa cushions, and other creations. With the help of a Cricut machine, you have the ability to effortlessly cut Christmas ornaments, party decorations, and even prints for glasses and mugs.

Jewelry. If you learn how to work with a Cricut die-cutter, you can also make your custom jewelry, like leather bracelets, custom earrings, pendants, and so much more! You can also make a custom pet collar, and do countless other DIY projects!

Business and office. A Cricut allows you to make your very own personalized, brand calendars, stickers, bullet journals, planner designs, and business cards. If you own a business or you're planning to start one, you can use a Cricut to put your brand name, logo, and business information on all sorts of promotional products, like keychains, mugs, coasters, and other items.

What Can't You Do or Make With a Cricut Machine?

Your projects will depend on the specific possibilities of the Cricut model you choose. That being said, there are a couple of general limitations that apply to all Cricuts:

Printing. Your Cricut won't be able to print images. However, you can use it for pen writing and apply numerous types of pens and ink for drawing. This gives you the possibility to choose text, colors, font, and size for any writing you wish to put on paper, even though you cannot print exact images. Instead, you'll have to provide a layout with the chosen color, pattern, or image to cut in the desired shape and apply the writing. This entails some careful thinking when making your designs. Keeping in mind that any images you wish to include are going to have to be printed in advance, you can later cut them using a Cricut. This way, you can apply a chosen image or pattern in the form of a sticker or transfer it onto the material before you start cutting more shapes and writing.

Sewing and gluing. Your Cricut can produce pieces for your project and decorate them with the type of writing you choose if you pick a more advanced model. However, your project will require further planning when it comes to putting a piece of work together. This might sound mundane at first, but you can easily find yourself lacking tools, supplies, or time to finish a project if you rely on the machine too much.

Safety. Depending on the intended purpose of your project, all safety concerns are going to have to be thought through in advance. The safety and endurance of your finished piece will have to be accounted for when thinking about the size and shape of your design, as it strongly depends on the safety and sturdiness of the materials you use. For example, if you wish to cut out children's toys, you'll have to make sure that your design doesn't feature shapes that can be easily broken off or swallowed or that are too sharp and pointy. Likewise, it is up to you to ensure that the materials you use are suitable for the intended purpose of the final product. It might sound appealing to use a Cricut for home decorations or even cutlery, but equal attention is necessary when choosing the most suitable and safest materials that will endure the strain that will be put on the object you plan to create.

Quality. Similar to safety, the quality and the life span of your work will depend on your choice of materials. Decorative pieces might not require particular material pickiness, but if the objects you're making are going to have to be washed, folded, or handled frequently, you'd be wise to look into materials that are water and heat resistant, perhaps antibacterial, and even machine washable. Whether it's vinyl, leather, wood, or foil, it would be wise to make sure that your materials can endure a significant amount of distress to get the most quality use out of them.

You now know just how useful a Cricut can be. In this chapter, you learned that you can use a die-cutter for arts and crafts, to make useful tools, to create decorations and accessories for your home, to make jewelry, and to create gifts for yourself and your family—you can even create entire pieces of clothing! A Cricut also gives you the possibility to make your own office supplies and promotional brand products—that is, if you choose the right one.

Since you know how a Cricut machine works, as well as what you can and can't use it for, it's time to choose the one that works best for you. The next chapter will review the most popular Cricut die-cutter models so that you can choose the one that has the exact features and functions you need.

Things I wish I Knew When I Bought My Cricut

The most common consideration when it comes to the Cricut Machine is the price. Depending on where you purchase your Cricut Machine, it can get to be pretty pricey. But that shouldn't be a drawback, especially if you are ambitious about the projects you wish to pursue. Consider that it can pay for itself if you plan to use it as part of a business.

That being said, it's important to consider that the Cricut Machine is ideal for those who carry out projects regularly. As such, if you are not a regular hobbyist or crafter, you might think twice about getting one of these machines. But if you are a serious hobbyist, then the Cricut Machine is a great way for you to bring your ideas to life.

The device itself is certainly worth it, especially when you can see everything it can do. The types of designs you can make with this machine are nearly impossible to make with other means. You can produce original creations in such a manner that no one else will be able to produce. That alone makes the machine worth its cost.

On the flip side, if you do want one of these devices but are unsure about investing in them, you might want to consider picking up a used one. Depending on the price, it could be a good option for you. You can try it out and see if it's right for you. The important thing is to make sure you don't overpay it as there is no guarantee regarding the condition it might be in. Nevertheless, these are pretty reliable and robust machines. As such, picking up a used one might not be the craziest idea.

Final Verdict

The Cricut Machine is ideal for serious hobbyists and crafters. Also, it's great if you are planning on using it for business purposes. It's the type of machine that can take a heavy workload. It will also make a good investment, especially when you consider how much it would cost you to get these types of creations made elsewhere. It can also provide a great means for family fun and entertainment.

On the whole, the Cricut Machine is the type of device that you can rely on. While it might get a bit pricey, the cost-benefit relationship for this machine makes spending the cash worthwhile. The only consideration in this regard would be to avoid spending too much money on it, especially if you are only a casual crafter or don't plan to use it very often. Otherwise, you can bet that this device will provide you with the type of versatility you need to make the most of your imagination. In the end, you will have the opportunity to truly set your imagination free. If you are on the ropes, you go for it! The worst thing that can happen is that you fall in love with the creations that you produce.

Chapter 4: - Cricut Tools and Accessories

Tool Kits

Basic Tool Kit

All the 5 essential tools in one package;

- A scraper to clean and polish

- Spatula to lift

- Micro-tip scissors

- Weeder for vinyl

- Tweezers

Basics Starter Tool Kit

Another set of essential tools including;

- Scraper and spatula

- Point pens in metallic

- Scoring stylus

- Deep Cut Housing and 1 blade

Essential Tool Kit

Made for Cricut Explore models, this 7-piece set includes;

- Trimmer and replacement blade

- Scoring stylus

- Scraper for cleaning and polishing

- Spatula

- Micro-blade scissors

- Weeder

- Tweezers

Paper Crafting Tool Kit

This 4-piece set is perfect for professional paper crafting and includes;

- Craft mat

- Distresser for edges

- Quilling tool for spirals

- Piercer for small piece placement

Sewing Tool Kit

Sewing essentials are all in one place. This set includes;

- Thimble made of leather

- Measuring tape

- Pins and pincushion

- Seam ripper

- Thread snips

- Fabric shears

Weeding Tool Kit

A set of 5 tools for elaborate cutting and vinyl DIY crafts includes;

- Hook tweezers

- Fine tweezers

- Hook weeder

- Weeder

- Piercer

Complete Starter Tool Kit

Perfect for the beginning Cricut user, this set includes;

- Black window cling

- Cutting mat

- Point pens in metallic

- Scoring stylus

- Deep Cut Housing and 1 Blade

- A scraper to clean and polish

- Spatula to lift

- Micro-tip scissors

- Weeder to remove negatives

- Tweezers

Single Tools

XL Scraper

Clean mats quickly and easily or adhere sizeable projects to an assortment of surfaces with this tool. Great for vinyl and can be used with all Circuit models.

Portable Trimmer

Precision cutting is achieved with the 12-inch swinging arm, and the storage for a replacement blade makes this an extra-functional tool. Swiftly insert materials, cut, and measure from both directions with the dual-hinged rails.

Scoring Stylus

3-dimensional projects, boxes, cards, and envelopes' lines can be scored in 1 step with this tool that holds the blade for cutting and the stylus. This tool is best for Cricut Maker and Explorer models.

Applicator and Remover

Remove or apply textiles easily and make the cutting mat last longer with these functional tools. Ideal for the Cricut Maker, these tools are sold together to make working with fabric that much easier (applicator is also known as a brayer).

Scraper and Spatula

Lift and clean easily with these two tools. Made especially for the cutting mat for all sorts of projects.

Scissors

Make clean cuts with micro-tip scissors and store them safely with the included end cap and cover for the blades (you can use a medical scissor too).

Tweezers

Secure project pieces after lifting them with the reverse-grip of this tool. Perfect to use for little items like small cuts and intricate trimmings.

Weeders

Use this tool to remove small cuts and for separating iron-on pieces and vinyl from their liners.

Accessories

Similar to the tools available for the Cricut, there are also a variety of accessories that can be purchased to compliment whatever model of Cricut you choose. Below is a list that highlights some of the available accessories and their functions. Consider purchasing them individually or take advantage of the different bundles and sets offered.

Functional Support Accessories

Specially designed accessories are made to enhance the experience of using a Cricut machine with function and style.

- Mats
- Light grip
- Standard grip
- Strong grip
- Fabric grip
- Scoring and Blades
- Rotary blade
- Fabric blade-bonded
- Deep cut blade
- Fine-point blade
- Premium blade made of German carbide
- Scoring stylus

Pens

- Variety of colored pens
- Extra fine tip-colored pens

- Ultimate fine tip-colored pens

- Washable fabric pen

- Variety of colored markers

Tapes

- Glitter tape

- Adapters and Tech

- Cartridge adapter

- Pen adapter

- Bluetooth adapter

- Accessory adapter

- USB cable

- Power cord

- Keyboard overlay

For the crafter on the go or in need of stylish and functional storage, these accessories are the perfect fit.

Pouches

- Accessory pouches for tools

- Totes and Bags

- Crafters shoulder bag

- Rolling crafters tote

- Machine tote

- Machine Add-On's

Cricut machines can accomplish many great things, but sometimes they could use a sidekick. That's where these machines come in.

Easy Press

Achieve the iron-on results like a professional in less than a minute! Simple to use and light to carry, this accessory is perfect for Cricut users who want t-shirt transfers to last.

Easy Press Bundles:

- Bulk

- Ultimate

- Everything

Cuttlebug

Cut or emboss almost any material on the run with this handy machine. Achieve the professional, clean cuts you want with ease.

Cuttlebug Add-ons:

- Mats

- Dies

- Materials

- Spacer plates

- Cutting mats

Bright Pad

This durable, light pad offers a soft, adjustable light to make tracing, cutting, and easier and more comfortable on the eyes.

Cricut Software

Design Space

Design Space is for any Explore machine with a high-speed, broadband Internet connection that is connected to a computer or an iOS device. This more advanced software allows full creative control for users with Cricut machines.

Craft Room

Some machines, such as the Explore and Explore Air, cannot use Craft Room, but many other models can. Craft Room users also have access to a free digital cartridge, which offers images that all Cricut machines can cut.

Chapter 5: - How to Use a Cricut Material

So, you have all your materials on hand, which is fantastic, but how do you use a Cricut machine? Well, that's what you're about to find out. If looking at your Cricut machine makes you feel all sorts of confused, then continue reading – here, we'll tell you how to use your new Cricut machine in a simple yet effective manner.

Setting Up the Machine

First, you'll want to set up the Cricut machine. To begin, create a space for it. A craft room is the best place for this, but if you're at a loss of where to put it, I suggest setting it up in a dining room if possible. Make sure you have an outlet nearby or a reliable extension cord.

Next, read the instructions. You can often jump right in and begin using the equipment, but it can be very tedious with Cricut machines.

Make sure that you have ample free space around the machine itself because you will be loading mats in and out, and you'll need that little bit of wiggle room.

The next thing to set up is, of course, the computer where the designs will be created. Ensure that whatsoever medium you're with has an internet connection since you will want to download the Cricut Design Space app.

Using Cricut Software

So, Cricut machines use a Cricut Design Spaces program, and you'll need to make sure that you have this downloaded and installed when you're ready. If it's not hooked up already, make sure you've got Bluetooth compatibility enabled on the device or the cord plugged in. To turn on your machine, hold the power button. You'll then go to settings, where you should see your Cricut model in Bluetooth settings. Choose that, and from there, your device will ask you to put in a Bluetooth passcode. Just make this something generic and easy to remember.

Once that's done, you can now use Design Space.

So, what I love about Design Space is that it's incredibly easy to use. They know you're a beginner, so you'll notice it's very easy to navigate.

Now, I like to use the app for Design Space since this will allow you to have every design uploaded to the cloud to reuse your designs. However, suppose you want to use them without having an internet connection. In that case, you'll want to make sure that you download them and save them to the device itself, rather than relying on the cloud.

When you're in the online mode, you'll see a lot of projects that you can use. For this tutorial, I suggest making sure that you choose an easy one, such as the "Enjoy Card" project you can get automatically.

So, you've got everything all linked up – let's move onto the first cut for this project.

<u>Inputting Cartridges and Keypad</u>

The first cut you'll be doing involves keypad input and cartridges, usually done with the "Enjoy Card" project you get right away. So, once everything is set up, choose this project, then you can use the tools and the accessories within the project.

You will need to set the smart dial before you get started doing your projects. It is on the right side of the Explore Air 2, and it's the way you choose your materials. Turn the dial to whatever type of material you want since this helps ensure you've got the right blade settings. There are even half settings for those in-between projects.

For example, let's say you have some light cardstock. You can choose that setting or the adjacent half setting. Once this is selected from in Design Space, your machine will automatically adjust to the correct setting.

You can also choose the fast mode, which is in the "set, load, go" area on the screen, and you can then check the position of the box under the indicator for dial position. Then, press this and make your cut. However, the fast mode is incredibly loud, so be careful.

Now, we've mentioned cartridges. While these usually aren't used in the Explore Air 2 machines anymore, they help beginner projects. To do this, once you have the Design Space software and everything is connected, go to the hamburger menu, and you'll see an option called "ink cartridges." Press that bad boy, and from there, choose the Cricut device. The machine will then tell you to put in your cartridge. Do that, and once it's detected, it will ask you to link the cartridge.

Remember, though, that you can't use it with other machines once you link this – the one limit to these cartridges.

Once it's confirmed, you can go to images and click the cartridges option to find the ones you want to make. You can filter the cartridges to figure out what you need. You can check out your images tab for any other cartridges purchased or uploaded.

You can get digital cartridges, which means you buy them online and choose the images directly from your available options. They aren't physical, so there is no linking required.

<u>Loading and Unloading Your Paper</u>

To load paper into a Cricut machine, you'll want to make sure that the paper is at least three inches by three inches. Otherwise, it won't cut very well. You should use regular paper for this.

Now, to make this work, you need to put the paper onto the cutting mat. You should have one of those, so take it right now and remove the attached film. Put a corner of the paper to the area where you are directed to align the paper corners. From there, push the paper directly onto the cutting mat for proper adherence. Once you do that, you just load it into the machine, following the arrows. You'll want to keep the paper firmly on the mat. Press the "load paper" key that you see as you do this. If it doesn't take for some reason, press the unload paper key, and try this again until it shows up.

Before you do any cutting for your design, you should always have a test cut in place. Some people don't do this, but it's incredibly helpful when learning how to use a Cricut. Otherwise, you won't get the pressure correct in some cases, so get in the habit of doing it for your pieces.

Is there a difference between vinyl and other products? The primary difference is the cutting mats. Depending on what you're cutting, you may need some grip or lack thereof. If you feel like your material isn't entirely sticking, get some Heat N' Bond to help with this since often, the issue with cutting fabrics comes from the fact that it doesn't adhere. But you may also need mats that are a bit thicker, too, to help get a better grip on these.

Selecting Shapes, Letters, And Phrases

When you're creating your design in Design Space, you usually begin by using letters, shapes, numbers, or different fonts. These are the basics, and they're incredibly easy.

To make text, you just press the text tool on the left-hand side and type out your text. For example, write the word hello, or joy, or whatever you want to use.

You can change the font size by pressing the drag and drop arrow near the corner of the text box or by going to the size panel near the top to choose actual font sizes. You can also choose different Cricut or system fonts too. Cricut ones will be in green, and if you have Cricut Access, this is a great way to begin using this. You can sort these, too, so you don't end up accidentally paying for a font.

The Cricut ones are supposed to be made for Cricut, so you know they'll look good. Design Space also lets you put them closer together so they can be cut with a precise cut. You can change this by going to line spacing and adjusting as needed. To fix certain letters, you go to the advanced drop-down menu to ungroup the letters, so everything is separate as required.

Cricut also offers different writing styles, which is a great way to add text to projects. To do this, choose a font made with a specific style, choose only the Cricut ones, and then go to writing. It will then narrow down the choice, so you're using the right font for writing.

Adding shapes is pretty easy, as well. In Design Space, choose the shapes option. Once you click it, the window will then pop out, and you'll have an incredible array of different shapes that you can use with just one click. Choose your shape, and from there, put it in the space. Drag the corners to make this bigger or smaller.

There is also the scoreline, which creates a folding line for you to use. Personally, if you're thinking of trying to make a card at first, I suggest using this.

You can also resize your options by dragging them towards the right-hand side. You can change the orientation by choosing that option and then flipping it around. You can select exact measurements, which is suitable for those design projects that need everything to be precise.

Once you've chosen the design, it's time for you to start cutting.

How to Remove Your Cut from The Cutting Mat

Removing your cut from the mat is easy but complicated. I ran into the issue of it being more detailed with vinyl projects since they love to stick around there. But we'll explain how you can create great cuts and remove them, as well.

The first thing to remember is to make sure that you're using the right mat. The light grip ones are good for very light material, with the pink one being one of the strongest, and only to be used with the Cricut Maker. Once the design is cut, you'll probably be eager McBeaver about removing the project directly from the mat, but one of the problems with this is that often, the project will be ruined if you're not careful. Instead of pulling the project from the mat itself, bend the mat within your hand. Push it away from the project since this will loosen it from the mat. Bend this both horizontally and vertically so that the adhesive releases the project.

Remember the spatula tool that we told you to get with your Cricut machine early on? This is where you use it. Use this spatula to lightly pull on the vinyl until you can grab it from the corner and lift it. Otherwise, you risk curling it or tearing the mat, which is what we don't want.

Now, with the initial cuts, such as the paper ones, this will be incredibly easy. Trust me, I was surprised at how little effort it took. Still, one of the biggest things to remember is that you have to go slow with Cricut machines when removing the material. Do this slowly, and don't get rushed near the end. Taking your time will save you many problems, and it will even save you money and stress, too!

Chapter 6: - Frequent Cricut Problems-How to Solve Them

<u>Material Tearing or Not Cutting Completely Through</u>

This is the biggest problem with most Cricut users. When this happens, the image is ruined, and you've wasted material. More machines have been returned or boxed up and put away due to this problem than any other.

But don't panic, if your paper is not cutting correctly there are several steps you can take to try and correct the problem.

Most important is this: Anytime you work with the blade, turn your machine off. I know it's easy to forget this because you're frustrated and you're trying this and that to make it work correctly. But this is an important safety precaution that you should remember.

Make simple adjustments at first. Turn the pressure down one. Did it help? If not, turn the blade down one number. Also, make sure the mat is free of debris so the blade rides smoothly.

Usually the thicker the material, the higher the pressure number should be set to cut through the paper. Don't forget to use the multi-cut function if you have that option. It may take a little longer to cut 2, 3, or 4 times, but by then it should cut clean through.

For those of you using the smaller bugs that do not have that option here is how to make your own multi-cut function. After the image has been cut, don't unload the mat just hit load paper, repeat last, and cut. You can repeat this sequence 2, 3, or 4 times to ensure your image is completely cut out.

If you are using thinner paper and it is tearing, try reducing the pressure and slowing down the speed. When cutting intricate designs, you have to give the blade enough time to maneuver through the design. By slowing it down it will be able to make cleaner cuts.

Clean the edge of the blade to be sure no fuzz, glue, or scraps of paper are stuck to it.

Make sure the blade is installed correctly. Take it out and put it back so it's seated firmly. The blade should be steady while it's making cuts. If it makes a shaky movement it's either not installed correctly, or there's a problem with the blade housing.

Be aware that there is a deep-cutting blade for thicker material. You'll want to switch to this blade when you're cutting heavy card stock. This will also save wear and tear on your regular blade. Cutting a lot of thick material will obviously wear your blade out quicker than thinner material and cause you to change it more often.

Machine Freezing

Remember to always turn your machine off when you switch cartridges. When you switch cartridges leaving the machine on it's called "hot swapping" and it can sometimes cause the machine to freeze. This is more of an issue with the older models and doesn't seem to apply to the Expression 2.

You know how quirky electronic gadgets can be, so give your machine a rest for five or ten minutes every hour. If you work for several hours continuously, your machine might overheat and freeze up.

Turn the machine off and take a break. Restart it when you come back and it should be fine. Then remember not to rush programming the machine and give it an occasional rest.

Don't press a long list of commands quickly. If you give it too much information too quickly it will get confused in the same way a computer sometimes does and simply freeze up. Instead of typing in one long phrase try dividing up your words into several cuts.

If you're using special feature keys, make sure you press them first before selecting the letters.

Power Problems

If you turn your machine on and nothing happens the power adapter may be at fault. Jiggle the power cord at the outlet and where it connects to the machine to make sure it's firmly connected. Ideally, you want to test the adapter before buying a new one. Swap cords with a friend and see if that fixed the problem. Replacement adapters can be found on eBay by searching for Cricut adapter power supply.

The connection points inside the machine may also pose a problem; here is how to test that. Hold down the plug where it inserts into the back of the machine and turn it on. If it powers up, then the problem is inside the machine and the connection points will have to be soldered again.

If the machine powers up but will not cut, then try a hard reset. See the resource section for step-by-step instructions on resetting your machine.

Here are a few tips especially for Cricut Expression 2users. Have you turned on your machine, you watch it light up and hear it gearing up but when you try to cut nothing happens? Or you're stuck on the welcome screen or the LCD screen is unresponsive.

Well here are two quick fixes to try. First, try a hard reset sometimes called the "Rainbow Screen Reset" to recalibrate your die cutter. If that does not resolve the problem you're going to have to restore the settings.

To help cut down on errors try to keep your machine updated. When an update is available, you should receive a message encouraging you to install the latest version.

For those of you using third-party software that is no longer compatible with the Cricut you probably already know that updating your machine may disable that software.

When you cut heavy paper and your Cricut Expression 2 shuts down try switching to the normal paper setting and use the multi-cut function.

Carriage Will Not Move

If the carriage assembly does not move, check to see if the belt has broken or if the car has fallen off the track. Provo Craft does not sell replacement parts, which is nuts, so try to find a compatible belt at a vacuum repair shop.

If the wheels have fallen off the track, remove the plastic cover, and look for a tiny screw by the wheel unscrew it. You now should be able to move the wheel back on track.

Unresponsive Keyboard

If you are sure you are pressing the keys firmly, you have a cartridge inserted correctly, and a mat loaded ready to go, but the keypad is still not accepting your selection, the problem may be internal.

You will have to remove the keyboard and check if the display cable is connected to the keypad and to the motherboard. If the connections are secure then you have a circuit board problem, and repairs are beyond the scope of this book.

An important reminder, please do not attempt any repairs unless your machine is out of warranty.

Weird LCD Screen

The LCD screen is now showing strange symbols or is blank after doing a firmware update. Try running the update again making sure your selections are correct.

When the image you choose is bigger than the mat or paper size you selected the preview screen will look grayed out instead of showing the image. So increase the paper and mat size or decrease the size of your image.

Also, watch out for the gray box effect when using the center point feature. Move the start position down until you see the image appear. The same thing may happen when using the fit to length feature. Try changing to landscape mode and shorten the length size until the image appears.

Occasionally using the "Undo" button will cause the preview screen to turn black; unfortunately, the only thing to do is turn the machine off. Your work will be lost and you have to start again.

Cartridge Errors

Sometimes dust or debris accumulates in the cartridge port, gently blow out any paper fiber that may have collected in the opening. Make sure the contact points are clean and that nothing is preventing the cartridge from being read properly.

With any electrical machine overheating can be a problem. If you get a cartridge error after using your machine for a while turn it off and let it cool down for about fifteen minutes.

If this is the very first time you're using the cartridge and you get an error, I'm sure you know the trick about turning the cartridge around and inserting it in backward.

If you thought you could use your Imagine cartridges with your Cricut Expression 2, think again. You will get an error message because you can only use the art cartridges that you can cut with, the color and pattern cartridges are for printing.

Even brand-new items fresh out of the box can be defective. If you see a cartridge error 1, 2, 3, 4, 5, 6, 9, or 99 call customer service and tell them the name, serial number, and error message number and they may replace the cartridge.

Chapter 7: - Maintenance of the Cricut Machine

Every Cricut machine needs to be cleaned and taken care of in order to keep it working for as long as possible. Here, you'll learn about the maintenance required for Cricut machines, and what you can do to keep your machine working efficiently.

Cleaning and Care

Cleaning your machine is very important, and you should do it regularly to keep everything in tip-top shape. If you don't take care of your machine, that's just money down the drain.

But what can you do to care for your machine? Well, I do suggest initially that you make sure to run maintenance on it as much as you can and keep it clean. There are a few other tips and tricks that can help prolong the machine's life. For starters, keep liquids and food away from the machine – never drink or eat while you use your Cricut machine. Set up your machine in a location that's free of dust and try to keep it away from excessive coolness or heat, so don't just throw it in the attic or an especially cold basement. If you're transporting your machine to use it at a different location, never leave it in the car. Excessive heat will melt the machine's plastic components, so be careful.

Finally, make sure the machine is stored away from sunlight. Keep it out of places in the home where sunlight hits it directly. For example, if you have an office that is very bright and the sun warms the machine for a long period of time, you'll want to move it so that it doesn't get damaged.

Be gentle with your machine. Remember, it is a machine, so you'll want to make sure that you do take some time and try to keep it nice and in order. Don't be rough with it, and when working with the machine parts, don't be too rough with them, either.

Caring for your machine isn't just about making sure that the parts don't get dirty, but you should also make sure that you keep everything in good working order.

Cleaning the Machine Itself

In general, the exterior is pretty easy to clean – you just need a damp cloth. Use a soft cloth to wipe it off, and keep in mind that chemical cleaners with benzene, acetone, or carbon tetrachloride should never be used on your Cricut machine. Any cleaner that is scratchy, as well, should be avoided at all costs.

Make sure that you never put any machine components in water. This should be obvious, but often, people may use a piece of a damp cloth, thinking that it'll be fine when in reality, it isn't.

You should consider getting some non-alcoholic wipes for cleaning your machine. Always disconnect the power before cleaning, as you would with any machine. The Cricut machine can then be lightly wiped down. Some people also use a glass cleaner sprayed on a cloth but do be careful to make sure no residue builds up. If you notice there is some dust there, you can typically get away with a cloth that's soft and clean.

Sometimes, grease can build up – you may notice this on the cartridge bar if you use cartridges a lot. Use a swab of cotton or a soft cloth to remove it.

Greasing the Machine

If you need to grease your machine, first make sure that it's turned off and the smart carriage is moved to the left. Use a tissue to wipe this down, and then move it to the right, repeating the process again.

From there, move the carriage to the center and open up a lubrication package. Put a small amount onto a Q-tip. Apply a thin coating, greasing everything evenly, and also clean any buildup that may have occurred. This is usually the issue if you hear grinding noise when cleaning the machine itself.

There are a few other important places that you should make sure to clean, besides the outside and the carriage. Any places where blades are should be cleaned; you can just move the housing unit of the blade to clean it. You should also check the drawing area, to make sure there isn't any excessive ink there.

Never use spray cleaner directly on the machine, for obvious reasons. The bar holding the housing shouldn't be wiped down, but if you do notice an excessive grease, please take the time to make sure that it's cleaned up. Remember to never touch the gear chain near the back of this unit, either, and never clean with the machine on, for your own safety.

When caring for a Cricut machine, try to do this more frequently if you're using the machine a lot, or twice yearly. If you notice strange noises coming from the machine, do get a grease packet. You can always contact Cricut and they'll help you figure out the issue, if there is one, with your machine.

Cricut machines are great, but you need to take care in making sure that you keep everything in rightful order.

Cutting Blade

Your blades will tend to dull over time, but this is usually a very slow process. The best way to prevent it is to have different blades to cut different materials. Having a different blade for each material is a really good idea.

You can get fine-point ones which are good for smaller items; deep-cut, which is great for leather and other fabrics; bonded fabric, so great for fabric pieces; a rotary blade for those heavy fabrics; and finally, a knife blade, which is good for those really thick items.

In order to maintain your blades, you should clean the housing area for every blade after each use, since they get gunky fast. Squirting compressed air into the area is a wonderful way to get the dust out of there.

As for the blades, remember foil? Use a little bit of that over the edges of the blade to help clean and polish them up. To polish them, you should put them on the cutting mat and from there, cut small designs on it. It actually does help with sharpening them, and it doesn't require you to completely remove them. You can do this with every single blade, too!

To change the blades in their housings, just open the clamps, pull up, and remove the housing within the machine. Put a new blade in, and then close it. That's all it takes.

Storing them is also pretty simple. There is a drop-down doorway at the front area of the machine. It's made for storing the blades within their housings. Put your loose blades in there first, then utilize the magnet to keep them in place. The best part about this storage is that your blades are always with the Cricut, even if you take the machine somewhere else.

There is also a blade organizer that you can use, too, made out of chipboard with some holders attached. This is also a wonderful means to store all of your items. Organizing your Cricut blades is very important, and understanding the best places to keep them is, of course, essential.

Cutting Mat

Your cutting mats need to be cleaned because if you don't clean them frequently, they will attract dirt and lose adhesiveness. That means you'll have to spend more money on mats, which isn't ideal. There are different ways to clean them, and we'll go over a few of the different means to clean your mats so you can use them for longer.

Cleaning the Mat Itself

First, if your mat is completely filthy, you need to clean it. Of course, you'll also want to do this for just general maintenance, too. Once it's been cleaned, you'll notice it's sticky again.

Typically, washing it down with either a magic eraser or a kitchen scrubber can do it. Sometimes, if it's really dirty, you might want to get some rubbing alcohol onto a wipe. If you notice a chunk of the debris left behind, however, is fabric oriented, then get some lint rollers or even just stick some scotch tape on there and pull it off. This can eliminate the issue.

But what about the really tough grime? Well, get some Goo Gone cleaner. Put a little bit on the troublesome spots and wipe it around, and then let the goo stick on there. From there, get an old card or something to get it off, and then wash the mat. Once it's dry, check to see if it's sticky. If it is, then great – you don't need to do anything more. But what if you notice that it's still not sticky? Well, why not restick the cutting mat itself!

Resticking The Mat

To do this, you need to make sure that you tape the edges, so you don't get adhesive near the edges, and mess with the rollers of the machine. Once that's there, use either spray adhesive or glue stick, and then let it dry. If you notice that it's still not sticky enough when you're finished applying the first coat, apply a second coat.

There are great adhesives out there, such as simple spray adhesive, easy tack, quilt basting, bonding, and also repositionable e glue. All of these are fairly effective, and if you notice that the mat is actually sticking pretty well, then you're in luck.

However, always make sure that you let this fully dry. If you don't let the adhesive dry and you start using the mat again, you will run into the problem of the material being stuck to it.

Once it's dried, try it out with some test material. If you find it too sticky at this point, but either your hands or a shirt on there to help reduce the tackiness.

Caring for Machines and Mats

Here are a couple of other tips to use with your cutting mats.

The first, use different mats. You may notice that you can get more out of one type of mat than another kind, which is something many people don't realize. Often, if you notice that you get a lot more out of the firmer grip mats, buy more of those.

Finally, halve your mats. You can save immensely by making sure that they're cut in half. This does work, and it helps pretty well.

You can expect anywhere from about 25 to 40 different cuts before you'll need to replace the mat, but cleaning after about half of that can definitely help with improving the quality of your cuts. The life of the mat, of course, does vary based on the settings and what materials you cut. When you can't get it to stick, try cleaning and resticking it, but if you notice that it's still not doing the job, you're going to need to get a replacement.

Taking care of your Cricut machine will get you more use out of it, so make sure you perform regular maintenance on all your machine's components so it can be used for years.

Chapter 8: - Comparison between Cricut Machines

The Difference between the Cricut Maker and Cricut Explore Air 2

 This section of the book will highlight the features of the Cricut Maker and the Explore Air 2

The following features are those of the Cricut maker that distinguishes it from the Explore Air 2: It is made up of the Rotary blade, which is mostly used for cutting fabrics. It is also used in cutting leather, silk, and other materials. In the Maker, the scoring pen is replaced by the scoring wheel, which has more delicate scored lines and sharper.

The Maker is made up of the knife blade used for thick and heavy materials such as the balsa wood and heavy chipboard. It is made up of the Digital sewing pattern library, which provides access to hundreds of fabric plans for an instant cut. It can cut hundreds of more materials ranging from the finest paper to heavy fabrics. Unlike the Explore Air 2, the Maker comes without the dial.

The Maker is also made up of a ridge that is used for placing your tablet devices as well as redesigned storage areas. In terms of cost, the Cricut Explore Air 2 offers the best value for money. It has lots of great features despite costing up to half of the price of the Maker.

It can be used for a variety of projects such as the patterned vinyl t-shirt, reverse canvas project, vinyl on glass water bottles, craft cutting, etc.

The Difference between the Explore Air 2 and the Explore Air

Both the Explore Air 2, as well as the Maker, can cut, score, and write twice faster than the Explore Air can.

Unlike the Explore Air that comes in the blue color, the Explore Air 2 does come in pastel colors.

Irrespective of their differences, they are similar in some areas:

•   Air and Air 2 are both made up of a dual carriage that allows cutting and writing without having to change any tools.

•   Another notable similarity between these machines is that they both work with the deep cut blades and fine points.

There are no considerable differences concerning the Cricut Explore family that may affect the result that it delivers. The machines are pretty much like iPhones. New versions get released often, but the newer ones do not perform more than the models that came before them. That being said, here are the distinct points that I noticed.

The Cricut Explore is no longer available, which means that if you are interested in purchasing this machine, you will have to look for a pre-loved one. Although that is not necessarily a bad thing, you should know that it is not wireless as well. You will have to connect the unit with a cable to your computer. It's not a big deal, but if you are like me who is firmly against cables, this will be an issue, and an upgrade may then be worth the extra money.

The Explore One is the most basic and the friendliest machine pocket-wise. The difference between this apparatus and the later models is that it does not have a dual carriage, and so it cannot do two things at once. E.g., score and cut in one go or write and cut.

Next up, we have the Cricut Explore Air, which is the next best thing after the Explore One. Personally, this upgrade is worth it as it has a dual carriage and can write and cut – or score and cut – at the same time. It's a time saver. Furthermore, it has Bluetooth, which means that there are no cables in sight except for the power cord! There aren't any wires that you will have to connect to your laptop either.

Lastly, there is the Cricut Explore Air 2. Now, there is no significant difference between this machine and the Explore Air. The former is faster and comes in a mint green color - that's it. For $50 more, the question remains whether the unit is worth the price or not. It's handy if you are tight on time and need to get those projects out quickly as it works nearly two times faster than the Explore Air. So, the usefulness of these features is entirely up to you and what you need in your Cricut machine.

 Pros

There are a lot of pros surrounding the Cricut Explore family. It is unlike the Cricut Cake, which is older and more difficult to work with.

The machine can cut nearly anything as well as draw on the material. It can cut more than 100 materials, which is pretty impressive. It is an upgrade from the Cricut Cake and Cricut Mini, for sure.

You do not need the software for your Cricut, even though it is necessary to set up and link your cartridges.

Cartridges aren't a must, and neither is the software. You can use whichever you prefer since both are quite easy to use. The cartridges are easier to use than the software but that's an entirely different issue.

It can connect to your mobile devices, which may come in handy later.

The Cricut Explore is an absolute powerhouse, and you do not need any other cutting machine if you have one. You won't get anything better for its price.

Cons

There are glitches and little to no information on how to fix the Cricut Explore or even tricks that will allow you to get the best results. While it is a weak point for nearly every Cricut machine, it seemed to me that the Cricut Explore family had the least amount of information on the glitches. You will have to rely on your wits to repair it. To clarify, this isn't to say that there will ever be a glitch. I've never experienced one myself, but I do know of someone who struggled with it so it is worth mentioning.

Fondant goes between the cracks. It can cut the material if you have the proper Cake Blade and mat, but the Cricut Cake is specifically designed to avoid those nasty bits of excess fondant from wedging themselves in every nook and cranny, which is different to the Explore. You will have to clean it out thoroughly after each use because once fondant heats up, it will create a sticky mess that might ruin the rest of your projects. No one wants fondant on a greeting card; that's why you should be very careful with this.

What is the best Cricut Machine to buy as a beginner?

This is the most important thing that comes to your mind while you learn everything about the Cricut Machine.

Buying the best Cricut machine would complement your creativity and would help you create crafts, designs, projects, and ornaments. First off, you need to know about buying Cricut machines is that all Cricut Machines work in the same manner.

The thing that sets them apart or creates a difference in the Cricut machine is the unique features that are designated to them. The similarity that every Cricut machine has is that each machine uses a free software called Design Space. It is important to know that every cutting machine has its software which is difficult to learn.

With that being said, if you are looking for a Cricut machine at a reasonable price, then I would recommend you to buy Cricut Explore Air 2. It would also be easy to use if you are a beginner. But if you have enough budget, then Cricut maker would be the best option.

Chapter 9: - Common Mistakes and How to Avoid and Solve Them

Why Can't I Weed My Design Lacking It Vehement?

There are two honestly public reasons for this kind of matter. Number one is dull blades. We have some tips on how to sharpen your blades, so just look for that! The second reason is a buildup of residues on your blades

Where Do I Go to Buy Materials?

When it comes to buying materials for your Cricut, there is nearly an unlimited number of places where you can get them. Since the Cricut is such a versatile machine with the ability to cut so many materials, you won't be able to go into any crafting or fabric stores without tripping over new materials you can use for your latest and greatest crafts.

As you continue to learn more about how Cricut works and what you can do with it, you will find which materials and brands best suit your needs. From there, you will often find what you need by shopping online to get the best prices and quantities of the materials you prefer, which will help you stretch your dollar as best as you can.

Do I Need a Printer to Use My Cricut?

In a word, no. Using your Cricut with the materials we've laid out in this manuscript doesn't require ink from a printer. However, there are some materials on the market for Cricut, which are specifically meant to be printed on before using.

If you're not using these items, then you will find that you can get the most out of your machine without that feature.

If you wish to print things and then cut them, this is known as the "Print then Cut" method, and there is a wealth of knowledge about this on the internet. You can make iron-on decals, tattoos, and so much more!

Where Can I Get Images to Use With My Cricut?

The beautiful thing about the Cricut Design Space and its ability to host so many different file types is that you can upload images from any source, so long as you have the legal rights to use that image.

Pulling images off of Google Image Search is done amongst crafters, but if you're selling the design in any way, you will want to make sure that the images you're using are either open license, or you've purchased them for use and distribution.

Do I Have to Buy All My Fonts Through Cricut?

Cricut Design Space has an option when looking through your fonts to use fonts that are installed on your computer.

This is called "System Fonts." Any font you can buy or download can be used through Cricut Design Space with little to no issues. There are many resources for this on the internet as well.

However, if there is a font you're using, do make sure that you have the license to use the font for the purposes you have in mind for that font! Fonts, just like pictures, do have copyrights and can be limited in what they allow you to do with them.

Why Is My Blade Cutting Through My Backing Sheet?

This can be due to improper seating on the blade in the housing, so just pop the housing out, re-seat the blade inside, reload, and try again. This can also be due to an improper setting on the material dial.

If you're cutting something very thin but have the dial set to cardstock, your needle could be plunging right through the whole piece of material and its backing!

Why Aren't My Images Showing up Right on My Mat?

It is possible when you click "Make It," that the print preview of your project doesn't look anything like how you have it laid out in Design Space. If this is the case, go back to Design Space, highlight all your images, click "Group," then click "Attach." This should keep everything right where it needs to be for all your project cutting needs!

I'm Just Getting Started; Do I Need to Buy All Of Cricut's Accessories Right Away?

No, you won't need all the accessories right at once, and some of them you won't ever need at all, depending on what crafts you intend to do with your Cricut machine. In fact, you can use crafting items you likely already have on hand to get started, buying tools and accessories here and there as you get more use out of your machine!

It is, by no means, necessary to spend a small fortune on accessories and tools just to do your first Cricut crafting project!

Which Cricut Machines Are Compatible With Design Space?

The Cricut models that are currently compatible are all of the motorized cutting machines they have on the market! This means the Cricut Explore, Cricut Explore Air, Cricut Explore Air 2, and the Cricut Maker. You can use all these tools with the current Design Space version to create countless projects for every style and occasion.

Outdated machinery will need to be tested with the application to see if they're compatible, as Cricut does provide regular updates for the application that could nullify that compatibility over time.

Do I Need to Be Connected to the Internet to Use Design Space?

Cricut Design Space is a web-based application that utilizes the cloud. Because of this, you do need an active, high-speed internet connection in order to make use of the application for your designs.

However, the cloud functionality gives you access to your account, your designs, your elements, and everything within the Design Space from any device, anywhere in the world, so long as you have an internet connection and your account credentials.

Is My Operating System Compatible With Cricut Design Space?

Cricut Design Space is currently compatible with devices operating in the latest systems for Windows, Mac, Android, and iOS. If you have questions about your device's compatibility with the latest plug-in for Cricut's Design Space, simply visit their page on system requirements and see what is listed there for you and the operating system you use.

Can I Use Design Space on More Than One of My Devices?

Yes, thanks to Cricut's web-based and cloud-based functionality, all of your designs, elements, fonts, purchases, and images are accessible from any device with an internet connection and your account credentials. This way, it's possible to start a design while you're out and about for the day and then wrap them up when you're back in your crafting space.

How Long Can I Use an Image I Bought on Design Space?

Any design asset or element you purchase through the design space is yours to use as many times as you'd like while you have an active account with Cricut Design Space!

Feel free to cut as many of every image you'd like!

I Accidentally Welded Two Images. How Do I Unweld Them?

Unfortunately, there is no dedicated unweld option currently available in Design Space.

If you weld an image, however, you can still click "Undo" if you have not saved the changes to your project. It is recommended that you save your images locally at each different stage, so you have clean images to work with for every project.

How Do I Set Design Space to Operate on the Metric System?

On your computer (whether it's Windows or Mac), click the three stacked lines in the upper left-hand corner. From there, click "Settings." In those settings, you'll see the option to set inches or centimeters as the default measurement.

If you're using Design Space on your mobile device, you will access your settings from the bottom of your screen. You may need to roll or jab to the left to view all your options, but this setting is available on mobile as well!

What Types of Images Can I Upload Through Cricut's Design Space iOS or Android Apps?

Any images saved in the Photos or Gallery app on your Apple or Android device can be uploaded! If you have SVG files saved, you can upload those as well. If you are trying to upload a .PDF or a .TIFF file, it should be noted that Cricut Design Space does not support these.

Can I Upload Images Through the Android App?

Yes! Cricut understands how crucial mobile accessibility is to its users, so this feature has been made available on all platforms where you can access Cricut Design Space, including Android!

Can I Upload Photos While I'm Offline?

Uploading images can only be done with an active high-speed internet connection. This is true of any platform you'll work with that is based on the web or the cloud. Once an image is uploaded, however, it can be accessed and downloaded onto other devices for offline use.

Do I Have to Buy a Bluetooth Wireless Adapter Purchasing a Machine to Explore?

If you bought the air Browse and explore atmosphere 2, you do not have to obtain a Bluetooth wireless adapter. But this is not the same for the Explore One, and so you can buy Bluetooth wireless adapter Cricut if that's what they want.

Cricut Makers Can Know the Sheet Loaded Without Smart Dialing. How?

The machine carriage moves to the right before cutting your project. This is called homing. In this case, the device will scan the page and find out what you have installed.

How to Download Software Explore Machines?

To do this, first, go to design.cricut.com on your laptop or computer and log on with your ID Cricut. You will be guided through the process of downloading the plug-in Space Design and install it.

It can also be used on your phone by downloading the application from Google Play Store if you are a user of Android, App Store if you are a user of iOS.

If I Upgrade From Maker Explore to Cricut, Will I Lose My Projects and Cartridges?

No, you will not. All your information is not linked to the Cricut machine. Instead, you connect to your Cricut ID cloud. While you are using the same ID, you can access all your information and projects when a new machine Cricut is obtained.

Should My Cricut Machine Be Connected to the Internet?

Your Cricut machine does not work alone, but instead must be connected to Design Space. Design Space uses an Internet connection unless you are using the offline version on your iOS device.

How Can I Use the Same Design Space for Both the Series and Cricut Explore Maker?

Your Design Space will not change, even if you are replacing a Cricut machine with another. Also, no matter which one you are using, you always have to use Design Space. But Cricut Maker has more benefits Design series exploring the area.

Chapter 10: -41+ Tips and Tricks

Want to enjoy your machine? Here are a few tips and tricks that will help you:

1.   De-Tack Your Cutting Mat!

Your Cricut Explore Air will arrive with a cutting mat upon which you will put your projects before cutting. When purchased newly the cutting mat is usually very sticky. I would advise that you prime the cutting mat before your first use. Priming makes it less sticky such that your paper projects do not get damaged. You prime the cutting mat by placing a clean dry fabric over the cutting stock over the cutting mat and pulling it out again.

2.   Keep Your Cutting Mat Clean

Use wipes to keep your cutting mat clean. Be careful with alcohol wipes as they could make the carpet lose stickiness. You can also use the plastic cover to store your cutting mat when it is not in use.

3.   Use The Proper Tools

Use the correct Cricut Tools. The best tools are the tools from the Cricut Tool Set. This toolset contains tweezers, scrapers, scissors, spatula, and a weeding tool. These tools make work go very smoothly.

4.   Start Your Cricut Journey With The Sample Project

It is best to start with the sample project and the material provided. The materials you will find in the package will be sufficient for you to start an initial sample project. Start with a simple sample project to have a feel of how the machine works.

5.   Always Test Cuts

When carrying out projects, it is advisable to do a test cut before running the whole project. You can designate a simple cut to test run your settings before cutting material for the project. If the blade is not well set the test cut will reveal it.

6.   Replace Pen Lids After Use

Replace the pen lids when you are done using your pens. This avoids it from drying out. It is a good thing that Design Space sends a notification that reminds you to put the lid back on!

7.   Link Your Old Cricut Cartridges

If you have cartridges you have used with your older machines, you can still hook them up with your new device.

8.   Bend The Cutting Mat To Get Materials Off The Cutting Mat

To remove cut materials from the cutting mat (incredibly delicate Vinyl); you can bend the carpet away from the fabric. That way, you can use the spatula to help get the cut material off the cutting mat.

9.   Use The Deep Cut Blade For Thicker Materials

Use the deep cut blade to cut through thick materials. These materials could be leather, cardboard or even chipboard. Get the edge and the blade housing.

10.   Always Replace The Pen Lids After Use

You should ensure you avoid forgetting your pen in the machine after you are done with a project. This might result in your cell drying out, so you should always remember to have the lid back on it after you are done.

11.   Linking Your Old Cricut Cartridges To Your Design Space Account

In a situation where you have old cartridges from previous machines, it helps hook this up with your new machine. It is to be noted that cartridges can only be linked once. In a situation where you are buying a second-hand cartridge, you will need to confirm if it has not been linked to a machine before.

12.   Get Materials Off The Cutting Mat

Getting the project peeled from the mat can cause curling; therefore, you can instead just peel the mat from the project. Just have the carpet bent away from the card rather than the other way round.

13.   Get The Deep Cut Blade

You are advised to order the deep cut blade. It is useful in cutting through thick cards, chipboard, leather, etc. It works perfectly with the Cricut Explore Air 2.

You should get the blade housing along with the blade.

14.   Always Replace The Blades

It is usual for Cricut blades to wear out after being used for sometimes. The blade will start to be ineffective and will no longer be smooth; at this point, it is necessary to have the blades changed. Some other signs that show that it's time for the blade to be replaced include when it starts lifting or pulling the vinyl off the backing seat, they start to tear the cards or vinyl and incomplete cutting process.

15. Keep Your Cutting Mat Clean

Use wipes to keep your cutting mat clean. Be careful with alcohol wipes as they could make the carpet lose stickiness. You can also use the plastic cover to store your cutting mat when it is not in use.

16. Use The Proper Tools

Use the correct Cricut Tools. The best tools are the tools from the Cricut Tool Set. This toolset contains tweezers, scrapers, scissors, spatula, and a weeding tool. These tools make work go very smoothly.

17. Start Your Cricut Journey With The Sample Project

It is best to start with the sample project and the material provided. The materials you will find in the package will be sufficient for you to create an initial sample project. Start with a simple sample project to have a feel of how the machine works.

18. Always Test Cuts

When carrying out projects, it is advisable to do a test cut before running the whole project. You can designate a simple amount to test run your settings before cutting material for the project. If the blade is not well set the test cut will reveal it.

19. Replace Pen Lids After Use

Replace the pen lids when you are done using your pens. This avoids it from drying out. It's a good thing that Design Space sends a notification that reminds you to put the lid back on!

20. Link Your Old Cricut Cartridges

If you have cartridges you have used with your older machines, you can still hook them up with your new machine.

21. Bend The Cutting Mat To Get Materials Off The Cutting Mat

To remove cut materials from the cutting mat (especially delicate Vinyl); you can bend the mat away from the material. That way, you can use the spatula to help get the cut material off the cutting mat.

22. Use The Deep Cut Blade For Thicker Materials

Use the deep cut blade to cut through thick materials. These materials could be leather, cardboard or even chipboard. Get the blade and the blade housing.

23. Use Different Pens Where Necessary

Like you should use different blades for different materials; you should use different pens for different uses. There are different pen adapters available which you can use with your machine.

24. Make Use Of Free Fonts

There are many free fonts you can use. You can make use of these fonts for free instead of purchasing fonts on Cricut Access. When you identify a desired free front, download it and install it on your computer. The font will appear on Cricut Design Space.

25. Use Different Blades For Different Materials

Do not use one single blade for all the different materials you will cut. For example, you can have one blade for cardboard, another for only leather and one for vinyl. It is best to have different blades for different materials because each material wears differently on the blade. A dedicated blade will be best because it will be tuned to the peculiarities of each material.

26. Use Weeding Boxes For Intricate Patterns

When cutting delicate or intricate patterns it is important to use weeding boxes in the process. Create a square or rectangle using the square tool in Cricut Design Space and place it such that all your design elements are all in it. Doing this makes weeding easier as all your design elements are grouped within the square or rectangle you have created.

27. Always Remember To Set The Dial

This sounds like stating the obvious setting the dial to the right material is something you can easily forget. The consequences of forgetting to set the dial to the appropriate material range from damaged cutting mats to shallow cuts on the materials. You can prevent these by always setting the dial before cutting.

28. Make Use Of The Free SVG Files

Apart from making use of the designs available in the Design Space store, you can have your SVG files created or employ other SVG files available on the internet. This will help you in saving a lot of money.

29. Other Pens Compatible with The Cricut Explore Air 2

Apart from the Cricut pens, we have other pens that are compatible with the Cricut Explore Air 2 machine and any other machine that uses the accessory adapter. These pens include American craft pens and Sharpie pens. Nevertheless, the Cricut pens, when compared to these other pens, are of higher quality.

30. Have the Mat Correctly Loaded

Before beginning the cutting process, it is crucial to ensure that your mat is successfully loaded. You have to ensure that it slips correctly under the rollers. In a situation where the mat is not correctly loaded, the machine may just start cutting before the grid top on the mat or may not cut at all.

31. **Label blades for use on paper, vinyl, fabric, etc., and only use those blades on that medium. This helps preserve the lifetime of the blades.**

32. **Learn the proper cutting methods and approved materials by reading the cutting guide on the Cricut website.**

33. **Spray paint is a great tool for coloring vinyl if ever in a pinch and do not have a required color on hand or the time for it to arrive.**

34. **Free fonts can be uploaded and used in the Cricut Design Space. Find free fonts on multiple font websites.**

35. **Personal images and pictures can be used for Cricut projects if the image is saved on the computer as a .PNG, .JPG, or .SCG.**

36. **Test out materials before printing and cutting a final project to be sure it will work as planned.**

37. **Pens other than Cricut pens work with the machine. Some brands to try include Sharpie, American Crafts, and Recollections.**

38. **Avoid paper curling by pulling the cutting mat from the project and not the other way around.**

39. **Lint rollers are great for removing leftover materials from cutting mats. If the mats need further cleaning, use soap and water and gently rub clean with soft cloth. Rinse with clean water and let air dry.**

40. **Go Button: This can also be called the "Cut" button. This is the button on the Cricut cutting or EasyPress machine with the green Cricut "C" on it. The button is pressed when a project is ready to be cut or pressed for the EasyPress models.**

41. **JPG File: A JPG file is a common form of the digital image. These image files can be uploaded for use with a Design Space project.**

42. **Kiss Cut: When the cutting machine cuts through the material but not the material backing sheet, it is called a Kiss Cut.**

43. **Libraries: Libraries are lists of images, fonts, or projects that have been uploaded by the user or maintained by Cricut Design Space.**

Conclusion

You have just become a professional Cricut user! However, it would help if you did not forget the most important things in this book. If you forget things quickly, have this book with you every time you want to work on your Cricut machine.

Using a Cricut machine should not be a new experience for you by now. However, it would be best if you kept an open mind to new updates. Cricut always gives its users many options to choose from, so try as much as possible to carry out extensive research about their products, materials, and subscriptions.

Cricut machines are designed to handle multipurpose tasks. A lot of work can be done on it without stress. You can write, score, and cut with the machine. A lot of Cricut users are yet to reach the maximum level of usage. With Cricut, people rarely over-utilize. Most people only underutilize.

I hope that you enjoyed this book and learned a lot! If you did, I would love to see your opinion and review on Amazon!

CRICUT MAKER

An Effective Step-by-step Guide to Start Making Real Your Cricut Project Ideas Today: 369 Illustrated Practical Examples, Original Project Ideas, and Tips & Tricks.

Introduction

The world of craft is filled with many design problems to solve, Cricut Machines come into aid to solve many of those problems.

A Cricut is a cutting system that helps you to cut and make beautiful and amazing crafts with materials that you didn't even know existed, that's the short answer. You can also sketch, emboss, and produce folding lines to realize 3D designs, birthday cards, boxes, etc. depending on the layout you have.

The Cricut device has several usages in addition to being a cutter machine for a scrapbooking design. It is possible to make use of the designs to produce items like welcoming memory cards, wall surface decorations, therefore a lot more. You need to think artistically. There are no borders, as well as they're all a figment of your creative imagination if there are actually.

There is a myriad of projects you can complete by using the Cricut Machine: you will discover the wonderful world of arts and crafts and you will make your project ideas become reality.

If you don't have much experience with these types of devices, don't worry. We've got you covered. You will find that the guidelines presented in this book are both easy to understand and simple to implement. You won't have to contend with complicated technical instructions written by some electronics nerd. You will find the information contained in this book in simple and plain English. This is what makes using the Cricut Machine so easy. Plus, you will find that it's much more fun when you don't have to deal with complex explanations.

Each of the chapters has been written to guide you through the process of deciding which machine to get through your first couple of projects. Best of all, you can take this information to make the best possible choice for you. After all, the sky's the limit when you use your imagination!

This book has been written with the average user in mind. All you need is the willingness to let your imagination fly. When you do so, you can make wonderful ideas become reality. Besides, there are thousands of project ideas you can use to make your creations come to life.

If that isn't enough to get you excited, then you ought to know that setting up the Cricut Machine is easy and doesn't require any special technical knowledge. All you need is a computer and the companion software that goes with it. This software is freely available when you purchase the Cricut Machine. You can use it on both your computer and a mobile device such as a tablet.

So, let's start with the wonderful creations you have in mind. Feel free to let your imagination wander. Ultimately, when you let your ideas take hold, you'll be able to render anything virtual to something possible.

Surely, you haven't seen anything like this before. Come on, let's get on with it! The sooner you start, the faster you can make your wildest ideas come to life.

Chapter 1: What Is the Cricut Machine

Several electronic die-cutting machines are prominent in today's world. Cricut machines are one of the best of this kind. It is widely used by card manufacturers, paper crafters, and scrapbookers.

A Cricut machine can cut materials from paper to fake leather, just to mention a few. The Cricut machine is also a very good option for those without handwriting. In other words, the Cricut computer can do a printer's job for you.

Designs written by loading the machine's accessory slot marker are always exceptional. More importantly, you don't need to use actual cartridges with some Cricut machine versions. Explore instance series is a typical example of the Cricut machine sort.

Ironically, the Cricut machine's exploring sequence also allows direct upload. Then, simply upload the specific design you want, and use the computer to cut it out. Cricut computers are a die-cutting tool. We can also be seen as a plotter-cutting machine. It's a printer that lets you create a design or image on your computer, send it to the Cricut, and it prints and cuts your design. You can also print and cut any content. The newer Cricut machine models can use materials like vinyl, paper, cloth, sticker paper, art foam, and even fake leather.

The Cricut machine can be used as a printer. There is an attachment slot in the computer that one can use to load a marker and then' draw' the template. If you're one with a love for handwritten quotes and so on, it's a perfect way to get your handwriting font on your craft.

Creatively, the Cricut can be used for various designs. All you need is an idea, imagination, room for your art, cutting materials, and a trusted Cricut machine.

How to Use it in Life

Here, we have listed all you can do with the manufacturer and why you could buy one for yourself. A lot can be done with a Cricut from great vinyl decals to advanced and powerful sewing patterns, particularly mostly with amazingly versatile Maker.

Dishes of Vinyl

Our number one hobby is to cut vinyl decals with stickers, and you can, of course, use the Cricut Maker to do this.

Manufacturing Cuts

One of the Maker's main sales outlets is the fact that the brand spanking new Rotary Blade is available.

Owing to its unusual gliding and rolling motion and the massive 4 kg of force behind the Cricut Builder, the machine can cut virtually any fabric.

Patterns for Sewing

Another talented pro is the entire extensive sewing model library, which you can access after you have purchased the computer. This includes hundreds of patterns, including Simplicity and Designs of Riley Blake, which ensures that you can easily pick the model you like, and the designer will cut it for you. Don't break patterns manually (but no more operator errors!) An easy cleaning fabric pen is also included that shows where the design parts will fit together.

Cuts of Balsa Wood

The Cricut Maker could even cut materials up to 2,4 mm thick thanks to the massive force of 4 kg and the utility knife (sold separately). That means that we now have large fabrics that were previously outside the limits of the Cricut and Silhouette machines. We can't wait for the wood to be cut!

Household Cards

Both paper crafters and the Manufacturer are not left out. The strength and accuracy of the system can make paper and card cuts quicker and more comfortable than ever. Your homemade cards have only gone up.

Ornaments of Christmas Tree

The Rotary blade, which promises to cut any fabric, is the perfect instrument for designing vacation decorations. Scour the Christmassy pattern sewing library (we have our eyes on the man's gingerbread ornament!); cut the sequence using felt or any fabric you want and sew it separately.

Dolls and Soft Toys Felt

One of the simple designs we have in the sewing method library is the pattern of felt doll and clothes. We know a few small boys and girls that would love to add a homemade doll to one's collection. Simply select, cut, and sew the pattern. Pretty easy!

Transfers of T-Shirt

Naturally, the Cricut Maker will cut your thermal performance vinyl to make your designs a factory. You just have to design a Design Space transfer, load the manufacturer with your thermal energy vinyl (or perhaps even sparkly HTV if you are adventurous), ask the machine to begin cutting, and iron the transfer on your t-shirt. Likewise, you can use the new single Cricut added strength to transmit the vinyl, which meets the efficiency of a heat press!

Clothes for Babies

Unfortunately, Cricut Maker's mat size is only 12 by 24, so you can't cut adult clothes models on this machine. This dimension must be big enough even to cut the patterns of baby clothing.

Signs of Calligraphy

The main selling point of the Cricut machine is its ability of the organism System. This is the component that keeps your maker forever. It is essentially a tool that not only matches all Explores instruments and blades but also fits all future devices and blades produced by Cricut. The copperplate pen is one of these instruments and it's ideal for making cards and signing!

Invitations to Marry and Save Dates

We all know how 'low' costs, such as invitations as well as STDs, can add to the enormous cost of the wedding. As producers, we know how to compensate for some of these risks by doing things like this by ourselves. Cricut Maker would be perfect for inviting people not only to cut out intricate designs of paper but also to use the calligraphy pen once more.

Wedding menus, Place Cards, and Favor Tags

Naturally, you aren't only limited to crafts before your wedding, so you can also use your maker for the great day. The sky is the limit, but it begins with crafting menus, putting cards, and encouraging labels. Seek to use a similar style to keep a theme in front and center for your paperwork.

Keyrings Fabric

There were also several simple designs for textile keyrings that caught our eyes in the sewing pattern library. Again, the manufacturer makes it easy – just cut out the pattern and sew it together.

Headbands and Covers of hair

Now that Cricut has launched a machine that can cut thick leather, we have an excellent idea for complicated, steampunk-inspired hair decoration, and even headbands. Do you know that it is so practical for great fashionable statements?

Cut Out Tree for Christmas

We know, we know, during the holiday season, everyone wants a real Christmas tree. If in your living room you don't have a place for an exalted tree, or you're allergic to pine, God forbid, you may want to create your tree. As the Cricut Maker can cut dense materials like wood, it is a great project to play with this year. When the Creator is at your beck and call, no laser is needed!

Toppers Cake

Know when Cricut pulled out the 'Cake' cutter? It was made of the maker; rubber paste and the like. Well, the maker is not a cake machine as Cake is, but you think it's just a machine for making small, complicated cakes with which we can adorn our cakes.

Refrigerator Magnets

Just like the machines from Cricut Explore, the manufacturer can cut out magnetic material. Excellent news for the magnet collectibles and those who like to jazz up their fridge!

Decals Window

Want to put on the windows an inspirational quote? Or maybe a cute tiny pattern on the back window of your car? No issue, with Cricut Maker-load the device with a window fastener and create your design.

Scrapbooking Updates

We are delighted to use our Maker for adornments that we could use when booking scrapbooks. Although the Cricut machines will always be quite good at cutting intricate designs, the new blades with an unusual reaction will make complexity the thing of the past, even if you cut delicate materials, like tissue paper!

Collars Peter Pan

So, we discussed earlier that baby and doll clothes speak about how large the clothing patterns you can cut on the Cricut Maker. Well, you can slice patterns on adult clothes accessories here, sorry! We find more than a few basic collars designs that fashionistas love.

The Craft of the Wall

We've talked a lot about the paperwork you can do with the creator, but we agree that wall art is a probability for you too. The precision level the Maker offers is so advanced that you can create everything beautiful and incredible with ease. Do not slip and tear or skip part of your design!

Cricut Explore Air 2

This is the youngest sibling of the Cricut Explore line. It is the best of the machines in this line. Explore Air 2 is efficient as the other ones, but it does its work even better. It has a better design, and comes in different colors.

Capability

The model features a Fast mode that speeds up the cutting process, primarily if you work with deadlines.

It also has the features in the other systems like the German carbide premium blade, inbuilt Bluetooth adapter, dual carriage, and auto-settings.

The great thing about the Explore Air is that it is ideal for both beginners and advanced users.

Materials

This machine can cut through a hundred materials or even more. This includes and is not limited to cotton, silk, tissue paper, corkboard, foil, foam, aluminum, leather, clay, chipboard, burlap, and even birch wood.

It also has the Smart Dial, which helps you manage the cutting width depending on the materials.

Cutting Force

The model is highly potent, and it makes use of the German carbide premium fine point blade, which comes with precision and speed. It can cut any material with a width of 11.5 x 23.5 inches.

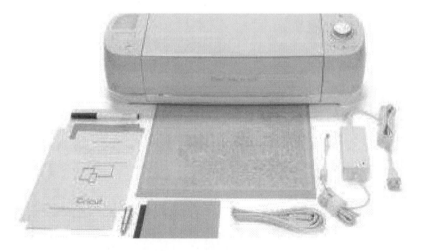

When you first purchase a Cricut Explore Air 2, you get a three months free subscription with access to premium features offered by Cricut!

The Cricut Design Space is also cloud-based for those using IOS devices. With this, you can work offline!

The only downside in this model is the slightly increased noise level, but this is expected because it works two times faster than the previous ones.

Cricut Maker:

The newest Cricut die-cutting machine is the Cricut Maker. If you thought that the Explore Air 2 was a great model, then you should get ready to be blown away.

The Cricut Maker is a rare unit amongst other die-cutting machines. The rotary blade is already enough to attract experienced users. And, for beginners, it provides an avenue for improvement and unlimited creativity.

Capability

The Cricut Maker, as an updated version of others, is very powerful and flexible. It comes with a toolkit that includes a rotary blade, knife blade, deep cut blade, and fine point blade. It also comes with a single and a double scoring wheel, as well as a collection of pens. The pens include a fine point pen, a washable fabric pen, a calligraphy pen, and a scoring stylus.

The machine also improves its efficiency by adding some unique features. We have the adaptive tool system, which means that the device can adjust the angle of the blade and the pressure of the blade automatically depending on the material. It doesn't need the Smart dial feature because the Cricut Maker determines your cutting force for you, and its decisions are usually accurate.

It has two clamps, one for the pen or scoring tool and the other for the cutting blade. This system is also unique because of its fast and precise mode. This works for any paper, cardstock, and vinyl.

Materials

As expected, the Cricut Maker can handle thicker materials than the machines in the Cricut Explore series.

From light materials to basswood and leather, this machine will exceed your expectations.

Cricut Design Space also provides a lot of benefits for Cricut Maker users. It allows .jpg, .gif, .png, .svg, .bmp and .dxf files.

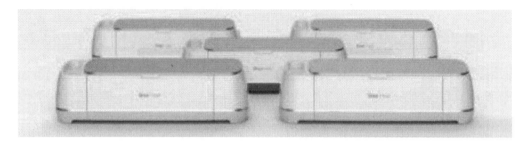

The system also supports wireless Bluetooth adapters. So, you can enjoy the Sewing Pattern Library if you own a Cricut Maker. The library contains 50 ready-to-cut projects, and it is a result of a partnership between Cricut and Riley Blake Designs.

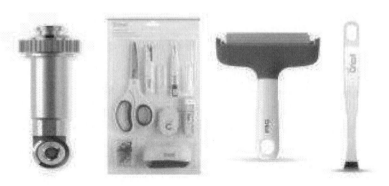

Another great benefit you get when using Cricut Maker with Design Space is that you get free membership of Cricut Access for a trial period.

The only downside of this model is working slowly with very thick materials, but that can be expected. It is also noisy because of the fast mode.

Tools and Accessories Needed to Work with Explore Air 2 Machine

Thanks to Cricut machines and all the blades you can use with different models, you are set to find out how crafting can be more rewarding, simpler, and easier with additional tools and accessories. Aside from blades and tips created and designed for different purposes, fabrics, and crafting materials, some Cricut tools, and accessories can make your crafting and DIY projects more successful and rewarding.

Weeding Tools

Some crafting projects just call for the use of weeders, a.k.a. weeding tools. There are several different Cricut weeding tools, each handy in its way, and proposed for different weeding techniques. Weeding tools are particularly handy if you are working with iron-on and vinyl, and you need to remove excessive material as you are working on your project. Weeding tools can also be very helpful for removing excess glitter and glue. Regular weeding tools available as a part of the Cricut toolset will do a great job to remove excessive material and adhesives from your projects. Another option is going for the hooked weeding tool that looks much like something you would find in a dentistry toolkit. Many crafters find this tool to be efficient and precise

Tweezers

What crafter wouldn't make good use out of a quality pair of tweezers. There are four different types of Cricut tweezers, each designed with a different angle so crafters may choose the most suitable tool for their projects' needs. If your projects require regular work with small parts and most of the work is "touchy" you will like the idea of owning a pair of fine tweezers. Reverse tweezers may seem a bit strange to a crafter used to working with regular or fine tweezers as these tweezers work in a reverse way. When you apply the pressure and squeeze the reverse tweezers, it opens instead of closing.

Cricut Scissors

Cutting but with no scissors in your toolkit? Your Cricut machine can do most of the cutting, but a crafter still needs their scissors, right? So, you don't need to buy Cricut scissors – if you have a pair of scissors that work great for you, there is no need for changing your tools. In case you decided to look for a pair of quality scissors, Cricut models may be suitable for your needs. Basic scissors have a rather small cutting part and might not be particularly comfortable to use. The second model, fabric scissors, has a 5-inch blade that is designed to cut through thick materials

Brayer

Every crafter uses adhesives, which makes brayer a rather handy piece of tool to add to your Cricut station. Cricut brayer has an ergonomic design, which means that it is pretty easy and simple to use while also very comfortable. You are set to love using brayer as you can easily avoid wrinkles and bubbles when applying adhesives to your fabric. The brayer is perfect for thick materials, while you can also use it for stamping and making prints. The brayer performs intended operations smoothly, including adhering fabric to your mat in case you are using mat Fabric Grip for your projects.

Scoring Tool

If you are planning to buy Cricut Maker or you already own this model, you won't need the Cricut scoring tool as Cricut Maker has a Quick Swap Scoring Wheel tip that can help you make folds and 3D projects. In case you are using one of the other available Cricut machine models and need a tool to help you with folding and scoring, you will love the scoring tool by Cricut. You can use the scoring tool manually for making folds, or insert it into the Cricut Explore tool cartridge.

Cricut Trimmer

As a part of the Essential tool kit by Cricut, you will get a trimmer that can help you cut different types of materials quickly and without much effort. Regardless of what type of projects you are working on, having a quality trimmer is helpful.

Cricut Spatula

In case you take your regular use of paper in crafting projects seriously, you will mark the use of spatula as necessary and even mandatory. The size of the Cricut spatula is suitable for larger pieces of material, while you can also work with smaller pieces of paper. To avoid tearing the paper pieces when removing the paper from the Cricut machine, you can easily slip the spatula between the mat and paper pieces. Once you start using a spatula, make sure to clean it often.

Cricut Mats

Every type of Cricut crafting material has recommended Cricut mats depending on which projects you are working on and what materials you are cutting. You can find recommended mats for your projects and make the best out of every cut you make with your machine. Mats aim to support your materials and fabrics. Therefore, it is important to choose your mats to match your preferred materials and specifications of the crafting project you are working on. It is important to learn which type of mat fits the requirements of your projects as Design Space won't suggest which mat to use for what project as it is the case with recommending blades.

Cricut Blades Maintenance and care

Use Your Blades with Recommended Materials

The life of your blades can be decreased in case you are not using your blades properly and as recommended. While you need to get a hold of which mat to use for which type of material by yourself, as Design Space doesn't recommend appropriate mats, Design Space will help you choose suitable blades based on the material you are using for your crafting project. Moreover, you need to make sure that the right blade is used on the material you are cutting as you can damage the blade in case you choose to cut the wrong type of material. Follow the advice from Design Space and make sure that each of your blades is used on an appropriate material or fabric.

Protect the Blades and Housing Gears

Quick Swap Scoring Wheel and blades for Cricut machines all have plastic covers. Make sure to keep these covers and use them to protect your blades when not in use. By properly storing your blades, you are protecting your tools from outside particles that can compromise the functionality of your tools, such as dust. The plastic cover protects blades and housing gears at the same time.

Store Your Blades Properly

When you are not using your blades, make sure to cover them and store them properly. You can keep your tools in storage pouch or a box. Blades can be safely kept in your Cricut machine. The machine is designed to provide storage for the blades you are not using, while the storage compartment also has a magnet to keep your blades neatly stored. You can keep your tools in the Cricut machine storage compartment as well. This way, you will always have all the blades and tools you need, accessible whenever you want to use them, but also protected and safe from damage.

How to Design

Log into your Design Space.

Select "New Project" and then, click on "Templates" in the top left corner. Choosing a template makes it easier to visualize your design to know how good or bad it will be on your T-shirt.

Choose "Classic T-Shirt" and pick your preferred style, size, and color.

You will see tons of beautiful designs for iron-on T-shirts. Browse through the entire images before you make your choice.

Remember, if your preferred design isn't available, you can upload your pictures to the Cricut Design Space. We have created a tutorial on how to upload your images to Cricut Design Space.

After you have selected the image, resize the image to fit the T-shirt. You can do this by clicking the resize handle in the bottom part of your design and dragging the mouse to enlarge or reduce.

When you are done, click the "Make it" button in the top right corner. You will be told to connect your Cricut machine.

Toggle the green "Mirror" button on. Toggling it on will make sure your design is not cut backward.

Face the shiny part of your vinyl design down on your cutting mat. Remember to move the smart set dial to the iron-on option.

Remove all the vinyl designs you don't want to be transferred to your project when it's ironed. Use your welding tool to remove those little bits that will jeopardize your beautiful design. This process is called weeding.

Transfer your design to your T-shirt when you are done weeding. You can either use an iron or an Easy Press. Preheat your Easy Press before use.

How to Clean a Cricut Maker

When the Cricut Maker was released by Cricut, it came with a new mat – the pink FabricGrip mat. We all know that the Cricut Maker is a specialized machine for cutting fabric (among a host of other materials) and to ensure perfect fabric cuts, the mat has to be in top shape.

A lot of crafters find it difficult to keep their pink mats clean because it is different from the other mats used by the Explore Air series.

Do Not Use Scrapper

With the pink FabricGrip mat, there is no need to use the scrapper because the adhesive on it is different from the others and can be scraped off the mat.

Keep your Hands off

Unlike other mats, the Cricut pink mat is made with delicate adhesive. Thus, if your hands are oily, they can easily break down the adhesive on the mat, resulting in the loss of its stickiness.

Be very careful with the mat and try as much as possible to avoid touching the adhesive. To adhere your fabric to the mat, use a Brayer, and do not apply too much force, just enough to get you to stick to the mat. Another way of keeping your hands off the mat is by using Tweezers to pick up pieces of materials from it. Desist from picking up a loose thread from the mat to – use Tweezers, if you really must pick.

Threads

Talking about threads, whenever you cut the fabric, you'll realize that you end up with a lot of threads on the mat. Leave them. In our minds, we believe that our mats have to be super clean because any form of a bump when cutting vinyl or paper can be detrimental to our project. However, the rotary blade is super awesome, it can cut through loose threads even if there is fabric over it

Tips for the Felt

Cricut Maker cuts felt perfect. Thus, if you intend to embark on this operation, there are a couple of options available for you to avoid damaging your pink mat with fuzz. First of all, you can use the older green mats and take off your pink mat. However, the green mat should have some stick. It is better to gunk up the old mat than to gunk with the pink mat with sticky fiber.

Save the Pink mat for Fabric.

You can opt to back your felt in transfer tape and stick that to the mat. You just have to peel it off after the cut. Depending on the material you're cutting, this option can be capital intensive because you'll be using transfer tape for every cut.

Do not Re-Stick the Mat

On the internet, there are so many tutorials on how to re-stick the Cricut mat, and they involve the use of baby wipes, water, painter's tape, GooGone, spray adhesive, and many others. However, you have to understand that the pink mat's adhesive is completely different from the adhesive on other mats, and if you use any of those materials to re-stick it, you'll end up damaging your pink mat. The pink mat's adhesive is designed to grip fabric but also release it easily.

Material that Can Be Used

Cricut machines, in general, can cut through over a hundred materials. Of course, we can't mention them all, but we will categorize them into six categories.

Paper and cardstock- this includes about 35 types of paper and cardstock.

Fabrics- including about 16 types of fabrics and textiles.

Iron-On- which includes about six types of iron-on materials.

Vinyl- which includes about ten types of vinyl materials.

Additional Materials- ranging from adhesive foil and adhesive wood to washi sheets and temporary tattoo paper, Cricut can cut them all.

Cricut Maker Special- this particular model of Cricut can cut through materials that the others can't like chiffon, cashmere, terry cloth, knits, jersey, velvet, tweed, and others.

Chapter 2: How to Use a Cricut Machine

Every machine has its own branded software. Using and uploading it into or onto your computer is free. Cricut also comes with an app that you can use. The software is user friendly, and you can upload photos and build designs. You can make your designs from scratch, or buy other designs. You can also upload images from the application and buy designs and change them to match your custom designs.

Cricut Design Space is a cloud-based framework. Therefore, to make the most of the application for your designs, you need a robust high-Speed Internet connection. The cloud functionality also allows you the access to your account, your designs, your apps, and anything inside the design room, from any computer anywhere in the world as long as you have your credentials and are connected to the internet

You now know the basics and also what a Cricut does. Your concern is probably what types of projects or designs you might do with them. We shall address this in this book later, as you can use it in hundreds of different ways. The capacitive stylus supports designs as well. Such a machine uses many devices for various purposes and tasks, and it is good to have your machine do exactly what you want.

A machine like this will not be a printer, but it can be that it comes close. If you use the "print, then cut" method, it will allow you to design your project and take it from there so that you can use it properly. It would be a little like making stickers if you want to think about it.

Setting up the Machine

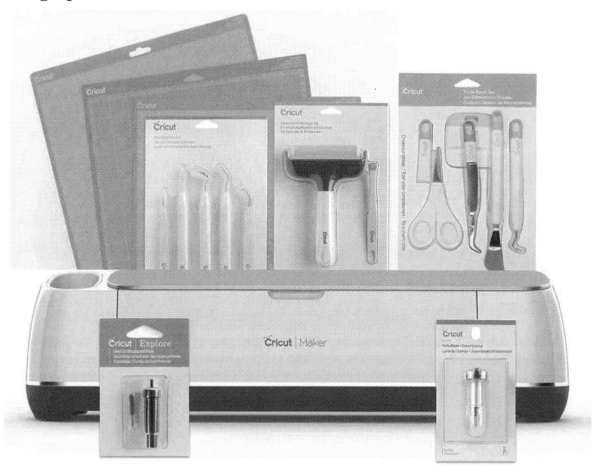

Before plugging in the machine, make sure that you have removed all the safety and travel packaging materials. These include foam around the blade housing, plastic tape strips to keep the compartments closed, and so on.

Go to www.cricut.com\setup for the step-by-step setup guide to get the machine connected to a device and Design Space.

Choose 'Cricut Maker'

The first screen will be the 'Welcome to the Cricut Family' screen.

Click the green 'Get Started' button.

If you have not as yet set up a Cricut ID, the next screen will prompt for this to be done.

If you do have a Cricut ID, at the bottom of the screen there is a 'Sign in' button beneath 'Already have a Cricut ID?'

The Cricut ID is required to work in Design Space to be able to create your projects.

Answer the next screen which is the 'Getting to know you' screen.

The next screen is the 'Connect machine' step which the program will take you through, step-by-step.

Make sure that the machine is positioned at least 10" from the wall.

Connecting the Cricut Maker With the USB Cable

Use the USB cable that was provided with the Cricut Maker machine. You can buy these separately, should anything happen to the one that came with the machine. Plug the small square side of the cable into the square USB port located next to the power port at the back of the Cricut Maker.

Plug the larger flat USB part of the cable into the USB port of the computer that will be connecting with the machine.

Plugging in the Maker

Use the power supply that comes with the Cricut Maker. Plug it into the wall socket with the power on the wall socket turned off.

Plug the other end into the power socket on the Cricut Maker, switch on the wall socket, then power up the Cricut Maker by pressing the power button.

Cricut Maker Firmware Update

When the machine syncs up with and is found by the software, the next screen will check the firmware version of the machine. The firmware contains updated drivers, features, commands, and so on.

There will be a section that will let you know what the current version is and what version is on the Cricut Maker. It is advisable to update the firmware if the machine's firmware is not the same, but older than the currently available firmware version.

When you update the firmware, the power button on the Cricut will change to red and the load/unload mat button will turn white. There will be a progress bar to show how far the update download is. The Cricut Maker will automatically reboot upon completion of the firmware update.

This section will also automatically register the Cricut Maker machine.

Click 'Continue' to take you to the next setup section.

Using Cricut Software

So, Cricut machines use a program called Cricut Design Spaces, and you'll need to make sure that you have this downloaded and installed when you're ready. Download the app if you plan to use a smartphone or tablet, or if you're on the computer, go to http://design.cricut.com/setup to get the software. If it's not hooked up already, make sure you've got Bluetooth compatibility enabled on the device, or the cord plugged in. To turn on your machine, hold the power button. You'll then go to settings, where you should see your Cricut model in Bluetooth settings. Choose that, and from there, your device will ask you to put a Bluetooth passcode in. Just make this something generic and easy to remember.

Imputing Cartridges and Keypad

The first cut that you'll be doing does involve keypad input and cartridges, and these are usually done with the "Enjoy Card" project you get right away. So, once everything is set up, choose this project, and from there, you can use the tools and the accessories within the project.

You will need to set the smart dial before you start making your projects. This is on the right side of the Explore Air 2, and it's basically the way you choose your materials. Turn the dial to whatever type of material you want, since this does help with ensuring you've got the right blade settings. There are even half settings for those in-between projects.

You can also choose the fast mode, which is in the "set, load, go" area on the screen, and you can then check the position of the box under the indicator for dial position. Then, press this and make your cut. However, the fast mode is incredibly loud, so be careful.

Now, we've mentioned cartridges. While these usually aren't used in the Explore Air 2 machines anymore, they are helpful with beginner projects. To do this, once you have the Design Space software and everything is connected, go to the hamburger menu and you'll see an option called "ink cartridges." Press that bad boy and from there, choose the Cricut device. The machine will then tell you to put your cartridge in. Do that, and once it's detected, it will tell you to link the cartridge.

Once it's confirmed, you can go to images, and click the cartridges option to find the ones that you want to make. You can filter the cartridges to figure out what you need, and you can check out your images tab for any other cartridges that are purchased or uploaded.

You can get digital cartridges, which means you buy them online and choose the images directly from your available options. They aren't physical, so there is no linking required.

Selecting Shapes, Letters, and Phrases

When you're creating your design in Design Space, you usually begin by using letters, shapes, numbers, or different fonts. These are the basics, and they're incredibly easy.

To make text, you just press the text tool on the left-hand side and type out your text. For example, write the word hello, or joy, or whatever you want to use.

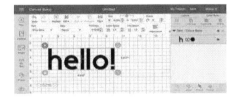

You can change the font size by pressing the drag and drop arrow near the corner of the text box, or by going to the size panel near the top to choose actual font sizes. You can choose different Cricut or system fonts, too. Cricut ones will be in green, and if you have Cricut Access, this is a great way to begin using this. You can sort these, too, so you don't end up accidentally paying for a font.

The Cricut ones are supposed to be made for Cricut, so you know they'll look good. Design Space also lets you put them closer together so they can be cut with a singular cut. You can change this by going to line spacing and adjusting as needed. To fix certain letters, you go to the drop-down advanced menu to ungroup the letters, so everything is separate as needed.

Adding shapes is pretty easy, as well. In Design Space, choose the shapes option. Once you click it, the window will then pop out, and you'll have a wonderful array of different shapes that you can use with another click. Choose your shape, and from there, put it in the space. Drag the corners to make this bigger or smaller.

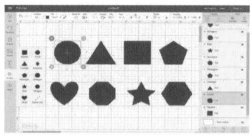

There is also the scoreline, which creates a folding line for you to use. Personally, if you're thinking of trying to make a card at first, I suggest using this.

You can also resize your options by dragging them towards the right-hand side, and you can change the orientation by choosing that option, and then flipping it around. You can select exact measurements as well, which is good for those design projects that need everything to be precise.

Once you've chosen the design, it's time for you to start cutting, and we'll discuss this next step below.

How to Remove Your Cut from the Cutting Mat

Removing your cut from the mat is easy, but complicated. Personally, I ran into the issue of it being more complicated with vinyl projects since they love to just stick around there. But we'll explain how you can create great cuts and remove them, as well. The first thing to remember is to make sure that you're using the right mat. The light grip ones are good for very light material, with the pink one being one of the strongest, and only to be used with the Cricut Maker. Once the design is cut, you'll probably be eager to remove the project directly from the mat, but one of the problems with this is that often, the project will be ruined if you're not careful. Instead of pulling the project from the mat itself, bend the mat within your hand, and push it away from the project, since this will loosen it from the mat. Bend this both horizontally and vertically, so that the adhesive releases the project.

Remember the spatula tool that we told you to get with your Cricut machine early on? This is where you use it. Use this spatula to lightly pull on the vinyl, until you can grab it from the corner and lift it. Otherwise, you risk curling it or tearing the mat, which is what we don't want.

Now, with the initial cuts, such as the paper ones, this will be incredibly easy. Trust me, I was surprised at how little effort it took, but one of the biggest things to remember is that with Cricut machines, you have to go slowly when removing the material. Do this slowly, and don't get rushed near the end. Taking your time will save you a lot of problems, and it will even save you money and stress, too!

Loading and Unloading Your Paper

To load paper into a Cricut machine, you'll want to make sure that the paper is at least three inches by three inches. Otherwise, it won't cut very well. You should use regular paper for this.

Now, to make this work, you need to put the paper onto the cutting mat. You should have one of those, so take it right now and remove the attached film. Put a corner of the paper to the area where you are directed to align the paper corners. From there, push the paper directly onto the cutting mat for proper adherence. Once you do that, you just load it into the machine, following the arrows. You'll want to keep the paper firmly on the mat. Press the "load paper" key that you see as you do this. If it doesn't take for some reason, press the unload paper key, and try this again until it shows up.

Now, before you do any cutting for your design, you should always have a test cut in place. Some people don't do this, but it's incredibly helpful when learning how to use a Cricut. Otherwise, you won't get the pressure correct in some cases, so get in the habit of doing it for your pieces.

The primary difference is the cutting mats. Depending on what you're cutting, you may need some grip or lack thereof. If you feel like your material isn't fully sticking, get some Heat N' Bond to help with this since often, the issue with cutting fabrics comes from the fact that it doesn't adhere.

Complex Operations Blade Navigation and Calibration,

To access these features, you can select one of the creative feature keys before or after you select your chosen letter, shape, or phrase, as long as the creative key is selected before pushing the cut button.

A size tip: If you make a two-inch shape and want a shadow for that shape to keep the size dial at two inches. This goes for all sizes up to 5.5 inches. The maximum size your Cricut Cutter machine can cut a letter shape or phrase is 5.5 inches so the shadow creature will not always work with the size dial set to 5.5 inches. If the Cricut Cutter machine cannot cut the letter, shape, or phrase a warning will appear on the LCD Display screen.

The blackout feature creates a shape, letter, or phrase that is completely solid with no gaps. Characters cut in the blackout feature appear like silhouettes. concerning the sizing of letters, an important factor is the Key Height Character. The height of the character is determined by measuring from the lowest point to the tallest point. The Key Height Character is the tallest character of all the other characters on the keypad.

Blade Navigation Buttons

Because you know few advanced processes, it is important to identify how many advanced keys and buttons function. In many projects, your blade may not be in the right place before cutting, to solve this use the Blade Navigation Buttons. These buttons are located around the Cut button on your Cricut Cutter machine. There is an up, down, left, and right button. These buttons move the blade on your machine to exactly where you want to begin cutting. Move your blade, if necessary, after selecting what you would like to cut and after selecting the Cut button.

Set Paper Size

The default size for paper in your Cricut Cutter machine is six inches by twelve inches in the standards Cricut Cutter machine. If you ever do a project that requires paper smaller than six inches by twelve inches you must select the Set Paper Size button to tell the machine what size paper, you are using.

Load Last

Another key that will come in handy often is the Load Last button. This button, when selected, tells the blade to cut where it last stopped cutting. This key is useful if you want two shapes or letters to be a continuous item or if your Cricut Cutter stopped cutting at some point and you need it to continue to select the Load Last button.

Paper Saver

For more environmentally conscious crafters or those that would like to reduce waste, there is also the Paper Saver button. The paper saver button, when selected before the cut button, rearranges the way the cut will be made. The new arrangement should appear on the LCD Display Screen of the Cricut Cutter machine. This button will always put your shapes, letters, or phrases into the best arrangement to save paper. Once the Paper Saver button has been selected, the saving paper will become the default of your machine. To get your machine out of the Paper Saving mode select the Paper Saver button again. Make it a habit to always check the LCD Display Screen before pushing the Cut button to decrease the number of mistakes made and the amount of wasted material.

Speed Dial

The speed dial on your Cricut Cutter machine is used to regulate the speed at which the blade cuts. For thicker materials, the dial can be turned up to go faster but for thinner materials, it is recommended to turn the speed down for a slower cut. Also, the speed dial should be adjusted between cutting a simple cut and a complex cut. Simple cuts can be down very quickly and with ease, but more intricate, complex cuts should be done at a lower speed. When adjusting the speed of the cut it is recommended to test the new speed on a scrap sheet of material to make sure that it is correct and gives the wanted results. The speed will appear on the LCD Display screen each time it is adjusted. If ever your cut is ripped by the blade, decrease the speed of the cut; if the cut is still being torn, try adjusting the depth of the blade on a spare sheet of paper.

Pressure Dial

The pressure dial on the Cricut Cutter machine changes how hard the blade is being pushed into the material to cut it. As a rule of thumb, thicker materials like card stock and high fiber papers use a higher setting on the pressure dial and thinner materials like paper and vellum use a lower setting on the pressure dial. When you change the setting on the pressure dial, the new setting will appear on the LCD Display screen. It has been said many times in this book but always tests out new settings on scraps of material to make sure that the setting is correct.

Cricut Design Space

The Cricut Design Space can be accessed through web browsers on PC and Mac. When you first access design.cricut.com, it will download the plug-in it needs to function. If you have not done this already, it will prompt you to create an account. Everything you save and upload will be attached to this account. If you decide to upgrade your Cricut machine, everything you did on your previous one will be available in your account.

Design Space is also available as an app on both iOS and Android so that you can download it on your tablet or smartphone. If you have the Cricut Explore Air 2 or Cricut Maker, you can use the machine's built-in Bluetooth to connect it to your mobile device. This allows them to communicate so you can send a design right to the machine without any cables involved. The iOS version of Cricut Design Space has an offline mode that lets you send designs to your machine without an internet connection. Most of the instructions here will be based on the web version of Design Space for simplicity. However, it will largely be the same in the mobile apps, though things might be moved around slightly.

Linetype determines what will happen with the lines of your image or text. The options are Cut, Draw, Score, Engrave, Deboss, Wave, and Perf for the Maker, or Cut, Draw, and Score for the Explore. The option you choose will determine what the machine does to the lines. You can set different Line Types for different objects on the Canvas. If you choose Draw, you'll need to attach the writing to the layer you want it done on.

If you run into trouble with your Cricut machine identifying the cut sensor marks, there could be a few things causing the issue. Too much direct light or too bright light directed at the Cricut can impede the sensors. The material may not be in the right position on the mat. It should be placed in the top left-hand corner and be completely smooth. The cutting mat might not be inserted perfectly into position. If there are smudges or other marks on the mat near the cut sensor marks, it may affect the machine's ability to read them. If the design wasn't printed on white paper, the color or pattern of the paper might be impeding the sensors. Glossy paper can also affect it. Make sure there are no other marks on the material around the cut marks. If you're still having problems, check the cut sensor light for dust or debris. You can gently wipe it clean with a small dry paintbrush. Print then Cut is only compatible with inkjet printers because laser printers melt the toner to bind it to the paper, affecting the paper itself so that the sensor can't read the marks.

Cricut Pens

Cricut Pens and the Cricut Pen Adapter allow the Cricut to create designs that are not cut but drawn on to the material. These pens are non-toxic, acid-free, and are permanent. Cricut Pens come in a variety of colors and textures but can get somewhat expensive. More fiscally conscious crafters need to know that some Sharpie brand pens and markers can be used with the Cricut Cutter machine without damaging it. Some crafters do prefer the Cricut brand pens as they can come in more sizes and tip varieties than Sharpies. Cricut Pens can be a fine tip, medium tip, calligraphy tip, metallic, glitter, and just normal black pen. Regardless of the project, there is a pen out there that will be perfect for it. It is also important to note that if you are using the Cricut Design Space you must specify that you are writing and not cutting. To do this go to the panel on the right side and change the scissors icon to the write icon, then you're ready to cut.

Chapter 3: Design Space Software Secrets and the Design Space App

The "Weld," "Contour," and "Slice" functionalities:

These three tools will be activated at the bottom of the screen for designs that allow for these changes.

The "Weld" tool will allow you to merge two different designs to obtain one composite design, without any leftover seams and cut lines that might be present on the individual designs. It helps you in obtaining a single continuous cut for your design, so you do not need to glue and assemble multiple pieces to obtain the final design, for example, the creation of cake toppers, gift tags, and other decorations.

The "Contour" tool can be used to activate or deactivate any cut lines in any cut files, and thereby, allowing you to customize the image in various ways. So, imagine you have an image of a flower. You want to remove the details of the design and obtain more of an outline of the flower. You can do so by clicking on the "Contour" button at the bottom of the screen and selecting the different elements of the image that you want to turn on or off from the contour pop-up window.

The "Slice" tool can be used to slice a design from an image by cutting out or removing elements of the image, as shown in the picture below.

Use your search keywords wisely. The search functionality within the "Design Space" is not very dynamic, so your choice of keywords will make a big difference in the designs and projects that will be displayed to you. For example, if you search for images containing dotted designs and search with the keyword "Dots," you would be given around 120 images, but if you search with the term "Dot," you would see almost twice as many images. You should also search with synonyms and closely related terms of your target project idea. For instance, if you wanted to create a Halloween project, you can search with terms like pumpkin, costumes, and trick or treat, among others. It will ensure you are viewing any images of your project.

A treasure trove of free fonts and images. As a beginner, you would want to utilize a large number of free fonts and images to get your hands-on experience with your "Cricut" device. It is a great way to spend less money and still be able to create stunning craft projects. Within the "Design Space" application, you can click on the "Filter" icon next to the search bar (available within the images, fonts, and project tabs) and select "Free" to only view free resources within each category.

Use synchronized colors to save time and money. It is a great tool when you have designs that are either a composite of multiple images or inherently contain different hues of the same color. Instead of using five different shades of the same color, you can synchronize the colors, so you need to use only one colored sheet. To do this, simply click on the "Color Sync" tab on the "Layers Panel" on the top right corner of the screen. Then drag and drop the desired layer(s) of the design to your target color layer, and the moved layer will immediately be modified to have the same color as the target color.

Use the "Hide" tool to cut images from the Canvas selectively. When you are looking to turn your imagination into a work of art, you may want to view and take inspiration from multiple images while you work on your design. But once you obtain your desired design, you would not want to cut every other image on your canvas. It is where the "Hide" tool comes in handy, so you do not need to delete the images on the Canvas to avoid cutting them along with your project design. To hide the image, you just need to click on the "eye" symbol next to those specific image layers on the "Layers Panel." The hidden images will not be deleted from the Canvas but would not appear on the cutting mat when you click the "Make It" button to cut your project.

Ability to Change the Design Lines to be Cut, Scored, or Drawn.

With the latest version of the "Design Space" application, you can simply change the "Linotype" of design from its predefined type to your desired action, instead of looking for designs that have a predefined line type meeting your project need. For example, if your selected design is set at "Linotype" Cut, but you want the design to be "Linotype" Score, you can easily change the "Linotype" by clicking on the "Linotype" drop-down and making your selection.

You can Utilize the "Slice" Tool to Crop the Image.

The "Design Space" application still lacks the "Crop" functionality, so if you need to crop an image, you will need to get creative. A good tip is to use the "Slice" tool along with the "Shapes" to get your desired image.

Change the Position of the Design on the Cutting Mat.

When you are ready to cut your design and click on the "Make It" button, you will notice that your design will be aligned on the top left corner of the mat. Now, if you are using a material that was cut at its top left corner, you can simply drag and move the image on the "Design Space" mat to meet the positioning of your cutting material. You will be able to cut the image anywhere on the mat by moving the design to that specific position on the mat.

Moving Design from one Mat to the Other.

Yes! You can not only move the design over the mat itself, but you can also move the design from one mat to another by simply clicking on the three dots (…) on top of the mat and select "Move to another mat." You will then view a pop-up window where you can select from the existing mats for your project to be used as the new mat for your selected design.

You can Store the most Frequently Used Cut Materials on the "Cricut Maker."

Unlike the "Cricut Explore" series which has dial settings for a variety of commonly used cut materials, the "Cricut Maker" requires you to use a "Custom Materials" menu within the "Design Space" application that can be accessed using the button on the machine bearing "Cricut" logo, since there is no dial to choose the material you want to cut.

Choose to Repeat the Cut of the Same Mat or Skip a Mat from Being Cut Altogether.

By following the instructions on the "Design Space" and feeding the right color and size of the material to the machine, you will be able to get your design perfectly cut. You can change the order in which the mats are cut, repeat the cut of your desired mat, and even skip cutting a mat if needed. You can do this easily by simply clicking on and selecting the mat you would like to cut.

Adjust the Pressure with which the Material can be Cut.

You may want just to adjust the pressure with which the cut is made to obtain a clean and neat cut of the material, without needing to go through the process described above to adjust the cut setting of the material. On the cut screen, once you have selected the cut material, a drop-down option with the "Default" setting will be displayed.

Simply click on the drop-down button and adjust the pressure to "More" or "Less."

"Cricut Access Membership" – \

At a monthly fee of around $8 or an annual membership fee, you will be able to use a wider variety of fonts and images for free. You will be able to use more than 30K images, over 370 fonts freely, and thousands of projects, saving a lot of money in the long run, depending on your usage.

Best Projects You Can Do with Cricut Maker,

In case you're attempting to extend your innovativeness for utilizing the Cricut Maker, there are numerous tasks that you can take on with unlimited potential outcomes.

There are numerous extraordinary things about the Cricut creator machine that will make you need to utilize it to an ever-increasing extent.

Even though there's a wide assortment of undertakings, utilizing your creative mind for DIY activities will demonstrate that you have an imaginative mind and sharp eyes to use this machine.

Fabric

Blankets

The Cricut group has been making propels in bettering its design quality for blanket making.

Cricut has cooperated with Riley Blake Designs to give crafters a wide assortment of sewing designs inside the example library.

You can precisely remove the correct examples for sewing and make the ideal blanket easily.

Felt Dolls and Soft Toys

You might need to make toys without anyone else as a DIY. The Cricut producer effectively enables you to cut examples for delicate felt dolls and fragile toys. Aren't these two above unbelievably sweet!?

Infant Clothes

The Cricut Maker can slice boards up to 12 X 24. So, while it will be dubious about making grown-up garments with it, it is extraordinary for making infant dress.

Make and slice designs, so you can make child shirts, onesies, shirts and that's only the tip of the iceberg.

Doll Clothes

Since you're going to make dolls with the Cricut Maker, you can make them adorable little doll equips that will make them look increasingly one of a kind.

Make a multicolor doll dress that will make your Cricut dolls stand apart among your locally acquired dolls.

Texture Christmas Projects (Ornaments and Christmas Stockings)

Utilizing the Cricut Maker will make cutting texture for making decorations and Christmas leggings a breeze. This machine is ideal for designing unique texture adornments or potentially leggings.

The machine has an example library that you can use to mix various looks of Christmas or occasion improvements. Primarily utilize the machine to remove your example and after that sew it together.

Stick Cushions

It's conceivable you will do a ton of sewing with the Cricut Maker. As you get the majority of your lovely designs cut out, you're going to require a sticky pad to hold every one of your pins.

There are diverse stick pad designs in the example library. As it is, you can get imaginative and make your unique ones as well.

Pads and Cushions

Since the machine trims 12 X 24 estimated designs, you can make bunches of various pads and pads for your bed, chairs, lounge chairs, and niches. You can make a few incredible designs to tidy up your home.

Remember that you can remove iron-on vinyl on your producer as well, so why not take your pad design to the following level.

Glass

Raised Letters

Make a treat container or a personalized vessel to hold pretty much anything. It would be an extraordinary blessing thought for an educator, mother, father, or companion. Utilize a single word or a platitude to express your affections for the beneficiary. All you need is a compartment, a paste firearm or some raised letter-formed stickers, and some splash paint. Visit the Lettered Cottage to perceive how charming and straightforward this venture is.

Carved Drinking Glasses

You don't have to realize how to draw for this task, and you need to brush on some carving dissolvable. Particularly decent is the way that these are launderable, not only for looks. Perceive how to make these by visiting A Beautiful Mess.

Vintage String Holders

It is an ideal method to shield string balls from getting all hitched up. What's more, they are so adorable! It would seem that they're sucking up a long string of spaghetti. An incredible undertaking for children, as well. Locate the instructional exercise at Handmade Charlotte.

Sewn Jar Cover

Shirt yarn is utilized to make these stitched spreads that resemble little sweaters. You can undoubtedly make your shirt yarn using any old or undesirable shirts that you have. The stitch example is found at LVLY. It's an easy task thus charming with the additional lace.

Snowman Luminary

This little snowman looks cold with his soft snow finish. Put a battery-worked light inside, and it sparkles! Safe to utilize anyplace in the house or hold tight to the tree. Go to Club Chica Circle for the instructional exercise to make this winter light. Keep in mind, and the snowman is proper throughout the entire winter.

Pumpkin Jack-o-Lanterns

It is conceivable to think about pumpkin or a jack-o-light as being "exquisite," at that point that is the thing that I'd call this design. In case you're searching for an option in contrast to cutting pumpkins this year, consider this specialty venture for your Halloween party. Locate the instructional exercise at Chica Circle.

Tissue Decoupage Bottles

Would you like to include a touch of shading without a ton of cost? These tissue paper decoupage jugs will consist of the hues that you need in your stylistic theme with almost no time. You'll locate the instructional exercise at Crafting a Green World. So straightforward and easy, yet a lovely expansion to any room!

Hanging Mason jar Pendant Light

Okay, accept this is an upcycled old restroom vanity light strip? If you cherish this, you can locate a utilized vanity light strip at a carport deal, swap meets. Or second-hand shops and make your very own effectively. The directions are found at remodelaholic.

Turkey Jar

In addition to the fact that this is little turkey a social improvement, it can likewise hold confections, or nuts as a cute gift. Locate the instructional exercise at About Family Crafts.

Penny Lanterns

Here's an extraordinary thought for utilizing a portion of the pennies you no uncertainty have gathered in a heap someplace since it's a lot of issues conveying them with you. These little lights are appealing. Discover the guidelines at DIY Showoff.

Ocean Glass Votive

Make a rich votive by following the instructional exercise given at a Pumpkin and a Princess. A few of these ocean glass votives in various shapes and sizes would be stunning. If you don't have ocean glass, consider utilizing shells.

Wind Chimes

You'll locate the instructional exercise at Saved by Love Creations. Any globules may be utilized here, alongside old neckbands or bits of metal.

Blessing Purse

It must be so lovely to give a blessing. Think about all the little endowments that would be made significantly increasingly insightful in this sort of wrapping. Discover the guidelines at In My Style.

Group Lights

You can consider going to Home Talk for the instructional exercise. It would be an incredible expansion to a yard or patio. I can even envision it utilized as a Christmas adornment by including an occasion shaded strip and greenery.

Town Silhouette

It is such a straightforward however excellent thought for a Christmas focal point. It truly makes you incline that you're taking a gander at Christmas' past. Locate the instructional exercise at Shabby Art Boutique.

Exquisite Cloche

Change any old compartment into a minor ringer container to grandstand any gathering. Get more instructions on the most proficient method to make a cloche.

Container of Fireflies

Make getting fireflies overly easy by amassing this holder of artificial flickering bugs. Shine in obscurity paint, and a few catches give you the appearance of fireflies without the pursuing. Locate the instructional exercise at By Stephanie Lynn.

Paper-Based Cricut Projects

<u>Fruity Tray</u>

Supplies:

An octagonal tray, crealia coral, light yellow, white, and leaf green decorative paints.

One or two flat brushes

A pencil

A 10cm paper disc and brown

Black and glitter green poscas

Polish glue to varnish spray and masking tape.

Steps:

Draw disks on your board and paint them green (mix leaf green with light yellow) it will be necessary to make 2 layers. After drying, make yellow ovals in the center (light yellow and white) and paint in two coats too. All this can be done using a Cricut template

Trace the outlines of the discs in brown. Draw the green lines (see photo) in the green area and then the pips. Apply a spray varnish to prevent the posca from drooling in the glue varnish in the next step.

Stick the stickers with the varnish glue at the bottom of the tray. After drying, apply a little varnish in spray to prevent the ink of the stickers from dissolving in contact with the resin.

Using a glue gun, attach the small wooden fruit decorations.

Craft Paper Pencil Holder

Supplies:

Imitation leather kraft paper braiding tape - 9.5 cm

Self-healing cutting mat - 60x45 cm

Transparent ruler for creative hobbies 40 cm

Scissors

Mini high-temperature glue gun

Pencil

Salvaged cardboard, glass, and jar or compass

Steps

Take a glass and a jar with different diameters. Trace the outlines of the circles on recycled cardboard. Cut with a cutter. In addition to this, you need to know more about it.

Glue the cardboard discs together with the glue gun. Cut strips of kraft paper braiding 20 cm long. Glue them one by one in radiation. Superimpose them slightly at the base: the bands must be an edge to edge at the circumference of the cardboard disc. In addition to this, you need to know more about it.

Cover the larger cardboard disc in this way. Glue with a glue gun. Fold the braiding strips, then measure the circumference of the cardboard disc and cut 5 braiding strips of this size. In addition to this, you need to know more about it.

Slide a strip of braiding perpendicular under one of those welded to the cardboard base. Stick one end to it, as close as possible to the base. Pass it alternately under one vertical strip and over the next one. Attach a dot of glue to the glue gun under a few vertical stripes.

To close, glue the second end of the strip under the first end. In the same way, slip the second strip of braiding, mount a second row, tightening to avoid gaping spaces.

Set up the braiding of the pot with 5 strips in all. Fold a base strip towards the inside of the pot. Mark the fold in the pot to mark the length. Cut off the excess. In addition to this, you need to know more about it.

Cut a strip of braiding a little larger than the circumference of the pot. Glue to the top edge of the pot with a glue gun. Fold the strips one by one towards the inside of the pot. Glue them with a glue gun. R with a glue gun.9. The pot is ready to accommodate the pencils in your office.

Magnet Alphabet Fun with Iron-On Mosaic Squares

Materials

Cricut chipboard

Cricut holographic art deco permanent vinyl— this project uses red and green

Purple StrongGrip mat

Cricut Knife Blade

Weeding tool

Scraping tool or brayer tool

Pair of scissors for cutting the material to size

Hot glue gun

52 magnets 1" by 1" in size

Builder's tape

Directions:

Open a new project in Design Space.

Select 'Square' from the 'Shapes' menu on the left-hand side.

Change the background color to grey.

Unlock the shape and change it to 11" wide and 11" long.

Zoom the screen to 50%.

Select 'Text' from the menu on the left-hand side.

Choose a nice font that is clear for children like 'Arial Black.'

Type out the alphabet in capital letters.

Unlock the text and change the height dimension to 2".

Change the width dimension to 22".

Select the uppercase letters, and from the top menu, click on the little down arrow beneath the 'Advanced' menu option.

Choose 'Ungroup to letters.'

You will notice that all the letters now have their own cut layer on the right-hand side.

Starting from A, choose all the second letters of the alphabet and move them into the large grey square.

Once they have all been moved, select them and change the color to red.

Select the remaining letters and change the color to gold.

You can do the same for lowercase letters if you wish. For the sake of this project, there will only be the uppercase letters.

Move and delete the large grey square.

Save the project.

Click 'Make it.'

Design Space automatically puts the text onto two separate cutting sheets.

Select cut number 1 and position the text into 2 or more rows to ensure they are well spaced out.

Do the same for the second cut sheet.

When you have the letters correctly lined up for cutting, press 'Continue.'

Place the wooden board onto the purple cutting mat.

Take the red vinyl and cut it to the size of the wood.

Pull off the back of the vinyl sheet.

Place transfer tape over the vinyl sheet, smoothing it down with the scraping tool.

Apply the vinyl to the Cricut chipboard square and use the brayer or scraping tool to ensure it transfers correctly onto the chipboard.

Slowly pull the transfer tape from the back of the vinyl.

Carefully cover the corners of the wooden block with builder's tape to ensure the wood sticks to the purple cutting mat.

Change the Cricut blade to the knife blade.

Change the Cricut dial to the custom setting.

Move the star wheels to the right-hand side of the feeding bar.

Load the cutting sheet into the Cricut.

In Design Space, choose the correct materials and press 'Continue.'

When the Cricut is ready to cut, press 'Go.'

It will take a bit of time to cut the wooden cutouts.

When it is done with the first one, repeat the steps from 25 to 36 but use the green vinyl.

While the Cricut is cutting out the second wood sheet of letters, remove the letters from the excess clipboard and clean them up using the weeder, knife, and tweezers.

Glue the magnets onto the backs of each letter. Use 2 per letter, placing them strategically onto the wood.

When they are done, they will make a lovely gift.

Birth Announcement Card

Supplies/

The assortment of Parisian ties "newborn girl"

An assortment of 80 Parisian ties - Pink

Alphabet Glitter uppercase - Pink

25 Pollen folded cards 135x135 mm - White

Mahé sheet 30.5 x 30.5 cm white

Mahé sheet 30.5 x 30.5 cm pale pink

Tube of universal gel glue - Cultura - 30 ml

Precision cutter and 3 blades

Self-healing cutting mat - 30x22 cm

An assortment of 3 precision tools

Transparent ruler for creative hobbies 30 cm

Template to download and print

Steps:

To start, download, print, and reproduce the heart template. Hollow out the pattern using the cutter to create a stencil.

Cut an 11 x 11 cm pink square and a 10.5 x 10.5 cm white square.

Center the stencil on the square of white paper and secure it with adhesive paper, to prevent it from moving.

Place a few Parisian ties to guide you in their positioning, inside the cutout heart.

Using a precision cutter or paper punch, pierce your card and insert the Parisian clips.

Once the heart is filled, glue the white part on the rose.

Finish by pasting the desired text (first name ...) to finalize the card.

The invitation is ready.

Cloud Shelf

Supplies:

Créalia "Clouds" wooden shelf

Acrylic tube 120 matt white

3u7m, bkjFlat synthetic brush n ° 18

Straight scissors - 17 cm

Transparent ruler for creative hobbies 30 cm

Precision cutter and 3 blades

Self-healing cutting mat - 45x35 cm

Cardboard Stickers - Baby

Extra strong double-sided adhesive tape - 6mm x 10m

Steps

Paint the cloud shelf white. Let dry.

Download and transfer the templates to different papers from the collection and compose the decoration.

Glue the cut papers on the cloud shelf using the extra-strong double-sided tape.

Personalize the shelf with stickers from the collection.

Tip: the 30 x 30 cm block of paper offers visuals to frame to decorate your child's room or make scrapbooking albums.

The cloud shelf is ready to decorate your child's room

DIY Bookmark Cat-page!

Supplies:

block of 20 multi-colored cartoline sheets

Glue

Pouch of 24 decorated colored pencils

6 round movable eyes Ø 12mm

PERFO ROUND CLAMP 6MM

5m roll of Glitter masking tape - Green

5m roll of Glitter masking tape - White

Steps

Print the template and choose its paper colors.

Cut out the template along the lines.

Copy the drawing of the body, front legs, and back legs on the brown sheet, do the same in the purple sheet for the belly and cut out.

Glue the elements together with glue.

To facilitate the gluing put a little glue in a cardboard plate and use a brush to spread the glue well. Then clean the brush with warm water and soap.

Glue the movable eyes, glue a piece of masking tape to make the collar, cut a piece of pink paper in a triangle for the nose, and with a black pencil draw the mouth, mustaches, and legs.

With the hole punch, make a small circle in the yellow paper and glue it to finalize the cat's collar.

To get an easy triangle nose, first cut out a square and cut it in half diagonally.

Write your name on the cat's belly with a colored pencil.

And there you have a nice cat-page bookmark for your summer readings. I'm going to reread the adventures of the little wizard and what will you read?

You can even do it in other colors so that it isn't boring!

<u>Table Decoration</u>

Supplies:

Set of 6 Scrapbooking paper sheets - Tropical Paradise

Mahé Leaf - 30.5x30.5cm - petrol blue.

Mahé Leaf - 30.5x30.5cm - menthol green

Mahé Leaf - 30.5x30.5cm - lime green

Mahé Leaf - 30.5x30.5cm - spring green

Slate scrapbooking sheet - Mahé - 30x30cm

Sheet of 34 epoxy stickers - Tropical Paradise

8 cardstock polaroid frames - Tropical Paradise

Assortment of 40 die-cuts - Tropical Paradise

100m two-tone spool - Sky blue

16 mini clothespins 35 mm

Vivaldi smooth sheet A4 240g - Canson - white n ° 1

Precision cutter and 3 blades

Blue cutting mat - 2mm - A3

Black acrylic and aluminum ruler 30cm

Precision scissors 13.5cm blue bi-material rings

3D adhesive squares

Mahé Tools - Easy Mounter - scrapbooking

Pack of 6 HB graphite pencils

Steps

Gather the materials.

Using the template and a pencil, reproduce the palm tree on the papers in the collection.

Download and print the template here.

Cut out with a cutter or scissors.

Assemble the trunk of the palm tree. Glue the foliage. Using the template, reproduce the traces of the cocktail support on thin cardboard, following the dimensions indicated. Cover it with the collection paper.

Download and print the template here.

After having cut in the slate sheet: 1 x (8.5 x 8.5 cm). Choose a Polaroid. Glue the slate sheet to the back of the Polaroid. Using a chalk pen, write "Cocktail of the day". Decorate with the stickers. Fold the support at the dotted lines.

Using the templates and a pencil, draw the leaves and flowers on the Mahé paper and the collection paper. Draw.

Download and print the leaf and flower template.

Choose photos. Cut them to size: 8.5 x 8.5 cm. Stick to the back of the Polaroids.

Glue the leaves and flowers together. Cut the string to the desired dimensions and glue it to the back of the flowers. Glue the birds on the string and hang the photos using mini clips.

 And here is a pretty summer and tropical decoration! Beautiful evenings in perspective!

Clothespin Card

Supplies:

Clothespin

Glue

Painting

Color paper or illustrations to download

Decorations: eyes, sequins

Steps:

Start by painting your clothespins.

Cut out the illustrations or your colored paper in a heart shape.

Come and cut your shape in half in the middle.

Apply glue to the ends of your clothespin.

And stick your heart or your butterfly on your clothespin.

We now add glue to the back of your clothespin to be able to place the small text "I love you".

You can also add small decorations to further customize your clothespin. Your laundry card is ready!

Easter Special Containment

Supplies:

Rolls of toilet paper,

Colored sheets,

Markers and glue

Steps:

Cut the height measurements from your roll and glue by wrapping this paper around. With white glue or whatever you have at home.

Hold the paper with pins so that it sticks.

Then make a template to make ears that we transfer to a paper and that we cut.

With another paper, cut out the inside of the ears and glue them.

Now, we have to make eyes.... either you have moving eyes or you do them yourself like me... For that, we make circles by hand or with perforators.

Glue the eyes and ears.

Make bunny papattes, cut them, and glue them.

Draw the nose and whiskers with a felt tip pen.

Now we're going to make the paper chick ...

Cut 2 rectangles in the paper here 6x14 and 6x12

Staple the papers together to make rolls. And superimpose them as below.

Cut out some feet, glue them and your chicks are ready!!!

Dog Tags

Materials

Cricut aluminum

Purple StrongGrip mat

Engraving tip (this fits on the scoring tool)

Builder's tape

Jewelry ring

Directions:

Open a new project in Design Space.

Select 'Square' from the 'Shapes' menu on the left-hand side menu.

Change the background color to grey.

Unlock the shape and change it to 8" wide and 8" long.

Select 'Square' from the 'Shapes' menu on the left-hand side.

Leave the background as it is.

Unlock the shape and change it to 4.056" wide and 2" long.

Select 'Circle' from the 'Shapes' menu on the left-hand side.

Leave the background as it is.

Unlock the shape and change it to 0.516" wide and 0.516" long.

Duplicate the circle.

Unlock the duplicate circle and change its dimensions to 0.316" wide and 0.316" long.

Position the smaller second circle over the first one directly in the middle.

Right-click and select 'Slice.'

Select the circle, then remove and delete the two slices.

Move the circle with the hole in it to sit on the top edge of the small square. Place it in the middle touching the edge of the square.

Select the smaller square and the circle, right-click, and select 'Weld.'

Select 'Heart' from the 'Shapes' menu on the left-hand side.

Leave the background as it is.

Unlock the shape and change it to 2.378" wide and 2.504" long.

Rotate the heart until the rounded, curved side points to the right and the point of the heart points to the left of the screen.

Position it on the right end of the smaller square about halfway to the middle of the heart.

Duplicate the heart and move the duplicate heart to one side.

Select the smaller square and heart, right-click, and select 'Weld.'

Flip the duplicate heart horizontally so it mirrors the welded heart.

Repeat steps 22 to 24.

Move the dog bone onto the larger grey square.

Select 'Text' from the menu on the left-hand side.

Choose a font and type the dog's name on it. If you like, you can type a phone number, etc.

Duplicate the dog bone tag as you can fit two of these tags onto one metal sheet.

Change the text on the second dog bone shape.

Remove and delete the larger grey square.

Save project.

Click 'Make it.'

Put the engraver point on the rotary blade and place it into the Cricut machine.

Move the star wheels to the right side of the feeding bar.

Set the dial on the Cricut to custom.

Stick the metal onto the StrongGrip mat.

Stick the metal plate down with builder's tape around the edges so it is firmly attached.

Load the mat into the Cricut.

In Design Space, select the correct material and make sure the design lines up with the metal on the cutting mat.

Press 'Continue' and 'Go' on the Cricut when it is ready to cut.

Note that it does take quite a while to do the engraving.

When the Cricut is finished cutting, remove the metal from the cutting mat.

Pop the tags away from the excess metal and use the weeding tool as well as the tweezers to clean up the designs.

Place a jewelry ring through the top little loops on top of the dog tags, and they are ready to attach to the dog's collar.

Boat Garland

Supplies:

Marine origami papers 70 g / m², Clairefontaine

8mm wooden beads, Créalia

Two-tone blue and white twine, Toga

A folder

A paper piercer

A needle with a large eye

A cutter

A pair of scissors

Steps

Fold the different squares as shown in the small boat construction diagram below. At each step, remember to use a folder to facilitate folding and not to tear the paper

Using the paper punch, pierce the small boats at their tops.

Cut 1m of two-colored strings. Make a loop 50cm from the wire so that it is in the middle.

97

Using the needle, thread alternately a bead and then a small boat (from the smallest to the largest). Each element must be blocked with a small double knot. Finish with a double knot below the last boat and cut the excess thread that protrudes.

All you have to do is hang your garland!

Chapter 4: Maintenance of the Cricut Machine

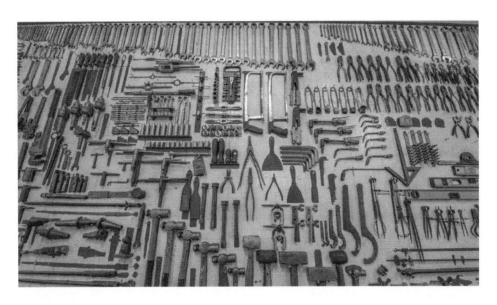

The Cricut Cutter machine needs to be kept intact in a variety of ways: the blade must be replaced, the cutting mats must be taken care of, and the machine, in general, must be kept clean.

Cutting Blade

Every single blade you use might get up to fifteen thousand individual cuts before it needs to be replaced. To prolong this number of individual cuts, place the aluminum foil onto the cutting mat and cut out a few designs. This process keeps the blade extra sharp and lengthens the life of the blade. This number of cuts can be greatly based on what types of materials that have been cut by the blade. If you are doing many projects in which thick materials need to be cut the blade will deteriorate quickly; the blade can also deteriorate quickly if you are cutting many materials on high pressure. A good way to know if your blade needs to be replaced is if the quality of your cuts starts to greatly decrease. If this happens it's best to replace the cutting blade. When replacing the blade, it is always best to get blades that are the Cricut brand. Generic blades are often not the best quality and will cause you to constantly replace your cutting blade.

To install the new blade once you've ordered the correct one, you need to first unplug your Cricut Cutter machine. Always unplug the machine before installing anything in your Cricut cutter. Next, you must remove the old, dull cutting blade from your Cricut Cutter machine. The process of how to do this has been mentioned numerous times in this book and the last chapter. Once the cutting blade assembly has been separated it is now time to eject the blade. Find the small silver button above the adjustment knob and press the button down; this will eject the cutting blade. Be very, very careful when doing this as the blade is extremely sharp and can easily cut through the skin. Keep all blades away from children and pets. To put in the new blade, insert the blade on the end of the blade assembly opposite of the blade release button. The blade will then be pulled up into the assembly.

Cutting Mat

The Cutting mat in addition to the cutting blade needs to be taken care of. One cutting mat can have a life of anywhere from twenty-five to forty cuts. The life of the cutting mat can vary from this amount depending on the pressure and speed at which the cuts have been made and the type of materials that have been cut on the mat. To prolong the life of your cutting mat, remove any debris from the mat after a cut and always avoid scraping the mat. If you scrape the mat, it can push any debris further into the mat. After each craft, it is best to run lukewarm water over the mat and dab it dry with a towel afterward. When a material cannot adhere to the cutting mat any longer then it is time to finally replace the mat. It is recommended to get many cutting mats and rotate between them to prolong the life of all the cutting mats. This extends the life of the mats because one cutting mat will not be cut on for many, many projects in a small amount of time. It is also recommended that you keep all of your cutting mats and all of your cartridges and blades in a very organized manner. Throwing the components haphazardly can destroy and deteriorate them so it is best to keep them in a very organized fashion. A benefit of keeping your Cricut Cutter components organized is you won't lose or damage the very expensive items that are necessary for several projects.

How to Clean a Cricut Mat

Sometimes it also depends on the materials you use that make your machine dirty. For example, using felt means you'd need to grab stray pieces using tweezers. Another great way to clean your Cricut machine is to use a lint roller across the entire machine to pick up debris, scrap vinyl, and pieces of felt. You can also use this roller on your mats.

To clean your mats, if there is any leftover residue on your mats, the general rule is to use bleach and alcohol-free baby wipes to gently wipe the mat clean and remove it from grime, glue, and dust. You can also get yourself GOO GONE. Spray this on your mat and let it sit for 15 minutes, then use a scraper tool to remove the adhesive. But do this only if your mat is very dirty. Otherwise, wet wipes will do.

Another tip to keep your mats clean is by putting a protective cover back over them when you are not using them.

Cleaning the Cricut Machine

The final thing to keep clean is the actual Cricut Cutter machine. The machine needs to be wiped down with a damp cloth. Only wipe down the external panels of the machine and with the machine unplugged. Always wipe down the machine with a dry cloth after cleaning the outside of the machine. Never clean the Cricut Cutter machine with abrasive cleaners such as acetone, benzene, and all other alcohol-based cleaners. Abrasive cleaning tools should never be used on the Cricut Cutter machine either. Also, never submerge any component of the machine or the Cricut Cutter machine into the water as it can damage the machine. Always keep the Cricut Cutter machine away from all foods, liquids, pets, and children. Keep the Cricut Cutter machine in a very dry and dust-free environment. Finally, do not put the Cricut Cutter machine in excessive heat, excessive cold, sunlight, or any area where the plastic or any other components on the Cricut Cutter machine can melt.

Maintaining Cricut

If you want your Cricut Machine to last for a very long time, you have to maintain it routinely. This means cleaning it properly and also maintaining the cutting mats and blades. When using your Cricut machine, over time, it will inevitably collect paper particles, dust, and debris. Also, grease in the device will begin to stick to the carriage track.

If you want your machine to last long, then you should clean it regularly, or else it can get damaged prematurely. Here are some cleaning tips to help you out when cleaning the machine.

Before cleaning your machine, disconnect it from the power outlet. This will prevent electrocution or any other accident that can damage the device or injure you.

When cleaning your machine, don't use any form of acetone. Acetone, like nail polish remover, will damage the plastic parts of the device permanently.

You can clean the machine using a glass cleaner instead. Spray it on a clean, soft cloth and wipe the device gently.

In the case of grease buildup on the carriage tracks, then you should use a tissue, cotton swab, or a soft, clean cloth to wipe it off gently.

There is also the case of a buildup of static electricity on your machine. This can cause dust, debris, and particles to form on the device. This can also be easily cleaned with a soft, clean cloth.

Application of Grease for the Cricut Explore Models

Disconnect the Cricut machine from the power outlet.

Push the Cut Smart carriage gently to the left.

Wipe the entire Cut Smart carriage bar with a tissue. The bar is the surface in front of the belt where the carriage slides on.

Push the Cut Smart Carriage Gently to the Right.

Repeat the cleaning process for the other side by cleaning the bar with a clean tissue.

Then, push the Cut Smart carriage to the center of the bar.

Take a lubrication packet, open it, and squeeze out a little grease. Put the amount of grease on a clean cotton swab.

Apply a small coating of the grease on the two sides of the Cut Smart carriage around the bar so that it will form a quarter-inch ring on both sides.

To make the grease become even in the carriage, push the Cut Smart carriage to both sides slowly and repeatedly.

Clean off any grease that stained the bar while you were greasing the machine.

You can purchase a grease packet from Cricut. This will work better than using a third-party grease packet so that the machine will not get damaged. This is especially if, after using another grease product, your Cricut machine is making a grinding sound.

This process is almost the same as greasing your Cricut Maker machine too.

Maintaining the Cricut Cutting Mat

You also have to clean and maintain your Cricut cutting mat because that is where the cutting takes place.

If the cutting mat isn't clean, it can stain the machine. Also, if your cutting mat has stopped sticking, it can spoil your designs and creations.

When your mat is no longer sticky because of debris and grime, cleaning it and making it sticky again will bring it back to life.

The solutions that I will mention are not ideal for the pink cutting mats, only for the green, blue, and purple.

Using Baby Wipes:

Make use of alcohol-free, unscented, and bleach-free baby wipes to clean your mat. You should use the plainest baby wipes that you can find so that you don't add lotions, cornstarch, solvents, or oils to your cutting mat. If not, you could affect the stickiness and adhesive of the mat. Also, after cleaning it, let it dry completely before using it.

Using a Sticky Lint Roller

You can also use a roll of masking tape if you don't find a sticky lint roller. Run the roll across the mat to get rid of hairs, fibers, specks of dust, and paper particles.

This form of cleaning can be done daily or between projects so that dust doesn't accumulate on the mat. This is a fast way to remove dirt apart from using tweezers or scrapers.

Using Warm Water with Soap

You can also clean the mat with soap and warm water. You should use the plainest soap possible too so that you don't mess with the mat. Use a clean cloth, sponge, soft brush, or a magic eraser. Also, rinse it thoroughly and don't use it until it is completely dry.

Using an Adhesive Remover

In the case of heavy-duty cleaning, then you should use a reliable adhesive remover to clean it properly. When using an adhesive remover, read the directions properly before you start.

Then, spray a little amount on the mat and spread it around with a scraper or anything that can act as a makeshift scraper.

Wait for a few minutes so that the solvent can work on the mat. Then, scrape the dirty adhesive off your mat with a scraper, paper towels, or cloth.

After this, wash the mat with warm water and soap in case there is leftover residue and let it dry properly.

How to Make Your Cutting Mat Sticky Again

After washing or cleaning your cutting mat, you have to make them sticky again.

The most advisable way to make your mat sticky again is by adding glue to it. Get a solid glue stick like the Zig 2-Way Glue Pen and apply it on the inner portion of the mat. Then, stroke the glue around the mat and ensure that there is no glue residue on the edges of the mat.

After about 30 minutes, the glue will turn clear. If the cutting mat turns out to be too sticky after you apply glue, you can use a piece of fabric to reduce the adhesive by pressing the material on the parts of the mat that are very sticky.

Cover the mat with a clear film cover after a few hours.

You can also use tacky glues or spray adhesives that are ideal for cutting mats.

Maintaining the Cricut Cutting Blade

You can use your Cricut fine point blade for over a year if you maintain it properly! The same goes for the other types of cutting blades. When maintaining your Cricut cutting blade, you have to keep it sharp all the time so that it does not get worn out.

Keeping your blade sharp is essential because if it isn't, it can damage your materials, and cause wastage. Also, if you don't maintain your blades, you will have to replace them often.

Keeping Your Cutting Blade Sharp

Spread a portion of aluminum foil on a cutting mat. Without removing the blade from the housing, cut out a simple design in the foil. This will sharpen the blade and remove any paper particles, or vinyl stuck on the blade. This can be used for any type of cutting blade.

In the case of heavy-duty cleaning, you should squeeze a sheet of aluminum foil into a ball. You need to remove the blade from the housing of the machine to use this method. Then, depress the plunger, take the blade and stick it into the ball of aluminum foil repeatedly. You can do this 50 times. This will make it sharper and also remove vinyl or paper particles on the blade.

How to Store Your Cutting Blade

The best way to store your cutting blade is to leave it in the Cricut compartment. You can place it in the drop-down door that is in front of the machine. That compartment is meant for storing the blade.

As for the blade housing, you can place it on the raised plastic points at the back of the machine. There are magnets in the front of the machine where you can stick loose blades.

When you put your blades in the Cricut machine, you never lose your blades.

Tips and Tricks to Make Cricut Easier and Efficient

Subscribe to Cricut Access

If you want to get a full range of use out of both your Cricut Explore machine as well as the Cricut Maker machine, we would recommend you subscribe to Cricut Access right away. There are two options for payment. This works out to be slightly cheaper on a month to month basis. This will give you access to thousands of different predesigned projects as well as Cricut Access exclusive fonts, that you would otherwise have to pay to use. If you are planning to use your Cricut a lot, this will save you a lot of money as opposed to buying every project an image individually. We can all agree it is a lot easier to pay one flat rate instead of having to figure out how much you are spending on projects.

De-tack Your Cutting Mat

The Circuit Explore machine will come with a green 12"x12" Standard grip cutting mat. The Cricut Maker machine will come with a blue light grip mat. As you already know, you will place your cutting material onto this mat before inserting it into the machine to cut. As you will come to find out, the green cutting mat is extremely sticky when it is brand new.

Keep Your Cutting Mat Covers

The cutting mats that you purchase for your projects will always come brand new with a plastic protecting sheet over it. You will want to keep this plastic cover as long as you have the mat.

Cleaning the Cricut Cutting Mat

It is very important to keep your cutting mat clean for it to remain sticky and be available for use over and over. Ideally, you would want to clean the mat every time after use if not at least every couple uses would suffice. All you will have to do is simply wiping down a clean mat with baby wipes to keep it clean.

Adhere Your Materials to Your Mats with Painter's or Masking Tape

You will find that, as your Cricut mats age, they will slowly lose their grip. Before completely giving up on your mat and throwing it out, considering lining the edges of your project with painter's tape or with masking tape. This will hold your materials in place while they're being cut and will save you the expense of a new mat for some time.

Command Hooks from 3M to Hang Your Cutting Mats When Not in Use

Utilizing your wall space for storage can be invaluable when you're storing something delicate and prone to bending, like your Cricut craft mat. Using Command hooks will ensure that your walls won't be damaged by the adhesive and your mats will always be within arm's reach and will never be hidden from you with this method!

Keep the Clear Plastic Sheet That Comes with Your Cricut Mats

When you buy a fresh Cricut mat, you will notice a semi-rigid sheet of plastic that comes stuck to the grip. After you complete each project, re-adhere this sheet to the front of your mat before hanging them up or putting them away! This will keep the grip from getting ruined by dust, hair, rogue glitter, or animal fur in the air!

Take Care of Your Mat

Many mats have met their ends in my care, and there are multiple reasons for this. If the material won't stick to it, the paper, vinyl, and others will all move around while the blade is trying to cut through, and it will end in a disaster.

Try Different Markers

Don't feel limited by the Cricut markers. That's right! When you are using your Cricut machine to write or draw on your project, any marker that will fit will work perfectly. Not only are there cheaper options but the colors and variety of styles are virtually endless. Don't let anyone tell you that you can only use the markers from the Cricut brand. Even though they are of better quality and made for the machine, you are not limited to using them. Just make sure your markers fit.

Double-Check the Settings

Just like the testers, this is annoying, but you have to make sure that all of your settings are correct and that you have selected the right material option. If you are not using the Cricut Design Space, this is easy to forget. When you utilize the software, there is a broad selection of tools to choose from. However, when you are only using a cartridge, the materials are limited. Still, regardless of which set-up you wish to handle the design, you should check your settings twice.

Keep Your Blades in a Good Condition

Preferably, get one for every material that you are going to cut. In the list of materials that are available to add to your Cricut purchase, you may see different kinds of blades available. A dull blade is never a good thing, and it will ruin your project as easily as a sharp one will cut it perfectly.

Cut Slits in the Edges of Your Transfer Tape

If you're transferring a decal onto something round, like a cup or mug, you will find it much easier to lay the decal flat if you cut intermittent slits in the transfer tape. You will find these cuts down on its reusability, but you will get more even, less bubbly designs on your products, more reliably.

Reverse Weeding

This is a technique that is best used on designs that have a lot of intricate or delicate letters or lines. The way it is done is, once you've run your vinyl through your Cricut machine, adhere the transfer tape to the front of that vinyl piece. Burnish it with your scraper tool, and then remove the carrier sheet or backing from the vinyl.

Leave Your Explore on Custom

On the Explore models of the Cricut, you will find that you need to specify what type of material your machine is cutting. This tells the machine how hard it needs to work to get those precise cuts for you. It is a very common problem among the Cricut community, to leave your machine in the wrong setting, forget to change it, and have a project that doesn't come out exactly as you expected because of it. The solution for this is a simple habit!

If you're not a fan of leaving your machine on "Custom," or you can't seem to get that habit down, make a reminder to stick on the side of your machine that will tell you to check your settings for each job! This could be a Cricut project in itself, making a vinyl cling for the side of your machine so you never forget again. Don't forget to cut slits in the edges of your transfer tape for those curved edges!

Remove Your Transfer Tape at an Angle

Removing your transfer tape at an angle can help to eliminate and minimize bubbling under your vinyl designs. How you do this is by peeling up one corner of your transfer tape and pulling diagonally, toward the opposite corner. When using this method, you can also use your XL Scraper to keep your letters down, as described in one of the tips above. This will help keep your letters on even ground when negative pressure is applied while removing the transfer tape!

Don't Remove Your Design from the Mat before Weeding

A common practice among new crafters is to remove the vinyl from the Cricut mat before starting the weeding process. However, weeding on the mat is far easier. With the grip from the mat keeping your project firmly in place, it's like having an extra set of hands when doing the hardest part of your project! Don't underestimate the power of your mat!

Chapter 5: Tips for Solving Cricut Design Space Problems

When we try to use something and things just continuously go wrong, we tend to lose interest and move onto the next thing in our lives. When technology gives us problems, we just abandon it because we don't know what to do about it. We don't know how to fix it so we just move on with our lives. Personally, calling someone for help is too much effort and quite frankly, I am too proud of it. So, I just suffer from my pride and do things on my own. But, luckily for people like me, some tips and tricks can be tried in these situations. Of course, many things can go wrong with your machine. It's electronic, of course, it will malfunction from time to time. Here are a few things that I have learned by dealing with these issues myself.

The Machine Doesn't Cut Through the Material

Check your blades to make sure that they are blunt. That is usually the reason why this happens.

Your pressure might be too low. To fix this, simply go to your Manage Custom Materials page on your account menu in Design Space. Try increasing the pressure by 2 and do a test cut. If this doesn't work, increase the pressure 4-6 times, doing test cuts every time.

You can try cutting a different material. Remember to adjust the setting to accommodate the new material and cut. If it works, then the problem is with your material, not the machine.

If all of these options fail, you might want to call the customer care line.

The Blade Isn't Detected

In Design Space, you will see that it recommends a blade in the Load tools step. This is on the Preview screen. Make sure that you have installed the right tool. When I don't have the right tool, I just unload the mat, select the Edit Tools option in the project preview screen, and select a different tool. This usually does the trick. Remember to use B-clamp.

You also have to make sure that the tool sensor is clean. Be very gentle about this and use a microfiber cloth. Any form of dust build-up can cause issues so best keep it squeaky clean all the time instead of struggling with it when you want to start projects.

The Machine Turns Off Unexpectedly

This usually happens when you cut metals or foil. The reason for this happening is that there is a buildup of static electricity. Dry environments can also cause this, so don't worry too much about this.

To solve this issue, you can spray some mist into the air to humidify it. Do not, under any circumstances, spray it directly onto the Cricut machine. When I go to a particularly dry area with my Cricut, I like to have a humidifier handy. This is very, very useful and it might be worth investing in if your machine continues to give you this problem.

Slow Internet Connection

Without saying much, you must understand that a slow internet connection is one of the main causes of Design Space problems. Poor internet connection translates into problems for the software because it requires consistent download and upload speeds to function optimally.

Several websites only require good download speeds e.g. YouTube, thus users on these sites can do away with slow upload speeds. However, unlike those sites, Cricut Design Space requires good upload and download speeds to function optimally because users are constantly sending and receiving information as they progress with their designs.

If you're using a modem, you're likely to have a more stable connection if you move closer to it.

Chapter 6: Best Software to Use

Design Space

Design Space is for any Explore machine with a high-speed, broadband Internet connection that is connected to a computer or an iOS device. This more advanced software allows full creative control for users with Cricut machines.

Craft Room

Some machines, such as the Explore and Explore Air, cannot use the Craft Room, but many other models can. Craft Room users also have access to a free digital cartridge, which offers images that all Cricut machines can cut.

New

New means that you will start a new project, and clicking the tab will redirect you to a blank canvas. Be sure to save all changes on your current project before you go to the new canvas. Otherwise, you will lose all of the progress you have already made on that design.

Templates

Clicking on Templates will allow you to set a template to help you visualize and work with sizing. It is very handy for someone who is not familiar with Cricut Design Space and doesn't know what sizes to set. If you are cutting out wearable items on fabric, you can change the size of the template to fit whoever will be wearing it. I'm sure you can agree that this feature is especially beneficial for the seamstresses out there.

Projects

Projects, meanwhile, will lead you to the ready-to-make projects so that you can start cutting right away. Some of the projects are not customizable, but others are when you open the template, which is pretty cool. Many of these are not free either, which irks me to a new extent. You can choose the "Free for Cricut (whatever machine you have)", and the projects that will turn up won't have to be paid for.

Upload

When you click the Upload tab, you can upload your images and transform them into cuttable pieces. This, along with the text, is the only reason why I still use Design Space. It is awesome to be able to use this feature.

Cricut Basic

This is a program or software designed to help the new user get an easy start on designing new crafts and DIY projects. This system will help you with image selection to cutting with the least amount of time spent in the design stages. You can locate your image, pre-set the projector font, and immediately print, cut, score, and align with tools that are found within the program. You can use this program on the iOS 7.1.2 or later systems as well as iPad and several of the iPhones from the Mini to the 5th generation iPod touch. Since it is also a cloud-based service, you can start in one device and finish it from another.

Sure Cuts a Lot

This is another third-party software that has a funny name which gives you the ability to take control of your designs without some of the limitations that can happen when using cartridges used within the Cricut DesignStudio. You will need to install an update to your software to use this program; you can download it for free. It allows for the use of TrueType and OpenType font formats as well as simple drawing and editing tools. You can import any file format and then convert it to the one that you need. There is an option for blackouts and shadows.

Cricut DesignStudio

This program allows you to connect with your software and provides you with much more functionality as far as shapes and fonts are concerned. There are various options for tools that provide you resources for designing more creative images. You will be able to flip, rotate, weld, or slant the images and fonts. However, you will still be limited in the amounts or types of fonts that you can use based on the ones on the cartridges. There is a higher level of software features that allow for customization.

Cricut Sync

This is a program designed for updating the Cricut Expression 2 as well as the Imagine machine and the Gypsy device. You just connect your system to the computer and run the synced program for an installation of updates on the features that come with your machine. This is also used to troubleshoot any issues that could arise from the hardware.

Make the Cut

This is a third-party program that works with the Cricut design software. It offers a straightforward look at the design features that Cricut has. This system can convert a raster image into a vector so that you can cut it. There is also a great way to do lattice tools. It uses many file formats and TrueType fonts. There are advanced tools for editing and an interface that is easy to learn and use. This system works with Craft ROBO, Gazelle, Silhouette, Wishblade, and others. It allows you to import any file from a TTF, OTF, PDF, GSD, and so on and convert them to JPG, SVG, PDF, and so on. It is flexible and user-friendly.

How to Make a Business with Your Cricut Machine?

Selling Pre-cut Customized Vinyl

As we have mentioned earlier, vinyl is a super beginner-friendly material to work with and comes in a variety of colors and patterns to add to its great reputation. You can create customized labels for glass containers and canisters to help anyone looking to organize their pantry. Explore the online trends and adjust the labels. Once you have your labels designed, the easiest approach is to set up an "Etsy" shop, which is free and very easy to use. It's almost like opening an Amazon prime membership account. If your design is in demand, you will have people ordering even with no advertising. But if you would like to keep the tempo high, then advertise your "Etsy" listing on "Pinterest" and other social media platforms. This is a sure-shot way to generate more traffic to your "Etsy" shop and turn potential customers into paying customers. An important note here is the pictures being used on your listing. You cannot use any of the stock images from the "Design Space" application and must use your pictures that match the product you are selling.

Selling Finished Pieces

You would be using your "Cricut" machines for a variety of personal projects like home décor, holiday décor, personalized clothing, and more. Next time you embark on another one of your creative journeys leading to unique creations, just make two of everything, and you can easily put the other product to sell on your "Etsy" shop. Another great advantage is that you will be able to save all your projects on the "Design Space" application for future use, so if one of your projects goes viral, you can easily buy the supplies and turn them into money-making offerings. This way, not only your original idea for personal usage will be paid off, but you can make much more money than you invested in it, to begin with.

Again, spend some time researching what kind of designs and decorations are trending in the market and use them to spark up inspiration for your next project. Some of the current market trends include customized cake and cupcake toppers and watercolor designs that can be framed as fancy wall decorations. The cake toppers can be made with cardstock, which is another beginner-friendly material, light in weight, and can be economically shipped tucked inside an envelope.

Personalized Clothing and Accessories

T-shirts with cool designs and phrases are all the rage right now. Just follow a similar approach to selling vinyl and take it up a notch. You can create sample clothing with iron-on design and market it with "can be customized further at no extra charge" or "transfer the design on your own clothing" to get traction in the market. You can buy sling bags and customize them with unique designs to be sold as finished products at a higher price than a plain boring sling bag.

Consider creating a line of products with a centralized theme like the DC Marvel characters or the "Harry Potter" movies and design custom t-shirts, hats, and even bodysuits for babies. You can create customized party favor boxes and gift bags at the request of the customer. Once your product has a dedicated customer base, you can get project ideas from them directly and quote them a price for your work. Isn't that great?!?!

Marketing on Social Media

We are all aware of how social media has become a marketing platform for not only established corporations, but also small businesses and budding entrepreneurs. Simply add hashtags like for sale, product, selling, free shipping, the sample included, and more to entice potential buyers. Join "Facebook" community pages and groups for handcraft sellers and buyers to market your products. Use catchy phrases like customization available at no extra cost or free returns if not satisfied when posting the products on these pages as well as your personal "Facebook" page. Use "Twitter" to share feedback from your satisfied customers to widen your customer base.

Another tip here is to post pictures of anything and everything you have created using "Cricut" machines, even those that you did not plan to sell. You never know who else might need something that you deemed unsellable. Since you will be creating these only after the order has been placed, you can easily gather the required supplies after the fact and get crafting.

Target Local Farmer's Market and Boutiques

If you like the thrill of a show-and-tell, then reserve a booth at a local farmer's market and show up with some ready to sell crafts. In this case, you are relying on the number of people attending and a subset of those who might be interested in purchasing from you. If you are in an urban neighborhood where people are keenly interested in unique art designs but do not have the time to create them on their own, you can easily make big bucks by setting a decent price point for your products.

One downside to participating in local events is the generation of mass inventory and booth displays, topped with expenses to load and transport the inventory. You may or may not be able to sell all of the inventory depending on the size of the event, but as I said earlier, you can still make the most of this by marketing your products and building up a local clientele.

Conclusion

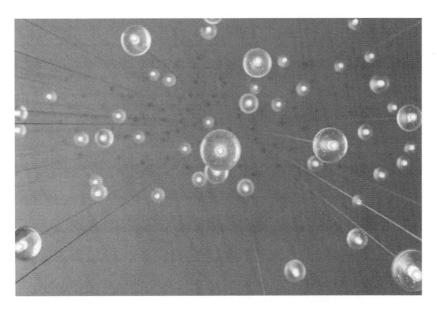

Thank you for making it to the end. Cricut maker is the handicraft enthusiast's best buddy, or for anyone who'd love to design and create. It supplies over 250 distinct designs in many sizes. The designs could be bigger compared to an inch or larger around one inch. The different cutting angles offer precision decrease - all of this together with templates that are attractive collectively with interlocking alphabets, provide considerably to select from.

Since Cricut machines are using skilled cutting equipment, no specifics are too detailed. Cut the most sophisticated shape, add ink with a "handwritten" note or score a pop-up card expertly. With the unrivaled precision of Cricut, every piece will always be exactly what you want. Cricut Basics makes a pleasure bringing together the pieces. From tweezers which handle delicate parts for foolproof iron-on to Cricut Easy Press, each essential makes a great project even bigger, every step of the way. This book is well articulated with amazing ideas of DIY crafts that can be made using Cricut.

Life can be great really! People also feel that the usage of a Cricut cutting procedure is simply restricted to the subject of scrapbooking. Just a few people know that the Cricut machine in addition to the cartridges along with the software tools might be used to find a significant selection of items. You will encounter a whole lot of Cricut projects it's very likely to utilize the Cricut cutting platform for and just your mind can limit what you could do.

Bear in mind, just your creativity can restrict what you do. These Cricut jobs may be used either for individual satisfaction or revenue-generating functions. Be imaginative with your favorite machine. You never know what crazy and angry ideas can pop into your own

As you gain more experience using the computer and try new features, you can solve almost all of these problems.

The next step is to find projects and materials that excite you and dive right in! It would be great to see you embrace the vast number of crafting opportunities that now lie ahead of you.

There is no imaginable limit to all the incredible things you can achieve with the powerful tools that you are going to use to create your next craft. These tools are versatile, and, with this combined with your creative ideas, there is no limit to what you can achieve.

Thank you!

CRICUT PROJECT IDEAS

A Sensational Step-by-step Guide to Craft Out Great and Amazing

Project Ideas for Cricut Maker, Cricut Explore Air 2 and Cricut Design Space.

369 Tips & Tricks for Beginners.

Introduction

Perhaps you've just purchased your first Cricut® or you've had one for some time but haven't tried it out yet, or you are fairly skilled but aren't sure how to use the Design Space. This book will teach you everything you need to know about using Cricut Design Space™ like a pro.

Some Cricut users have mastered the machine and they can make vinyl letters look as if they were painted onto the wood. The vinyl meshes so well that with the naked eye you won't be able to find a spot to lift one of the vinyl letters. That's how realistic it can look. And most vinyl is also weather-resistant. That means you can make all kinds of awesome things for outside use as well as inside.

Cricut has come so far since the days of die-cutting for scrapbooking, and although scrapbooking is still popular, you don't see as many sheets of stickers in stores, and in some stores, the scrapbooking section has shrunk since Cricut has become so much more than your scrapbooking partner.

If you are using a desktop computer, or a laptop you can select a Project Category from the drop-down menu located on the upper side of the screen, or if you know what you want, you can type what you need in the search bar.

There are plenty of decorations you can make using these machines, whether it's for Christmas, Halloween, or other seasonal-themed decorations. Perhaps you are looking for something more permanent, like unique hanging planters. For this one, you will need the Cricut Explore Air or Maker, a deep cut blade, a standard grip mat, chipboard, foam brushes, a glue gun, Deco Art Acrylic paint, sea glass, light masking tape and leather cording. Plus, you will need a plant (artificial one is better in this case), and a wire (but this is optional). If you choose the live plant, you will need a plastic recipient for soil and some small white gravel stones.

Whatever you desire you can make with a Cricut machine!

Chapter 1: What is a Cricut Machine?

A Cricut machine is a cutting machine. It has the unique functionality of being able to cut different materials which you will need for your crafts and DIY projects. Some of these materials include paper, vinyl, and even materials as thick as wood. Cricut machines are also dependent on their connection with your devices like mobile phones and computers.

Cricut machines are a very fun tool to make use of because they allow you to create art from materials you may not have known existed. They allow your creativity to take flight because with the use of Cricut machines, you are able to create new materials to aid your work, and these materials you create may not be found otherwise.

In a nutshell, you create designs and templates using the device which your machine is connected to (the phone or computer system). These designs are preloaded into the device which your Cricut is connected to, and you have full control of any changes or modifications with these designs. These designs are what you pre-load into the Cricut and make use of them to cut/print the material you are looking to print, just the way you want it to be.

When it comes to how a Cricut works, there are a lot to be learned about it, but having access to your own Cricut machine is like opening yourself up to a whole new world. There is literally no limit to the amount of awesome crafts you can make with the use of the Cricut machine.

The Latest Cricut Machines

The current Cricut machines for 2020 are listed below. They are compatible with most of the materials and tools of the previously released Cricut models.

Design Space is compatible and works with all the current Cricut machines.

Cricut Joy

The Cricut Joy is the latest addition to the Cricut family. It is a compact machine that can create larger-than-life crafting projects.

This little machine is designed to be used without a cutting mat which makes it able to produce cuts repeated for up to 20 feet in length. It can also cut a single design up to 4 feet. This makes it an excellent little machine to cut longer projects.

However, it does need to use some of its own accessories that are designed specifically for the machine due to its compact size. This means you will not be able to use the standard Cricut pens and some blades from the larger machines.

The little Cricut Joy is the best machine for children, beginners, scrapbookers, and greeting card makers. It can whip up small projects in no time and as it is so small, it is portable too.

The Cricut Joy can actually cut over 50 different material types. To make your life easier with the Cricut Joy, Cricut has designed "Smart Materials" for use with this mighty little machine. These Smart Materials do not need a cutting mat and as such, can be loaded directly into the cutting machine without the hassle of a cutting mat.

It should be noted though, that the Cricut Joy is not a commercial-grade cutter and it does require quite a few bits and bobs to get it going. Although the Cricut Joy can draw, emboss, do score lines, and cut, you can only do one function at a time. This means you will have to change tools a few times if you are cutting, drawing, and doing score lines in the same project.

Cricut Joy Dimensions and Weight

Dimensions = 5.5" x 8.40" x 4.25"

Weight = 3.85 lbs

Cricut Joy Color Options

The Cricut Joy only comes in Teal with White trim

What Comes with the Cricut Joy?

When you buy the Cricut Joy, it will come boxed with the following items:

The Cricut Joy Cutting Machine

Power adaptor for the Cricut Joy Cutting Machine

An all-purpose FinePoint cutting blade

The pre-installed Cricut blade housing

Standard grip 4.5" x 4.5" mat (green)

Cricut Joy Fine Point Pen (0.4mm) in Black

2 Sample materials; deluxe adhesive-backed paper and Smart Material vinyl

30-Day free Cricut Access trial membership

50 Projects that are ready to make and easily accessible online

Price

The price is approx. $ 180

Cricut Maker

The Cricut Maker is the ultimate machine of the Cricut family. It can do everything the other Cricut machines can plus a whole lot more. It is not an entry-level machine and, as it has commercial grade cutting machine functionality, it is made for serious crafters.

Cricut Maker Dimensions and Weight

Dimensions = 22.6" x 7.1" x 6.2"

Weight = 24 lbs

Cricut Maker Color Options

Blue

Champagne

Lilac

Mint

Rose

What Comes with the Cricut Maker?

When you buy the Cricut Maker it will come boxed with the following items:

Cricut Maker Cutting machine in the selected color

Rotary blade and drive housing for the blade

Premium Fine Point blade plus the drive housing for the blade.

Cricut Fine Point pen in black

1 FabricGrip mat (pink mat)

1 LightGrip mat (blue mat)

Sample materials; fabric and cardstock

30-Day free Cricut Access trial membership

25 Free sewing patterns

25 Free projects that are ready to make and easily accessible online

Price

The price is approx. $ 400

Cricut Explore Air 2

The Cricut Explore Air is one of Cricut's most popular cutting machines. It is the choice of many due to its fantastic capabilities, cutting quality, and the amount of material it can cut. Explore Air 2 has superseded the Explore Air, bringing with it all of the amazing features of its predecessor plus much more. The Explore Air 2 also works twice as fast as the Explore Air without compromising its precision cutting abilities.

Explore Air 2 Dimensions and Weight

Dimensions = 24" x 9.5" x 9.5"

Weight = 16 lbs

Explore Air 2 Color Options

Pink

Minty green

Baby blue

What Comes with the Cricut Air 2?

When you buy the Cricut Air 2 it will come boxed with the following items:

Cricut Explore Air 2 cutting machine in the color ordered

Getting started booklet

Power cord

USB Cable

Premium Fine Point blade and housing unit

Accessory adapter

1 Cricut Pen

1 Cricut StandardGrip cutting mat (green) — 12" x 12"

Sample cardstock cutting paper

Over 100 free images to use with projects

Over 50 ready-made free projects

Price

The price is approx. $ 250

Cricut Cuttlebug (discontinued)

The Cricut Cuttlebug is a small hand-operated machine that was designed to emboss. It is great for projects that need to have some texture to them. It is also a safe, easy machine for supervised children to learn on and is a great companion machine for scrapbookers. It was discontinued but can still be found in select stores.

Cuttlebug Dimensions and Weight

Dimensions = 16.10" x 3.69" x 7.3"

Weight = 5.25 lbs

Cuttlebug Color Options

Limited Blue edition with white trim

Green with white trim

Mint with white trim

What Comes with the Cricut Cuttlebug?

When you buy the Cricut Cuttlebug, it will come boxed with the following items:

The Cuttlebug cutting machine

User manual

1 A plate which is the spacer

2 B plates which are the cutting pads

1 6" x 8" Rubber embossing mat that is 0.09" thick

1 Simple flower embossing folder

Price

The price is approx. $ 150

Cricut EasyPress 2

The Cricut EasyPress 2 brings all the ease of its predecessor, the Cricut EasyPress, but it heats up twice as fast and reaches higher temperatures. The Cricut EasyPress is a very handy machine to have and can complement your crafts, especially if you are using heat transfers. These machines have thicker base plates than a normal iron does, so they tend to distribute weight more evenly.

Cricut EasyPress 2 Dimensions and Weight

There are 3 different sizes of Cricut EasyPress 2 machines available:

The larger press can be used for bigger projects like blankets, towels, banners, and so on.

Dimensions = 12" x 10"

Weight = 8.6 lbs

Cricut EasyPress 2 Color Options

Raspberry with white trim only.

What Comes with the EasyPress 2?

When you buy the Cricut EasyPress 2 it will come boxed with the following items:

EasyPress 2 machine in the size ordered

Safety base

Practice materials

Welcome booklet

Price

The price is approx. $ 200

Cricut EasyPress Mini

The Cricut EasyPress Mini is small, durable, easy to use, safe, and gets into those little places that the EasyPress 2 cannot. This little iron press is better than an iron for crafting materials and is not very expensive.

EasyPress Mini Dimensions and Weight

Dimensions = 3.25" x 1.92"

Weight = 0.8 lbs

EasyPress Mini Color Options

Raspberry with a white trim

What Comes with the Cricut EasyPress Mini?

When you buy the Cricut EasyPress Mini, it will come boxed with the following items:

Cricut EasyPress Mini

Protective heat base stand

Let's get started booklet

Price

The price is approx. $ 50

Materials to use

Adhesive Cardstock

Adhesive Foil

Adhesive Vinyl

Adhesive Wood

Aluminum Foil

Aluminum Sheets

Balsa Wood

Birch Wood

Burlap

Canvas

Cardboard

Cardstock

Chalkboard Vinyl

Chipboard

Construction Paper

Contact Paper

Copy Paper

Corkboard

Corrugated Paper

Cotton Fabric

Craft Foam

Craft Paper

Freezer Paper

Glitter Cardstock

Glitter Foam

Glitter Iron-On

Glitter Paper

Glitter Vinyl

Glossy Iron-On

Glossy Vinyl

Holographic Iron-On

Holographic Vinyl

Silk

Solid Core Cardstock

Stencil Material

Stencil Vinyl

Wool Felt

Wrapping Paper

Tools and Cricut Access

Cutting mats – Cricut offers a variety pack that has a 12 x 12 of the Light Grip Mat, Standard Grip Mat, and Strong Grip Mat, which are perfect to get started and complete most of the projects in this book.

Self-healing mat – Rather than a mat that goes into the machines, this is a mat you can cut on. Cricut has precision cutting bundles that include these mats and a precision blade.

Blades (Explore machines) – The Cricut Explore machines come with a fine-point blade, which you may need a replacement for after a long time of cutting. Also consider the Deep Point Blade, which is made for cutting magnet sheets, chipboard, rubber, thick cardstock, stiffened felt, foam sheets, and cardboard.

Blades (Maker machine) – The Cricut Maker comes with a premium fine-point blade and a rotary blade, which you may need replacements for after a long time of cutting. Also consider the Knife Blade, which can cut thicker materials such as balsa wood, basswood, leather, chipboard, matboard, and craft foam.

Essentials Tool Set – Cricut's essential set contains tweezers, a weeder, scissors, a spatula, a scraper, a scoring stylus, a paper trimmer, a replacement blade for the trimmer, and a scoring blade for the trimmer. This is a great starter set and will get you creating most projects. It even comes in different colors!

Cricut Pens – Cricut produces specialized pens that fit into the machines. They come in dozens of colors, finishes, and nib sizes.

Storage – Cricut sells rolling craft totes to carry supplies and accessories and machine totes for the Cricut machines themselves.

Cricut BrightPad – This is a light pad that makes it easier to weed your projects. The surface illuminates with a bright but diffused light. You can lay your projects on top of it to see where exactly you need to weed. It can also work well for tracing, paper-piecing quilt patterns, and jewelry making.

Chapter 2: Setting up your Cricut Machine on Design Space

On the Explore Air machines, you will find an "open" button that you can press and the whole machine will open up to expose its insides where the mat will go and where the settings will be. On the Cricut Maker, you will not find that button, instead you will find a little slot where your finger will fit. Merely lift the top lid and the bottom of the machine will drop wide open. Now, make sure that you remove the packaging innards from the machine. Do not leave anything inside because it can be harmful to your machine when you are trying to make something. You will see two slots. One is labeled "A" and will be empty. This is your accessory slot where you will be able to put your markers and so on. Next to it you will see another slot where the blades go. It is marked "B."

Mac/Windows

Once you have all of your parts and accessories set up and your machine is powered on, it is time to do the technical setup. This is fairly easy and not at all complicated. Here is how you set up your machine correctly and easily.

Connect your machine to your desktop or laptop. Turn on the Bluetooth on your computer and connect to your machine. You will instantly recognize the name of your Cricut machine so don't worry too much about that. Once you are paired, you are ready to move on to the next step.

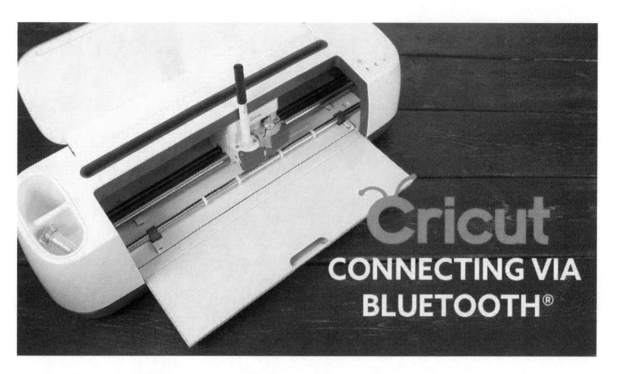

This will take you to a page where you will receive instructions to sign in with your premade Cricut account if you have one or create a new one.

Sign in with your Cricut ID

Use your Cricut ID for everything you do with Cricut

Email / Cricut ID

Password

Enter your password

Forgot?

☑ Remember me

Don't have an account yet?

Create A Cricut ID

Follow the steps to do either and this will take you to the next page where the next step will be explained.

On this page, download and install the Design Space plugin. You will automatically be prompted.

If not, reconnect your Cricut and reload the browser until it does. If you have an app blocking this, you might want to deactivate it for this purpose.

The setup will run itself and you will know that it is complete when you are prompted with a new page. This will tell you to create your first project.

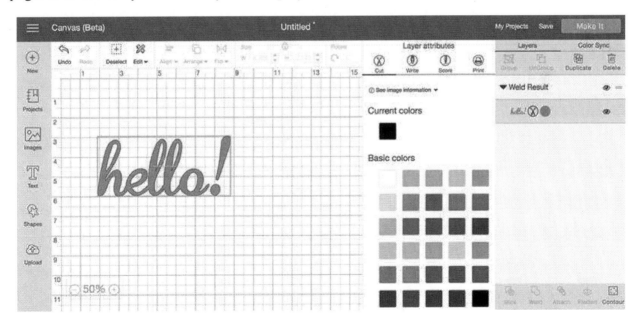

There you have it; your setup is done and dusted.

IOS/Android

Just like before, you can plug in your machine and power it up.

In the same way that you paired your desktop to your machine, you are going to pair your mobile and Cricut machine. Simply pair your two devices with Bluetooth and you are golden.

Now, you want to download the Design Space app from the App Store on iOS and Google Play on Android.

Once you have it downloaded, you are going to launch the app and log in using your Cricut ID. If you do not have one yet, you will be prompted to create one.

Welcome to Cricut Design Space®

New Machine Setup

Connect your Cricut
machine to the app.

App Overview

Get a quick overview
of key features.

Sign in

Sign in with Cricut ID.

Now, select the option called "Machine Setup App Overview." Once there, select "New Machine Setup."

The prompts will be easy and simple for you to follow, so do that and your machine will be set up to use from your mobile phone in no time. Like setting it up on your desktop, you will know that your machine was successfully set up when you are prompted to make your first project.

Why get the Design Space

The Cricut Design Space is an integral part of the creation process and you will need for a range of different things, especially the more complicated projects you will soon be an extra in. For example, it lets you combine pictures from several capsules (packs) you've got and combine them into a single layout. It is also possible to organize your layout before you put it to a cartridge. It allows you to perform actions like weld letters collectively, shrink or enlarge images, specify a photograph on a diagonal, then extend, rotate, or remove. Perhaps you want to stop and save your layout before it is finished, then return later to complete it. At any moment you've got the layout just how you need it; you can begin creating. When your Cricut reaches the point where it requires a different capsule, then it will alert you so that you could swap the capsules. When you complete a project, you can save your layout in your personal computer or flash drive and share it or get feedback from your friends or other Cricut enthusiasts.

Another benefit of Design Space is it's possible to check every accessible layout in the whole Cricut library, even if you happen to have obtained the cartridge or not. Just type in keywords to look for a specific picture or phrase, and you're in a position to ascertain just how it may appear in your endeavors. This will allow you to decide if you want to obtain a specific cartridge or maybe not. You might also preplan your style and store it till you are ready to proceed with the project.

Tips to help you start

You Can Customize Make It Now Projects

When you are initially getting started in Design Space, the level of choice and options can feel a bit overwhelming. It is often best to start with a "make it now" task that has already been designed and guides through the process. This way you won't have to discover everything all at once.

Of course you can still customize a Make It Now project. Click on the image of the project you intend to make. It will open up and reveal the materials you need and also instructions.

You Can Find Even More Ready-Made Projects in The New Cricut Community

If you like the idea of projects that are already created, you may wish to have a look around the community of Design Space. Did you know that you can create a profile and share your developments? It's a reasonably brand-new feature that users have enjoyed immensely. They know are able to see what various other Cricut users do and what they create. They work just like the Make It Now projects, yet they are made by Cricut individuals instead of Cricut itself.

Know How to Read the Images

When looking for photos, there are a number of things you may wish to look at. If the image is included in the Cricut Access registration it will have a little eco-friendly banner and an "an" in the top left corner. Near the bottom in the left edge is the rate, or it will say "bought" if you have actually previously acquired it.

Contour to Hide Parts of an Image.

If there is an image that has parts in it that you don't desire, you can erase them! The shape feature enables you to get rid of and cut (or create) lines from a picture.

Modification Project Copies # Instead of Copy as well as Paste.

There might be times you need a lot of one photo or more than one whole task cut. You can duplicate as well as paste, however, the easiest means to make more than one of something is to make use of the "project copies" feature instead.

As soon as you have your photo or job ready, proceed and send it to cut. In the leading left edge, you can enter in the amount of the job you want, and it will instantly place that number on the cutting floor covering.

Move as well as Hide Images on Cutting Screen.

In some cases, relocating a cut will assist you conserve much more materials, or you may want to conceal a picture, so it won't reduce. Once you get to the cut display, you can rearrange images, move them from one floor covering to another and even conceal them.

Chapter 3: Cricut Projects with Synthetic Leather

Fancy Leather Bookmark

Materials

Cricut metallic leather

Cricut holographic iron-on

Purple StrongGrip mat

Cricut Fine-Point Blade

Weeding tool

Pair of scissors for cutting the material to size

Brayer, or scraping tool

Cricut Knife Blade

Thin gold string, or ribbon

Swing design

Directions

Cut the leather to the size you want it to be.

Each leather holder is approximately 2' wide by 6' high.

Cut the holographic paper to the size you want it to be this will depend on the size of the font and the wording you choose for the bookmark.

Create a new project in Design Space.

Select 'Shapes' from the left-hand menu.

Choose the square, unlock it, and set the width to 2' with a height of 6'.

Choose a triangle from the 'Shapes' menu and set the width to 1.982' and the height to 1.931'.

Position the triangle in the rectangle at the bottom. Make sure it is positioned evenly, as this is going to create a swallowtail for the bookmark.

Select the circle from the shapes menu and unlock the shape. Set the width and height to 0.181'.

Duplicate the circle shape.

Move the one circle to the top right-hand corner of the bookmark, and the other to the left. These will be the holes to put a piece of ribbon or fancy string through.

Align the holes and distribute them evenly by using the 'Align' function from the top menu, with both circles selected.

Select the top left hole with the top of the rectangle and click 'Slice' in the bottom right menu.

Select the circle and 'Remove' it, then 'Delete' it.

Select the top right circle with the top of the rectangle and click 'Slice' from the bottom right menu.

Create a 'New Project' in Design Space and choose a nice fancy font. Do not make it any bigger than 1.5' wide and 3' high.

'Save' the project.

Click on 'Make It' and choose the correct material.

Now you are ready to iron on your design.

Your bookmark is now ready to use or give as a personalized gift.

Pendant with Monogram

Materials:

Necklace chain

Jewelry pliers

Cricut gold pen

Cricut Explore Air 2

Cricut strong mat grip

Cricut faux leather

Jump ring

Fabric fusion

Instructions

Start by opening the Cricut Design Space. Choose the size that you want the pendant to be. This can be a circle pendant. Using the machine, make another circular-sized pendant.

Attach the jump ring here later after the circles have been made.

Next, open the text section in the Design shop and type in the exact initials that you would like to use.

Select the section that has a writing style option from the menu and adjust the font of the lettering to whatever you wish.

Drag your letter to the center part of the circle and resize it to fit the appropriate size.

Be sure to make a front and a back. This will ensure both sides of the piece look like leather.

Create your circle so that it matches the other one minus the letter.

Make this an attached set.

Using the Cricut pen, begin to cut the pieces. As it is cutting the leather, it will print the initials.

Use your fabric fusion glue to join the two pieces of leather together making the pendant.

Using the pliers for jewelry, you can twist on the ring for the necklace.

Attach your pendant and jump ring together and then string it onto the chain.

The pliers can close the jump ring off.

Feather Earrings with Faux Leather

Materials:

Fabric fusion

Paintbrush

Washi tape

Metallic paint

Cricut Explore Air

Cricut faux leather

Cricut standard cutting mat

A hole puncher

Additional supplies needed:

Jewelry pliers

Jump ring

Chain

Additional earring supplies:

Earring findings

Jewelry pliers

Instructions:

Follow these directions to complete the craft project:

Use the cut file for the jewelry that you would like to cut for the pattern. Cut two pieces for each piece of jewelry.

Make sure that you have two pieces per item so that you can glue them together. This makes them look like leather on both sides.

Mirror the pieces so they match.

Using your washi tape, mark off a section that is the top half of the faux leather piece. Press this tape firmly in place so that you can prevent the leakage of the paint.

Paint the end that you would like to be painted. After it is painted, let it completely dry. Repeat for the other pieces that you are painting.

Once it is dried out, remove your washi tape.

Now, use the fabric to fuse together the two pieces of each mate. These pieces should flawlessly fit together. Use the directions on the bottle to adhere these pieces together.

Using a strong needle or a micro puncher, make a hole that is small but big enough to attach the hardware.

Use the pliers to open the jump ring and then loop it into the earrings. Attach the jewelry to the earring pieces or the necklace pieces.

Leather Cuff Bracelet

Materials:

A small piece of leather

A bracelet or piece of chain or cord, and small jump rings

Needle-nose pliers for jewelry

Deep cut blade for the Cricut Explore

Instructions:

Your first step is to choose the design image that you would like to use on your leather bracelet. This can be found inside the *'Image Files'* under Lace, or any other design file that you already have.

Next, verify that the sizing is appropriate for a bracelet by cutting it on paper. You definitely do not want to cut the leather the wrong way. This would waste the materials.

Once the size is perfect, you are able to begin your project.

Place the leather on the mat with the smooth side down and push the *'Cut'* button.

After the leather piece is cut, you will need to adjust your chain, or rope to the appropriate size that is needed for the wrist of the person that it will be fitting.

Connect the leather to the chain with the jump rings.

Attaching the links to the leather is perfectly fine, but it may tear the leather, so using the jump rings is a great alternative.

Leather Foil Gift Tag Keychains

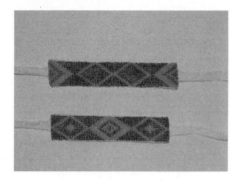

Materials:

Cricut Iron-on Foil in rose gold

Cricut EasyPress 2 Small

Cricut EasyPress Mat

Cricut Bright Pad

Cricut Essential Tools

Cricut True Control Knife

Cricut Self-Healing Mat

Keychain Lanyards

Cricut Normal and Strong Grip Cutting

Instructions:

Start by opening up Cricut Design Space

Design Space comes with many font, pictures, and characteristics so that it can be used immediately after you plug into it. You can easily upload your images, but the project today will only use a Cricut fountain.

Create and open a textbox to a new canvas. Specify your name, and in the dropdown list, select the ZOO DAY font. The all-caps fonts are perfect for this. It works great. When the name has been written down, the letter space is decreased so that the letters start to touch each other. Bring them together before and after each letter.

Select and solder every single name. All letters will be merged into one solid piece.

After soldering, the background is solid, and each name is solid. Choose and sweat or join all the blue names. Repeat the yellow names soldering.

Click on the button to make it.

On two separate mats, you will bring up the sold or attached words.

Mirror the frontend mat picture. Then, with a glittering side, place the iron-on vinyl on your mat. Set the Iron on the Foil configuration of the machine.

Click on the "C" button and insert it into the Cricut Maker. It will cut the picture with the fine dot blade beautifully.

Remove the vinyl iron and trim the edges once cut. Set it above your Bright Pad Cricut and see where you should weed. To remove excess vinyl, use the weeding tool.

Get the leather ready for the second mat. Leather cutting is incredibly easy with the Blade and the Builder Knife.

To help protect your cutting mat against leather, use the contact paper. Remove the leather packaging and turn it roughly onto it.

Place the paper and securely paste it on clear contact paper. Cut the leather in plastic.

Slide onto the machine and put the chrome blade in the machine to the right.

Make certain you have calibrated the blade previously.

Put the leather-covered contact paper right on the strong grip mat.

Where to Find Materials

Cricut Brand Products

Cricut.com – This is the official Cricut website and the place to find the entire line of products. All the current selections are available on the website but be sure to check back often for more! They also offer bulk orders to save money on a large number of materials.

Amazon.com – You can find almost anything on Amazon, including Cricut brand materials. They are often at a discounted price. You may also be able to find older materials that are no longer on Cricut's website. It can be, however, hard to tell the dimensions, feel, and components of the fabric when shopping online.

Craft stores – Craft stores such as JoAnn's and Michael's carry a variety of Cricut products. The in-store selection usually isn't as big as online, but you have the convenience of getting them on the same day without shipping costs, giving you a chance to see and feel the material before purchasing it.

ExpressionsVinyl.com – This website has several different types of vinyl at lower prices. One of their biggest advantages is that you can buy vinyl by the sheet, while in other places, you can only buy it by the roll.

MyVinylDirect.com – This is another online store with reasonably priced vinyl that is available both in rolls and sheets. There's a large selection, but it's similar to Amazon. However, you should check the reviews before you make a purchase. The quality can vary.

PaperAndMore.com – This website offers a huge selection of paper. Shop by searching what you'd like or by category. An advantage of this site is that you can keep narrowing down the categories, so you can find the specific paper you'd like while browsing. You can narrow down their categories by type of paper, material, size, and brand. They even offer custom printing and cutting services.

Office supply stores – Most office stores have a large paper section. They'll sell packages of cardstock in at least a few different colors and finishes.

Joann Fabrics – Joann is a national chain that has stores in most cities. It is focused on sewing and textile art, though they do carry a selection of other craft and art products as well. This will probably be the best in-person fabric selection you can find.

Spoonflower.com – Spoonflower is quickly growing in popularity. It has a huge selection of fabric in patterns and designs that you won't find anywhere else. You can even create custom fabric. Many of the designs are created by artists who get a portion of the sales. They are a bit pricey, but they have very high quality.

FabricDirect.com – This is a website that sells fabric at wholesale prices. It's a great place to save money by buying in bulk. You can also find smaller quantities of fabric at low prices.

Chapter 4: Great Cricut Explore Projects

Personalized Water Bottles

Materials:

Smooth Outdoor Vinyl Water Bottle

Transfer Tape Scraper or Brayer Blank Water Bottles

Instructions:

This is such a simple project to do.

Open Cricut Design Space and design your text, then add a name using an outline. Create a second text box smaller than the first one. Attach these two layers to separate your initial and name and resize to suit your water bottle.

To stick the initial name to your water bottle you will use your transfer tape.

Carefully peel your transfer tape, and you are done. Even though you used outdoor vinyl, you might still handwash the bottles. This way, you are sure to make them last as long as possible.

Hologram Party Box Tumblers

Materials

Hologram stick-on vinyl

Clear tumblers

Green StandardGrip mat

Cricut Fine-Point Blade

Weeding tool

Scraping tool or brayer tool

Pair of scissors for cutting the material to size

Directions:

Open a new project in Design Space.

Select 'Square' from the 'Shapes' menu on the left-hand side menu.

Change the background color to grey.

Unlock the shape and change it to the width and height of the tumbler. The hologram will run from about 1" below the lip of the tumbler to 1" above the base.

To accurately measure the width of the hologram paper, wrap it around the tumbler and cut it.

Lay it flat on the cutting mat to get the hologram paper's dimensions.

Select 'Text' from the menu on the left-hand side.

Type in the person's name that the tumbler is for.

Select a nice chunky font that will work for the cutout.

Position the font onto the middle of the square on the screen.

Stretch it to fit across the square.

Select both the square and the text.

Right-click and choose 'Slice.'

Select the first layer of the name text, move it off to one side, then delete it.

Select the second layer of the name text, move it off to one side, then delete it.

If you like, you can add an image and repeat steps 13 to 16 for the shape or image.

When the hologram image is ready, select 'Make it.'

Make sure the fine-point blade is loaded.

Make sure the hologram vinyl is correctly stuck to the cutting mat.

Select the correct material and press 'Go' once the Cricut is ready to cut.

Once it has cut, leave the vinyl on the cutting board and weed out the middle of the image and text.

Place the transfer sheet over the vinyl and use the scraper or brayer tool to smooth it out.

Remove the back sheet.

Carefully place the hologram paper around the tumbler.

Use the scraper to ensure it is on properly.

Remove the transfer sheet.

T-Shirts (Vinyl, Iron On)

Materials:

Cricut Machine

T-shirt

Iron on or heat transfer vinyl

Fine point blade and light grip mat

Weeding tools

EasyPress (regular household iron works fine too, with a little extra work)

Small towel and Parchment paper

Instructions:

In preparing for this project, Cricut recommends that you prewash the cloth without using any fabric softener before applying the iron-on or heat transfer vinyl on it. Ensure that your T-shirt is dry and ready before you proceed.

On Cricut Design Space, create your design or import your SVG as described in the section on importing images.

If you are using an SVG file, select it and click on "Insert Images". When you do this, the image will appear in the Design Space canvas area.

Then, you need to resize the image to fit the T-shirt. To do this, select all the elements, then set the height and width in the edit panel area, or simply drag the handle on the lower right corner of the selection.

After this is done, select all the layers and click "Attach" at the bottom of the "Layers" panel, so that the machine cuts everything just as it is displayed on the canvas area.

Once you are satisfied with the appearance of your design, click "Make It". If you have not connected your machine, you will be prompted to do so.

Now, it's time to cut. To cut vinyl (and other such light materials), you should use the light-grip blue mat. Place the iron-on vinyl on the mat with the dull side facing up. Ensure that there are no bubbles on the vinyl; you can do this using the scraper.

Install the fine point blade in the Cricut machine, then load the mat with the vinyl on it by tapping the small arrow on the machine. Then, press the "make it" button. When the machine is done cutting the vinyl, Cricut Design Space will notify you. When this happens, unload the mat.

Wait for the design to cool off a bit, then peel it off while it is still a little warm.

Ensure that you wait for at least 24 hours after this before washing the T-shirt. When you do wash it, be sure to dry it inside out. Also, do not bleach the T-shirt.

3d Paper Flowers (Paper)

Materials:

Cricut Machine

Cricut mat

Colored scrapbook paper

Hot glue gun and glue sticks

Instructions:

To make flowers, you need an appropriate shape for the petals. To make such a shape, you can combine three ovals of equal size. To create an oval, select the circle tool, then create a circle. Then click the unlock button at the bottom of the shape. Once this is done, you can reshape the circle to form an oval.

Duplicate this oval twice and rotate each duplicate a little, keeping the bottom at the same point, as shown in the picture.

Set your material to cardstock on Design Space or on the machine, depending on the model of your machine, then cut the petals out.

After you cut out the petals, remove them and cut a slit about half an inch long in the bottom of each one. Place a bit of glue on the left side and glue the right side over the glue for each petal.

The next thing to do is to place the petals on the circle base. For large flowers, you need three circles of four petals each. For small flowers, you need five circles on the outside and three on the inside. Put a bit of hot glue on the petal and add to the circle as described above.

For the center of the flowers, search Cricut Access for "flower" and chose shapes with several small petals. Cut these out using a different color of cardstock and glue to the center of the flowers.

Luminaries

Materials:

Luminary Graphic (From a Cricut Project)

Sugar Skull (SVG File)

Cricut Explore Air or Cricut Maker

Cardstock Sampler

Scoring Stylus

Glue Stick

Battery-Operated Tea Light

Instructions:

The first step is to open your Luminary graphic on the Design Space.

Then go ahead to upload the SVG file of your Sugar Skull and adjust its size to around 3.25" high. After doing that, move the Sugar Skull to the bigger part of the Luminary graphic (in the middle of the two score lines) and center-align it.

Select the Sugar Skull and the Luminary Graphic and then go ahead and click on "Weld".

Try selecting every graphic on the design space and click on "Attach." Then copy and paste the selected graphics on the same page (duplication).

Select "Make It" at the topmost right-hand corner, and then ensure everything is positioned correctly. Click on "Continue." If you notice the files being cut on two different mats, just move them back together on one single mat by simply clicking on the three dots located at the graphic corner.

Select "Light Cardstock" under the "Materials" menu, and then start loading the Mat and Cut. Also ensure that your Scoring Stylus is in Clamp A. This will automatically change your machine settings from scoring to cutting.

When the cut-out is done, fold it along the Score lines. Then start gluing the small Flap to the interior part of the lantern's back.

Switch on the Battery-Operated Tea Light, and then place your lantern on top of it.

Shamrock Earrings

Materials:

Cricut Maker

Earring (from a Cricut Project)

Rotary Wheel

Knife Blade

FabricGrip Mat

StrongGrip Mat

Weeder Tool

Cricut Leather

Scraper Tool

Adhesive

Pebbled-Faux Leather

Earring Hooks

Instructions:

First, open the Cricut Project (Earring). You can now either click on "Make It" or "Customize" to edit it.

Once you've selected one, click on "Continue."

Immediately the Cut page pops up, select your material and wait for the "Load" tools and Mat to appear.

Make your Knife blade your cutting tool in clamp B. This will be used on the Leather.

On the StrongGrip Mat, place the Leather and make sure it's facing down. Then load the Mat into the machine and tap the "Cut" flashing button.

When the scoring has been done, go back to the cutting tool and change it to Rotary Wheel so that you can use it on the Faux Leather.

Similarly, place your Faux leather on your FabricGrip Mat, facing down. Then load the Mat into the machine and tap the "Cut" flashing button.

Take away all the items on the Mat with your Scraper tool. Be careful with the small fringes though.

Make a hole on the top circle by making use of the Weeder tool. Make sure the hole is large enough to make the Earring hooks fit in.

If necessary, you may have to twist the hook's end with the pliers to fit them in.

Close them up after you have looped it inside the hole that was made inside the Earring.

Finally, you should glue the Shamrock to the surface of the Earring with adhesive. Wait for it to dry before using.

Glitter and Felt Hair Bow Supplies

Materials:

Hair bow project file in Cricut Design Space

Cricut Felt

Glitter Iron-on Vinyl

Hair Clips (large and small)

Cricut Mat

Glue Gun

Scissors and Weeding tools

EasyPress

Instructions:

To start, in Cricut Design Space, open the design (hair bow); then, click "Make it now". If you would like to make any modifications to the design, click "Customize".

Insert a regular blade into the Cricut machine. Then place the materials and the appropriate board on the Cricut mat.

Send the document to the Cricut machine and cut it out.

After the Cricut machine has cut out the felt and the iron-on, proceed to remove the excess vinyl, then cut around each of the bows using scissors.

Heat up your EasyPress. For the appropriate settings, check the EasyPress Guide.

Remove the transfer paper and repeat this for all the other bows.

Use the glue to stick one side of the bigger bow piece (the piece without the sharp edges) to the other side. This will form a circle.

Apply glue on the inside and on the middle of that bow piece. After this, fold the piece so that it forms a bow.

Stick the bow to its back piece.

Fold the small bow piece to the middle of the bow. Fold it in the back and glue it also.

Glue the bow to the bigger or smaller bow clips to have your bow.

Hand Lettered Cake Topper

Materials:

Glitter Card Stock

Gold Paper Straw

Cutting Mat

Hot Glue Gun

Instructions:

Create your design in Cricut Design Space or download your desired design and import it into Cricut Design Space using the instructions for how to import designs.

Resize the design as required.

Click the "Make it" button.

Select Glitter card stock as your material in Design Space and set the dial on your Cricut machine to "Custom".

Place the glitter card stock on your Cutting Mat and load it into the Cricut machine.

When this is done, press the "Cut" button on your Cricut machine.

After the machine is done with cutting the design, remove it from the mat. This can be done much more quickly using the Cricut Spatula tool.

Finally, using hot glue, stick cut out design to the Gold Paper Straw and stick it in the cake as shown in the picture.

Unicorn Free Printable

Materials:

Printables

White Card Stock

Cricut Mat

Crepe Paper Streamers (varied colors)

Gold Straws

Glue Stick

Hot Glue Gun

Scissors

Instructions:

Import the printable image into Cricut Design Space, following the instructions under the "Tips" section of this book.

Resize the PNG image and make it 5″ wide.

With your Cricut machine, cut the unicorn head using the white cardstock. Also, print and cut out the "stickers."

After cutting out the pieces, stick the horn and the other elements using the glue stick.

In each color, cut out strips of crepe paper, about 2'' wide; then, cut each strip into thirds.

On the reverse side of the unicorn head, glue the strips on the back edge (of the head), then glue on the top by the horn. Ensure that only half the length of each strip is on this side, as you are going to glue the other half on the other side of the unicorn head.

Turn the unicorn head back over and glue the crepe streamers in place.

Turn the head over yet again and use hot glue to stick the gold paper straw onto the unicorn head reverse side to use as party props.

Back to School Supplies

Materials:

Vinyl

Standard Grip Mat

White Paper

Markers (including black)

Pencil Case

3 Ring Binder

iPad Pro (optional)

Apple Pencil

Cricut Design Space App

Drawing app (e.g. ProCreate)

ProCreate Brushes

Instructions:

The first thing to do is to convert your kid's drawing into an SVG file that Cricut Design Space recognizes. This will be done by tracing it in the ProCreate app.

Get your child's design – it should not be too complex, to minimize weeding.

Open the Procreate app on your iPad.

Create a new canvas on ProCreate. Click on the wrench icon and select "IMAGE".

Next, click "TAKE A PHOTO". Take a picture of the design. When you are satisfied with the image, click "Use it".

On the Layer Panel (the two squares icon), add a new layer by clicking the plus sign.

In the layers panel, select the layer containing the picture and click the N. Also, reduce the layer's opacity so that you can easily see your draw lines.

From your imported brushes, select the Marker brush. To avoid the need to import a brush, choose the inking brush. You can resize the brush in the brush settings under the "General" option.

On the new layer, trace over the drawing.

Click on the wrench icon, click "Share", then "PNG".

Next, save the image to your device.

Alternately, use your black marker and trace the drawing on a blank piece of paper, then take a picture of it, using your iPad or phone.

The next stage is to cut the design out in Cricut Design Space

Open up the Cricut Design Space app on your iPad.

Create a new project.

Select "Upload" (located at the screen's bottom). Select "Select from Camera Roll" and select the PNG image you created in ProCreate or the image you traced out.

Follow the next steps.

Save the design as a cut file and insert it into the canvas. Here, you can resize the design or add other designs.

Next, click "Make It" to send it to your Cricut.

Choose "Vinyl" as the material.

Place the vinyl on the mat and use the Cricut to cut it.

Now, you can place the vinyl cutouts on the back to school supplies to make your child stand out!

Chapter 5: Christmas Cricut Projects

Penguin Christmas card

Materials:

Your Tacky glue is also needed

Hot glue

Two dimes or tinny weights.

7" piece of wire, tweezers or even a hooked took like a crochet hook or something else.

Cricut machine

Patterns or cut SVG files from free resource library or your own designs.

Instructions:

First, you upload the SVG file on Design Space. You click on the *Ungroup* button then change the two red layers having the score lines to *score*, next you would choose the red score layer plus its following black cut layer then click Attach. There is a need for you to join both sides of the red scored layers and the black cut layers also. This would allow the score lines to appear in the right places.

You start first by folding the top of the headpiece. This is the smaller round piece that doesn't have a hole in the middle. Then you would fold the other side from the tab inwards. You should not forget to crease each tab to get that good fold. There is also a need for you to fold in the triangle pieces also. Then you should fold the rubber band tabs in then up.

Next, you should reach for the inside with the hook you have been able to make from the other part. Then you'll get the rubber band and wrap it around the last end of the band holders.

It is at this moment you will let go of the head, and it should pop out into place immediately.

You flatten the head one more time and turn it over. You should be sure that the mechanism is sticking out. There might be a need for you to reach in and pull it out. Then you can allow the protruding side of the mechanism to capture that part of the bottom; this will keep it flat.

Now drop it, it is time to work on the surface mechanism on the other side down. Check to be sure that there is nothing impeding the mechanism from being pushed, especially when it lands on that work surface.

Next, you will fold the two halves on the penguin's body.

Glue down the triangles, as well as the side reinforcements pieces as well as the rubber band holders. The same way you did for the head pieces.

 Attach the glue on the white body pieces. You should watch closely, the arrangement of the black body pieces. You can do the same orientation just like the photos.

Now insert that hook and a size 18 rubber band into the body in the same way you did for the head.

Then you will paste the orange feet so that they stick out on both sides of the white part of the body.

Next, you will stand your penguin up, and you will paste the wings on both sides of its body. You should make use of strong glue so that the wings do not brush the ground. Furthermore, this will help the penguin when it jumps.

Another way you can increase stability is by placing two dimes glued onto the bottom. This will help it stabilize its weight when it pops up.

Paper star ornaments

Materials:

Cricut machine

Cricut glitter vinyl

Transfer tape

Scraper tool

Weeding tool

Ribbon

Ornaments

Instructions:

Log in to the Cricut Design Space and start a new project.

Click on the Input icon.

Type in your Christmas greetings.

Change the text font.

Ungroup and adjust the spacing.

Highlight and "weld" to design the overlapping letters.

Select the parts of the text you do not want as part of the final cut.

Readjust the text size.

Select the file as a cut file. You will get to preview the design as a cut file.

Approve the cut file.

The text is ready to cut.

Load the mat into the machine.

Custom dial to vinyl.

Cut the image.

Peel back the vinyl paperback.

Apply the vinyl onto the glass ornament.

Go over the applied vinyl with a scraper tool to remove air bubble underneath the vinyl.

Christmas Ornament

Materials:

Cricut machine

Cricut glitter vinyl

Transfer tape

Scraper tool

Weeding tool

Ribbon

Ornaments

Instructions:

Log in to the Cricut Design Space and start a new project.

Click on the Input icon.

Type in your Christmas greetings

Change the text font.

Ungroup and adjust the spacing.

Highlight and "weld" to design the overlapping letters.

Select the parts of the text you do not want as part of the final cut.

Readjust the text size.

Select the file as a cut file. You will get to preview the design as a cut file.

Approve the cut file.

The text is ready to cut.

Place the vinyl on the cutting mat shiny side down.

Load the mat into the machine.

Custom dial to vinyl

Cut the image.

Use the weeding tool to remove excess vinyl after the image is cut.

Apply a layer of transfer tape to the top of the cut vinyl.

Peel back the vinyl paperback.

Apply the vinyl onto the glass ornament.

Go over the applied vinyl with a scraper tool to remove the air bubble underneath the vinyl.

Slowly peel away the transfer tape from the glass ornament.

Chapter 6: Valentine Cricut Project Ideas

Butterfly canvas wall heart

Materials:

4 or more sheets of 8.5 by 11 paper. (we used seafoam green)

1 A sheet of 12 by 12 paper. This can be in any color that you want to create. You make use of it to make that heart template.

A canvas, board, or sign. (In this project I was able to use 16 by 20 stretched canvas on a frame)

The Cricut machine

Instructions:

Get your butterfly designs from online downloads, or you can construct yours by arranging these designs on the Cricut design space and give them a uniform measurement. We also made a large heart design to house these butterflies. To add that touch of beauty to it, you should use several types of butterflies in this heart like: the blue morphos, emerald swallowtails, monarchs, and even the scarlet peacocks.

Load the images on your Cricut machine and cut them out.

Fold the butterfly wings

Trace the heart or other shapes on the canvas with a pencil. Make sure that the traces are very light.

Glue those paper butterflies on the canvas forming any pattern you choose.

Mini **love note**

Materials:

Frost spray paint

Clear enamel spray

Holographic vinyl

Vinyl transfer tape

Cutting mat

Weeding tool or pick

Fairy lights

Instructions:

Spray the entire glass block with frost spray paint and let it dry.

Spray the glass block with a coat of clear enamel spray and let it dry.

Open Cricut Design Space and create a new project.

Select the "Text" button in the Design Panel.

Type "Live Love Laugh" in the text box.

Use the dropdown box to select your favorite font.

Arrange the words to sit on top of each other.

Place your vinyl on the cutting mat.

Send the design to your Cricut.

Use a weeding tool or pick to remove the excess vinyl from the design.

Apply transfer tape to the design.

Remove the paper backing and apply the words to the glass block.

Smooth down the design and carefully remove the transfer tape.

Place fairy lights in the opening of the block, leaving the battery pack on the outside.

Enjoy your decorative quote!

Valentine's Gift Tags

Materials:

Cricut Machine Design Space

Your preferred card inventory

Gold pen

Instructions:

Follow onscreen instructions to draw and cut each layer as required.

Glue the two layers of paper together, aligning the heart shaped hole atop the tag.

Add the vinyl

If you don't have glitter vinyl, you can attempt using the transfer tape, but the glitter tends not to stick with it.

So, if you are having trouble with the operation, you can thoroughly remove and apply each piece of vinyl cut.

Add twine or ribbon to the tag and attach the tag as you like. You can write a short message or a symbol at the back (maybe a unique signal to your special someone).

Alternatively, instead of using glue, you can bind the two cutouts together. Add these Valentine tags in your charms, embellishments, and accessories.

Draw a beautiful accent design with your gold glitter pen.

Add glitter vinyl word art to your Valentine tag.

You can use this pleasant Valentine's Day Cricut project to produce all kinds of custom tags or use parts to make other types of projects. Change colors, materials, and wording at your will.

Valentine's Day Classroom Cards

Materials:

Cricut Maker

Card Designs (Write Stuff Coloring)

Cricut Design Space

Dual Scoring Wheel

Pens

Cardstock

Crayons

Shimmer Paper

Instructions:

Open the Card Designs (Write Stuff Coloring) on the Design Space, and then click on "Make it" or "Customize" to make edits.

When all the changes have been done, Cricut will request you to select a material. Select Cardstock for the Cards and Shimmer Paper for the Envelopes.

Cricut will send you a notification when you need to change the pen colors while creating the Card, and then it will start carving the Card out automatically.

You will be prompted later on to change the blade because of the Double Scoring Wheel. It is advisable to use the Double Scoring Wheel with Shimmer Paper; they both work best together.

When the scoring has been finished, replace the Scoring Wheel with the previous blade.

After that, fold the flaps at the Score lines in the direction of the paper's white side, and then attach the Side Tabs to the exterior of the Bottom Tab by gluing them together.

You may now write "From:" and "To:" before placing the Crayons into the Slots.

Place the Cards inside the Envelopes and tag them with a sharp object.

Valentine's Day Treat Bags

Materials:

Cricut Machine (Explore or Maker as you will be scoring)

Design Space App

Valentine's Day Treat Bag project file

Paper (your choice)

Scissors

White glue

Plastic food bags

Instructions:

Log into Design Space and find the Valentine's Day Treat Bag project. You can do this by typing in the keywords into the search bar.

Load the paper you will be using. Please make a note of the size for each of the bags so that the paper matches the size.

First, you will print the letters on the bag using any of the pens for the Cricut Machine.

Then, you will score the bags so that you will have the creases on which you will fold the bags.

After, follow the instructions on the project to cut out the heart-shaped letters in the center of the treat bag.

Once you have cut the bag, go ahead and glue the plastic food bag on the inside of the treat bag. At this point, the treat bag has only been folded but is still open.

Now, close off the treat bag entirely by gluing the crease that makes the folds.

Also, don't forget to fold the bottom and make sure it is on tight.

Lastly, fill the treat bag with its contents and close off at the top. These can be sealed with colored tape or even ribbon.

In this particular project, the word "love" is cut into the middle of the bag using a heart shape. You can alter the word perhaps to suit the occasion. For instance, you can change the word to "baby" if it's a baby shower, or "congrats" if this is some type of celebration. Please remember that the sky's the limit with this project.

Chapter 7: Spring Project Ideas

Hello Beautiful Cosmetic bags

Materials:

Cricut Cutting machine

EasyPress and Mat

Cricut Cutting machine

Canvas Zipper Bag

Iron-on Vinyl

Instructions:

Put the iron on the matt, plastic shiny side on the mat

Then weed the image with excess vinyl.

Heat the EasyPress canvas bag up and then put the picture up while still warm.

Right on top of the towel bag, place EasyPress for a specified time. Add a little pressure while heating, too. It's lighter than the larger, so it's a bit more press induced.

Cooldown vinyl a bit and peel off the sheet of the carrier.

Repeat for as many bags as you have! Again, this project is so fun and makes a great fast gift!

Clutch Purse

Materials:

Two fabrics, one for the exterior and one for the interior

Fusible fleece

Fabric cutting mat

D-ring

Sew-on snap

Lace

Zipper

Sewing machine

Fabric scissors

Keychain or charm of your choice

Instructions:

Open Cricut Design Space and create a new project.

Select the "Image" button in the lower left-hand corner and search for "essential wallet."

Select the essential wallet template and click "Insert."

Place the fabric on the mat.

Send the design to the Cricut.

Remove the fabric from the mat.

Attach the fusible fleecing to the wrong side of the exterior fabric.

Attach lace to the edges of the exterior fabric.

Assemble the D-ring strap.

Fold the pocket pieces wrong side out over the top of the zipper and sew it into place.

Fold the pocket's wrong side in and sew the sides.

Sew the snap onto the pocket.

Lay the pocket on the right side of the main fabric lining so that the corners of the pocket's bottom are behind the curved edges of the lining fabric. Sew the lining piece to the zipper tape.

Fold the lining behind the pocket and iron in place.

Sew on the other side of the snap.

Trim the zipper so that it's not overhanging the edge.

Sew the two pocket layers to the exterior fabric across the bottom.

Sew around all of the layers.

Trim the edges with fabric scissors.

Turn the clutch almost completely inside out and sew the opening closed.

Turn the clutch all the way inside out and press the corners into place.

Attach your charm or keychain to the zipper.

Carry your new clutch wherever you need it!

Sugar Skulls

Materials:

Printer

Toothpicks

Standard cardstock

12x12 standard grip mat for Cricut

Sugar skull print, then cut image

Cricut Explore machine

Cricut Design space software

Glue

Instructions:

Use your Cricut Design Space you need to log in.

In the Cricut Design Space, you will need to click on Starting a New Project and then select the image that you would like to use for your sugar skulls. You can use the search bar on the right-hand side at the top to locate the image that you are wishing to use.

Next, click on the image and click Insert Image so that the image is selected.

Click on each one of the files that are in the image file and click the button that says Flatten at the lower right section of the screen. This will turn the individual pieces into one whole piece. This prevents the cut file from being individual pieces for the image.

Now, you want to resize the image so that it is the size that you wish it to be. This can be any size that is within the recommended space for the size of the canvas.

If you want duplicates of the image for the sheet of sugar skulls, then you should select all and then edit the image and click copy. This will allow you to copy the whole row that you have selected. Once you have copied, you can then edit and paste the multiple images to make a sheet. This is the easiest way to copy and paste the image repeatedly.

Follow the instructions that are on the screen for printing, then cut the sugar skull images.

Using glue, piece the front and back of the sugar skull together to create the topper with the toothpick inserted into the center of the pieces.

Planner Stickers

Materials:

Cricut printable sticker paper

Cricut Explore Air machine or Cricut Maker

Cricut standard cutting mat grip

Printer with ink

Instructions:

Choose the sticker designs. You can choose from the Design shop or upload your own.

Start by opening the Design Space program and click on the image option. Then head to the search function and locate the planner stickers. Locate which one you want to use.

Place the choices on the canvas and arrange them in the order that you would like them to be.

Click the "Make It" option and the Design Space will direct you to begin printing the image. Follow the directions to print the images.

And to proceed, place the stickers in the Cricut to cut the stickers out.

Woodland Fox Bookmark

Materials:

Cricut weeding tool

Multiple colors of cardstock

Adhesive

Standard cutting mat grip

Cricut machine

Instructions:

Open your Design shop and use the design file that you have created for this bookmark.

You may have to purchase the file that is needed to design this bookmark.

Cut two pieces for the bookmark. One for each side of the bookmark. This helps it to be sturdier.

You will need to glue the two identical pieces together.

Once you send the image to the Cricut machine, you can begin to place the color for your paper on the mat. Then cut it out. Continue to do this until all the pieces and colors have been cut.

Weed out any unnecessary pieces that come out with the fox.

Glue the fox together and then glue it to the bookmark backing. You do not want to use too much glue. This will keep the cardstock from being soggy.

Use a heavy book and place the bookmark in between the pages to get the glue to set and the bookmark not to wave.

Chapter 8: Halloween Cricut Project Ideas

Halloween Spiders

Materials

SVG Spider web file

Cricut machine

Adhesive

Black paper

Pieces of parchment paper

Instructions

Place the SVG file into the Design Space and proceed to cut into different web sizes.

Place the parchment papers on the work area.

Arrange the spider web just how you want it to look on the worktable.

After the arrangement of the web, move onto joining the edges of the webs with your adhesive. You have to be careful here to make sure that you get only the edges joined together.

Wait for a few minutes to get it properly dried.

Hang it around the house, and you have your perfect Halloween Spider web design!

Halloween Sleep Eye Mask with Eyes

Materials

Cotton material

Elastic lace to match the color of the eye mask

Fusible Thermolam

Holographic heat transfer vinyl (color of your choice)

Pink Cricut Fabric mat

Green StandardGrip mat

Cricut EasyPress (or iron)

Cricut Fine-Point Blade

Rotary blade

Weeding tool

Brayer tool

Pair of scissors for cutting the material to size

Directions:

Open a new project in Design Space.

Find a picture of a sleeping mask and upload it to Design Space.

The mask's dimensions should be approximately 7.125" wide and 4" high.

Duplicate the mask and make another two copies of it. Position them one below the other.

Make two masks the same color and one white for the Thermolam.

Choose 'Text' from the left-hand menu.

Type the word 'Asleep' in a nice bold font.

Position the text in the mask and stretch it to fit across the middle of the mask.

Save the project.

Click 'Make it,' and you will find three different cuts waiting in the queue.

For the cut with the one mask on it, cut out a piece of Thermolam using the measurements on the screen.

Stick the Thermolam onto the pink fabric cutting mat.

Load it into the Cricut.

Click 'Continue.'

Set the dial to custom.

Choose felt for the material setting.

Make sure the rotary blade is loaded into the Cricut in place of the fine-point blade.

Press 'Go' when the Cricut is ready to cut.

When the cutting is finished, remove the Thermolam and tidy up the eye mask cutout.

Stick the cotton material onto the pink fabric board.

Check which cutting board will print next in Design Space, and load that board into the Cricut.

Set the material to the correct fabric setting, and when the Cricut is ready to cut, press the 'Go' button.

Unload the material part of the eye mask and clean them up.

Load the holographic heat transfer vinyl onto the green mat.

Set the material to the correct setting.

Click 'Mirror' to mirror the text.

Change the blade to the fine-point blade.

Press 'Go' when the Cricut is ready to cut.

When it has finished cutting, remove the vinyl from the Cricut.

Sew the eye mask together with the Thermolam in the middle of the two cotton pieces.

Measure, cut, and sew the elastic lace onto the mask.

Using the Cricut EasyPress or an iron, heat the eye mask.

Place the holographic vinyl with the text on it facedown onto the front of the eye mask.

Use the heated Cricut EasyPress or iron to press down on the back of the transfer design.

Hold it in place for 30 seconds.

Use the brayer tool to roll the transfer to make sure it is in place.

Carefully pull the backing paper off the holographic vinyl.

Your mask is ready.

Cut DIY Halloween treats

Materials:

Strong or Tacky Glue

Halloween Candy

Cricut Explore machine

The SVG file or you can make use of your own personal design

Heavy White Cardstock. (recommended 110 lb weight)

Instructions:

Get your supplies, download the SVG file, and upload it to your Cricut Design space or construct your own design and make sure you save it as print files. Don't forget to resize the image to contain the candy. I made use of 5.8 by 6.7 in this project. Then cut the images. Note that they are front and back for each character.

After you have printed it out, you glue the front and back to make it a single piece.

Place the candy bar on the character. Wrap the *arms* of the character around it so that it looks as if it is holding it. Then you make use of the double-sided tape to hold these together.

Repeat this process for each character, the pumpkin man and the witch.

Halloween T-Shirt

Materials:

T-shirt Blanks

Glam Halloween SVG Files

Cardstock

Transfer Sheets (Black and Pink)

Butcher Paper (comes with Infusible Ink rolls)

LightGrip Mat

EasyPress (12″ x 10″ size recommended)

EasyPress Mat

Lint Roller

Instructions:

Import the SVG files into Cricut Design Space and arrange them as you want them on the T-shirt.

Change the sizes of the designs so as to get them to fit on the T-shirt.

Using the slice tool, slice the pink band away from the hat's bowler part (the largest piece). Make a copy of this band, and then slice it from the lower part of the hat. With these done, you will have three pieces that fit together.

You can change the designs' colors as you would like them. When you are done with the preparation, click "Make It".

Ensure that you invert your image using the "Mirror" toggle. This is even more important if there is text on your design, as infusible ink designs should be done in inverse. This is because the part with the ink is to go right on the destination material.

Click on "Continue"

If necessary, use the lint roller on the T-shirt again, after which you should heat your shirt with the EasyPress. Do this at 385 degrees for 15 seconds.

Turn the part where the design faces on the T-shirt. Place the butcher paper on the design, ensuring, again, that the backing does not overlap the design.

Place the EasyPress over the design and hold it in place for 40 seconds. Do not move the EasyPress around so that your design does not end up looking smudged.

Remove the EasyPress from the shirt and remove the transfer sheet.

To layer colors, ensure that your cutting around the transfer sheet is done as close as possible, then repeat the previous three steps for each color.

Halloween Nail Art

Materials

Vinyl

Nail polish – your color of choice

Top coat – to make the polish and nail art last longer.

Instructions

Again, you need to take a look at the Cricut Design Space and create the design that you want to appear on your nails.

There is virtually no limit to the design you can create!

Place a piece of vinyl into your cricut machine and send the design to the machine. It will cut the intricate shapes for you.

You need to make sure they are the right size for your nails.

You could use a glue to attach the vinyl but this could leave you in a mess! Start by placing the design on your nail and removing any excess vinyl.

You can then paint over it with your top coat. This will hold the vinyl in place.

The alternative is to hold the design in place and paint the nail a different color. The design will be left unpainted; all you have to do is carefully remove the vinyl. Again, a top coat should be added to protect the art on your nail.

DIY float koozies

Materials:

Blank Koozies

Any Weeding Tool

Cricut Maker

Heat Transfer Vinyl. Siser Easyweed was what I used here.

Iron

Pool Float SVG Designs

Multi-purpose paper. Which would contain parchment paper or that think cotton Fabric

Instructions:

You will need to cut out each layer of the design from the color of the vinyl.

Make sure you use the top layer to help with the lower layers. So, when you are laying the heat transfer vinyl, you will not only need the iron to lay for some few seconds which you will need to get it to stick since the layer will need more heat plus the application of an extra layer.

After using each layer, you are expected to remove the clear plastic backing then you can cover it with multi-use paper or the parchment paper or that thin cotton cloth which will protect the already spread over layers.

And there you have it! After the final layer has been applied, your koozie is ready to be used and to keep your drinks cool!

Chapter 9: Drawing Projects

Geometric Lampshade

Materials:

White cardstock

Metallic cardstock if you prefer

Ribbon or string

Hot glue gun

Instructions:

In Design Space, go into the library and enter the "Make It Now" unit. Find the project labeled "Geo Ball."

Once the project loads, place your cardstock on your cutting mat and send it to score the fold lines.

Once your paper is scored, glue the metallic and white pieces of paper together. Begin folding the paper to create the geometric shape. Place a line of glue along one edge and bring the project into its final shape.

If you are hanging your pendant, make sure to attach your ribbon or string to the bottom of the shape and hang it from your ceiling!

Takeout-Style Boxes

Materials:

Sticker paper for labels or stickers

Cardstock

Hot glue gun or glue dots

Instructions:

If you are going to add labels of stickers to your boxes, design them in Design Space with the image or text that you prefer. Consider adding the title of the event and the date to the label so guests know right away how long they have the leftovers for in their fridge. Create a variety of sizes so they will fit over the cardstock boxes you are about to create or other containers you might need to use.

Once your stickers or labels are created, send the file to print and cut.

Search in the Design Space library the template for Chinese Take Out Boxes and load it into a new workspace. Choose a variety of sizes. Load your cardstock onto your cutting mats and send the file to cut.

Fold your cut cardstock along the score lines. Apply glue along the edges to assemble the box and reinforce the seams.

If you are adding stickers to your boxes, add them now. For other containers, keep the stickers nearby or apply them onto them as well. You are ready to send your guests away in style now!

Cricut Foil Streamers

Materials,

Cricut party foil in colors of your choice

Green StandardGrip mat

Cricut Fine-Point Blade

Weeding tool

Scraper tool

Directions:

Start a new project in Design Space.

Select 'Images' from the left-hand side menu.

Search for image #M7D2D9CA.

Choose 'Square' from the 'Shapes' menu on the left-hand side menu.

Click 'Make it.'

Position the spiral in the middle of the board to give the Cricut enough cutting room.

Cut the party foil to the size of the cutting mat and stick it onto the mat.

Use either the brayer or scraping tool to ensure the foil is smooth and stuck down properly to the mat.

Make sure the fine-point blade is loaded into the Cricut.

Load the cutting mat with the foil into the Cricut.

Set the Cricut dial to custom.

In Design Space, click 'Continue.'

Select 'Party foil' as the material.

Click 'Continue.'

When the Cricut is ready to cut, click 'Go.'

When the Cricut has finished cutting, unload the cutting mat.

Carefully remove the excess foil and use the weeding tool to weed the small starts on the foil.

Use the spatula to gently remove the streamer from the cutting mat.

Latte Stencil

Materials:

Cardstock or vellum

Coffee in a mug and a dusting material

Instructions:

Measure the top of your mugs or your favorite mug that you use often. In Design Space, create a circle or shape that will rest over the lip of your mug and add another small circle to the side of it to be the tab that you will hold while the stencil is in use.

Write your message or create your image on your stencil. Make sure to place your image in the center. Send the file to cut on your vellum. Weed the small pieces in the center of your design and peel away the outside vellum or cardstock you do not need.

When your latte is ready and still nice and hot, place the stencil over your mug and dust your favorite topping over it to create the design. Gently lift the stencil away to reveal your barista design. If you used vellum, wash the stencil off and lay aside to dry for your next coffee creation!

Paper Flower Wreath

Materials:

Wreath base

Colored cardstock

Hot glue gun

Coordinated fabric, if desired

Instructions:

In Design Space, find a variety of different flower and leaf projects. Aim for about three or four different flower designs that are different in size. Try to make as many as possible in different colors

195

and sizes. Follow the instructions for compiling the petals and creating the flowers. Pinch the leaves or fold the bottoms over to add dimension to the leaves. A good goal is to have about 30 different flowers and 15 different leaves to start.

If you decided to wrap your wreath with fabric, add a little glue to one end of the fabric to the wreath and begin wrapping it around the wreath and securing the other end with hot glue when it is covered. You do not need to cover the whole wreath with fabric or use it at all, just make enough flowers and leaves to cover any exposed wreath base that you do not want to be seen.

Begin adding your flowers to your wreath with your hot glue gun. Make sure you are mixing shapes and colors on your wreath. Once all the flowers are added to your wreath, fill in with the leaves. Add other embellishments if you want. When the glue is dry, get ready to hang it.

Easy Lacey Dress

Materials:

Dress of your choice

White heat transfer vinyl

Cricut EasyPress or iron

Cutting mat

Weeding tool or pick

Instructions:

Open Cricut Design Space and create a new project.

Select the "Image" button in the lower left-hand corner and search "vintage lace border."

Choose your favorite lace border and click "Insert."

Place your vinyl on the cutting mat.

Send the design to your Cricut.

Use a weeding tool or pick to remove the excess vinyl from the design.

Place the design along the hem of the dress with the plastic side up. Add lace wherever you like, such as along the collar or sleeves.

Carefully iron on the design.

After cooling, peel away the plastic by rolling it.

Dress your child up in her adorable lacey dress!

Dinosaur T-Shirt

Materials:

T-shirt of your choice

Green heat transfer vinyl

Cricut EasyPress or iron

Cutting mat

Weeding tool or pick

Instructions:

Open Cricut Design Space.

Select the "Image" button in the lower left-hand corner and search "dinosaur."

Choose your favorite dinosaur and click "Insert."

Select "Image" again and search for "fossils."

Choose your favorite fossil and click "Insert."

Copy the fossil once so that you have two of them.

Place your vinyl on the cutting mat.

Send the design to your Cricut.

Use a weeding tool or pick to remove the excess vinyl from the design.

Place the dinosaur in the center of the t-shirt, and a fossil on each sleeve, with the plastic side up.

Carefully iron on the design.

After cooling, peel away the plastic by rolling it.

Show off the cool dinosaur t-shirt!

Flower Garden Tote Bag

Materials:

Canvas tote bag

White heat transfer vinyl

Cricut EasyPress or iron

Cutting mat

Weeding tool or pick

Instructions:

Open Cricut Design Space and create a new project.

Select the "Image" button in the lower left-hand corner and search "flowers."

Choose your favorite flower and click "Insert."

Continue with a variety of flowers, lining them up together to form a straight edge at the bottom.

Place your vinyl on the cutting mat.

Send the design to your Cricut.

Use a weeding tool or pick to remove the excess vinyl from the design.

Place the design along the bottom of the tote bag with the plastic side up.

Carefully iron on the design.

After cooling, peel away the plastic by rolling it.

Carry around your new garden tote bag!

Decorate a Mug

Materials:

Adhesive vinyl

Cricut machine

Weeding tool

Scrapper tool

Instructions:

Log in to the Cricut Design Space.

Create a new project.

Click on "upload image".

Drag the image to the design space.

Highlight the image and "flatten" it.

Use the Make It button.

Place vinyl to the cutting mat.

Push up against the roller.

Custom dial the machine to vinyl.

Load the cutting mat into the machine.

Push the mat up against the rollers.

Cut the design out of the vinyl.

Weed out the excess vinyl.

Apply a thin layer of transfer tape on the vinyl.

Peel off the backing.

Apply the cut design on the mug.

Smoothen with a scraper tool to let out all air bubbles.

Carefully peel away the transfer tape.

Chapter 10: Projects to Create with Paper

Wedding invitation

Materials:

Cricut Maker

Cutting mat

Decorative paper

Crepe paper

Fabric

Home printer

Instructions:

Log into the "Design Space" application and click on the "New Project" button on the top right corner of the screen to view a blank canvas.

Let's customize an already existing project by clicking on the "Projects" icon on the "Design Panel" and selecting "Cards" from the "All Categories" drop-down then type in "wedding invite" in the search bar.

For example, you could select the project shown in the picture below and click "Customize" at the bottom of the screen to edit and personalize the text of your invite.

Click "Text" on the "Designs Panel" and type in the details of the invite. You can change the font, color and alignment of the text from the "Edit Text Bar" on top of the screen and remember to change the "Fill" to "Print" on the top of the screen.

Select all the elements of the design and click on "Group" icon on the top right of the screen under "Layers panel". Then, click on "Save" to save your project

Art journal

Materials:

Glue

Colored thread

Large needle

Paper piercer or something to poke holes in your paper

Various cardstock in interesting prints

Various paper in interesting colors and prints

Instructions:

In Design Space, create a square on your canvas. Round the corners. You may want to ungroup the layers and delete the bottom layer. Also, adjust the size of your square to the size of your final notebook. For example, in this example, the notebooks are 5" x 7". This means your square will need to measure 10" x 7".

Add your score line to the middle of the square or rectangle shape. You will find this line under "lines." Adjust the size to fit your project and then select "Align" and "Center." This should automatically adjust the line, so it is directly in the middle of your project.

Next, add notches to your center score line to tell you where to pierce your paper. You can place another score line at 90 degrees from the centerline and scale it down, so it is small. Alternatively, you can place a very small circle over the place you want to pierce your paper and have the machine cut the little spot out for you. Measure down about one inch from the top and bottom to place your holes or notches.

When you are done designing your pages, send your file to print, cut, and score your cover and pages. Follow the prompts to load your paper and tools into your machine.

Thread your needle with the colored thread. Pass your needle through the holes and tie a slip knot. Tighten your knot as tight as possible and then tie off with a regular knot. You can tie on the outside of the journal or the inside. Trim the threads as short as you want.

Personalized Envelopes

Materials:

Envelope 5.5' by 4.25'

Cricut pens in the color of your choice

Green StandardGrip mat

Spatula

Instructions:

Create a 'New Project' in Design Space.

Choose the square from the 'Shapes' menu.

Unlock the square, set the width to 5.5' and the height to 4.25'.

Choose 'Text' from the right-hand menu.

This will be the name and address the envelope will be addressed to.

Choose a font and size it to fit comfortably in the middle of the envelope.

You can choose a different color for the font.

Move the text box to the middle of the envelope.

When you move the card around the screen, the address text will move with the envelope.

Load the envelope onto the cutting board and load it into the Cricut.

In Design Space, click 'Make It'.

Choose the material like paper.

When the project is ready, press 'Go' and let it print.

Flip the card over and stick it onto the mat.

 Use a piece of tape to stick the envelope flap down.

Load it into the Cricut.

Change the text on the envelope to a return address, or 'Regards From'.

Change the color of the pen if you want the writing in another color.

When you are ready, click on 'Make It'.

Make sure the material is set to the correct setting.

When you are ready, press 'Go'.

Once it has finished cutting, you will have a personalized envelope.

Paper Bouquet

Materials:

Cardstock

Glue gun

Lightstick cutting mat

Weeding tool or pick

Green pipe cleaners or floral wire

Instructions:

Open Cricut Design Space and create a new project.

Select the "Image" button in the lower left-hand corner and search for "paper flowers."

Select the image with several flower pieces and click "Insert."

Copy the flowers and resize for variety in your bouquet.

Place your cardstock on the cutting mat.

Send the design to your Cricut.

Remove the outer edge of the paper, leaving the flowers on the mat.

Use your weeding tool or carefully pick to remove the flowers from the mat.

Glue the flower pieces together in the centers, with the largest petals at the bottom.

Bend or curl petals as desired to create multiple looks.

Glue the flowers to the ends of the pipe cleaners or sections of floral wire.

Gather your flowers together in a vase or wrap them with tissue paper.

Enjoy your beautiful bouquet!

Easy Envelope Addressing

Materials:

Envelopes to address

Cricut Pen Tool

Lightstick cutting mat

Instructions:

Open Cricut Design Space and create a new project.

Create a box the appropriate size for your envelopes.

Select the "Text" button in the lower left-hand corner.

Choose one handwriting font for a uniform look or different fonts for each line to mix it up.

Type your return address in the upper left-hand corner of the design.

Type the "to" address in the center of the design.

Insert your Cricut pen into the auxiliary holder of your Cricut, making sure it is secure.

Place your cardstock on the cutting mat.

Send the design to your Cricut.

Remove your envelope and repeat as needed.

Send out your "hand-lettered" envelopes!

Watercolor Heart Sign

Materials:

Watercolor paper

Watercolor paints and paintbrush

Glue

Lightstick cutting mat

Weeding tool or pick

Frame

Instructions:

Paint your watercolor paper in soft gradients. Use a lot of water and gradually blend two or three colors into each other. Set aside to dry.

Open Cricut Design Space and create a new project.

Select the "Image" button in the lower left-hand corner and search for "heart."

Select the heart of your choice and click "Insert."

Place your watercolor paper on the cutting mat.

Send the design to your Cricut.

Remove the outer edge of the paper, leaving the heart on the mat.

Use your weeding tool or carefully pick to remove the heart from the mat.

Glue your heart to the center of a blank piece of paper, cut to fit your frame.

Place your sign into your frame.

Set or hang wherever you need a little color!

Chapter 11: Projects to Create with Vinyl

Vinyl Chalkboard

Materials:

Cricut Maker or Cricut Explore

Standard Grip mat

Cricut Linen vinyl in desired colors

Weeder, transfer tape

Chalkboard and chalk pen

Instructions:

Log into the *'Design Space'* application and click on the *'New Project'* button on the top right corner of the screen to view a blank canvas.

Click on the *'Projects'* icon and type in *'Vinyl Chalkboard'* in the search bar.

Click on *'Customize'* to further edit the project to your preference, or simply click on the *'Make It'* button and load the vinyl sheet to your Cricut machine and follow the instructions on the screen to cut your project.

Using a Weeder tool, remove the negative space pieces of the design.

Use the transfer tape to apply the vinyl cuts to the chalkboard. Then use the scraper tool on top of the transfer tape to remove any bubbles, and then just peel off the transfer tape.

Lastly, use chalk pen to write messages.

Vinyl Herringbone Bracelet

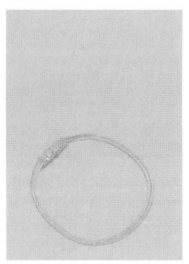

Materials:

Cricut Maker or Cricut Explore

Standard Grip mat

Vinyl (midnight)

Weeder

Scraper

Transfer tape

Metal bracelet gold

Instructions:

Log into the *'Design Space'* application and click on the *'New Project'* button on the top right corner of the screen to view a blank canvas.

Click on the *'Images'* icon on the *'Design Panel'*, and type in *'#M33278'* in the search bar. Select the image and click on the *'Insert Images'* button at the bottom of the screen.

Using a Weeder tool, remove the negative space pieces of the design. Use the transfer tape to apply the vinyl cuts to the bracelet. Then use the scraper tool on top of the transfer tape to remove any bubbles, and then just peel off the transfer tape.

Customized Makeup Bag

Materials:

Pink fabric makeup bag

Purple heat transfer vinyl

Cricut EasyPress or iron

Cutting mat

Weeding tool or pick

Keychain or charm of your choice

Instructions:

Open Cricut Design Space and create a new project.

Measure the space on your makeup bag where you want the design and create a box that size.

Select the "Image" button in the lower left-hand corner and search "monogram."

Choose your favorite monogram and click "Insert."

Place your vinyl on the cutting mat.

Send the design to your Cricut.

Use a weeding tool or pick to remove the excess vinyl from the design.

Place the design on the bag with the plastic side up.

Carefully iron on the design.

After cooling, peel away the plastic by rolling it.

Hang your charm or keychain off the zipper.

Stash your makeup in your customized bag!

Oogie Boogie Treat Packs

Materials:

Burlap Support Packs

Black Warmth Exchange (Press On) Vinyl

Treats/Treats

Cricut machine

Heat Press or Iron

Instructions:

Open Oogie Boogie record in Design Space.

Change the extent of your Oogie Boogie face to accommodate your packs.

Duplicate outline until the point when you have the same number of appearances as you do packs.

Load warmth exchange vinyl gleaming side down on light grasp slicing mat and send it to cut.

Weed overabundance vinyl from around appearances and separate faces (the fundamental toolbox proves to be useful with this).

Preheat burlap sacks before squeezing (either with an iron or warmth press for no less than 5 seconds).

Slowly peel plastic support from the left corner.

Fill your treat packs with fun treats.

Non-Slip Fun Socks with Heat Transfer Vinyl

Materials

Heat transfer vinyl - ThermoFlex (color of your choice)

Green StandardGrip mat

Cricut Fine-Point Blade

Weeding tool

Scraping tool or brayer tool

Pair of scissors for cutting the material to size

Pair of cotton socks

Directions:

Open a new project in Design Space.

Select 'Template' from the menu on the left-hand side.

Choose the 'Flip flops' template. There is not a socks template, and the flip flops give you a better idea of the sock shape.

Unlock the template and change it to the size dimensions of your socks.

Select 'Text' from the left-hand menu.

Change the font to a nice chunky font or one of your choosing.

Type "Left Foot Goes Here." Change the color to match the color of your HTV.

Type each word on a different line.

Make the font nice and big to fit in the front part of the sock just below the toes.

Duplicate the text and type "Right Foot Goes Here" in the second text box.

Save the project.

Click 'Make it.'

Mirror the image.

Choose the correct material.

Make sure that the fine-point blade is loaded.

Load the vinyl on the cutting mat.

Load the cutting mat into the Cricut and press 'C' when it is ready to cut.

Unload the cutting mat when it has been cut.

Pull the front of the vinyl off to leave the cutout shapes.

Use the weeding tool to clean up the letters.

Use the pre-heated iron or EasyPress to press the socks nice and flat.

Place the vinyl with the weeded design onto the socks where you want the design to be transferred to.

Place the heated iron or EasyPress onto the sock for 30 seconds.

Remove the press or iron and let it cool down.

While it is cooling down, do the second sock.

Pull the backing sheet off and your socks are done.

Party Plates

Materials

Gold Cricut foil (or color of your choice)

Transfer tape

Paper plates in the color of your choice

Green StandardGrip mat

Cricut Fine-Point Blade

Weeding tool

Scraping tool or brayer tool

Pair of scissors for cutting the material to size

Directions:

Open a new project in Design Space.

Select 'Template' from the menu on the left-hand side.

Change the background color to match the color of your plates.

Unlock the shape and change it to the same dimensions of your plates.

Choose 'Text' from the menu on the left-hand side.

Type "Happy Birthday."

Resize the text to fit on the top of the plate.

Change the text color to gold and choose a font you like.

Choose an image you want from 'Images' or upload your own.

Resize it to fit beneath the "Happy birthday" and set the color to gold.

Select both the text and image, right-click, and select 'Attach.'

Save the project.

Click 'Make it.'

You may have more than one plate to make. The cutting screen is a great place to make copies of the party plate image.

At the top left-hand corner of the screen, you will see 'Project copies.'

Next to the text, there is a scroll box with the number 1 on it.

For a standard-sized dinner plate, you should be able to get around 4 images per 12" by 12" cutout.

Set the number of project copies to 4.

Four copies of the design will appear on the page.

Position them with enough space around them for a comfortable cut. If there is room for more, increase the number of copies.

Check that the fine-point blade is loaded in the Cricut.

Set the Cricut dial to custom.

Cut out the foil to size and stick it to the cutting mat.

Load the cutting mat into the Cricut.

In Design Space, select the correct material.

When the Cricut is ready to cut, press 'Go.'

When the Cricut is finished cutting out the shapes, unload the mat.

Foil is a bit trickier than other materials to use.

Carefully remove the piece that is no longer needed.

You can gently use the weeding tool, but some tape like soft plumber's tape may work better.

Once you are happy with the cleaned-up image, cut them out into separate squares.

Use a piece of transfer tape the same size as the image square to place over the image.

Use the scraper or brayer tool to smooth it out and ensure there are no bubbles.

Pull the backing sheet off the image and stick it to the party plate.

Use the scraping tool or brayer tool to make sure the image is completely pressed onto the plate.

Gently pull off the transfer tape.

Your party plate is ready to use.

Chapter 12: Projects to Create with Fabric

Tassels

Materials:

12" x 18" fabric rectangles

Fabric mat

Glue gun

Instructions:

Open Cricut Design Space and create a new project.

Select the "Image" button in the lower left-hand corner and search "tassel."

Select the image of a rectangle with lines on each side and click "Insert."

Place the fabric on the cutting mat.

Send the design to the Cricut.

Remove the fabric from the mat, saving the extra square.

Place the fabric face down and begin rolling tightly, starting on the uncut side. Untangle the fringe as needed.

Use some of the scrap fabric and a hot glue gun to secure the tassel at the top.

Decorate whatever you want with your new tassels!

Monogrammed Drawstring Bag

Materials:

Two matching rectangles of fabric

Needle and thread

Ribbon

Heat transfer vinyl

Cricut EasyPress or iron

Cutting mat

Weeding tool or pick

Instructions:

Open Cricut Design Space and create a new project.

Select the "Image" button in the lower left-hand corner and search "monogram."

Select the monogram of your choice and click "Insert."

Place the iron-on material shiny liner side down on the cutting mat.

Send the design to the Cricut.

Use the weeding tool or pick to remove excess material.

Remove the monogram from the mat.

Center the monogram on your fabric, then move it a couple of inches down so that it won't be folded up when the ribbon is drawn.

Iron the design onto the fabric.

Place the two rectangles together, with the outer side of the fabric facing inward.

Sew around the edges, leaving a seam allowance. Leave the top open and stop a couple of inches down from the top.

Fold the top of the bag down until you reach your stitches.

Sew along the bottom of the folded edge, leaving the sides open.

Turn the bag right side out.

Thread the ribbon through the loop around the top of the bag.

Use your new drawstring bag to carry what you need!

Paw Print Socks

Materials:

Socks

Heat transfer vinyl

Cutting mat

Scrap cardboard

Weeding tool or pick

Cricut EasyPress or iron

Instructions:

Open Cricut Design Space and create a new project.

Select the "Image" button in the lower left-hand corner and search "paw prints."

Select the paw prints of your choice and click "Insert."

Place the iron-on material on the mat.

Send the design to the Cricut.

Use the weeding tool or pick to remove excess material.

Remove the material from the mat.

Fit the scrap cardboard inside of the socks.

Place the iron-on material on the bottom of the socks.

Use the EasyPress to adhere it to the iron-on material.

After cooling, remove the cardboard from the socks.

Wear your cute paw print socks!

Night Sky Pillow

Materials:

Black, dark blue, or dark purple fabric

Heat transfer vinyl in gold or silver

Cutting mat

Polyester batting

Weeding tool or pick

Cricut EasyPress

Instructions:

Decide the shape you want for your pillow and cut two matching shapes out of the fabric.

Open Cricut Design Space and create a new project.

Select the "Image" button in the lower left-hand corner and search "stars."

Select the stars of your choice and click "Insert."

Place the iron-on material on the mat.

Send the design to the Cricut.

Use the weeding tool or pick to remove excess material.

Remove the material from the mat.

Use the EasyPress to adhere it to the iron-on material.

Sew the two fabric pieces together, leaving allowance for a seam and a small space open.

Fill the pillow with polyester batting through the small open space.

Sew the pillow shut.

Cuddle up to your starry pillow!

Car Keys, Wood Keyring

Materials:

Wooden tags (L = 3.15" x W = 1.57" x D = 0.11")

1 medium-sized jump ring hoop (gold)

1 keyring hoop (gold)

14" to 5" gold link chain

Green StandardGrip mat

Cricut adhesive vinyl (color of your choice)

Cricut transfer tape

Cricut Fine-Point Blade

Weeding tool

Spatula

Brayer, or a scraping tool

Pair of scissors, for cutting the material to size

Instructions:

Open a new project in Design Space.

Choose *'Square'* from the *'Shapes'* menu.

Unlock the shape, and size it to the length and width of the wooden key tag.

Position the rectangle at the top corner of the screen, leaving some bleeding room for the Cricut.

Find a cute picture of a car, or search for one after choosing *'Images'* from the left-hand window.

Unlock the image, and scale it to the size you want it to be. For instance, if you want to position it at the bottom right corner of the wooden tag, you will need to make it a suitable size to fit that corner. Change the color of the image to the one you want to use on the key ring. Make it the same color that you are going to use for the text for this project.

Choose *'Text'* from the left-hand menu and type *'Car Keys'*.

Select the font that you like and set it to the same color as the image.

Unlock the font, position it where you want it to sit on the key ring; then resize it to fit perfectly.

You might want to rotate the text, so it runs long ways on the key ring.

Select the rectangle and delete it.

Select the image and the text, then click *'Attach'* from the bottom right-hand menu (or right-click).

As you should not waste any pieces of vinyl, you can do a few of these key ring signs at a time.

From the *'Shapes'* menu, select the *'Square'* and unlock the shape.

Set the shape size to 12" by 12" and set the *'Fill'* color, to a light grey.

Click on the *'Arrange'* top menu item and send the grey box to the back.

Move the Car Keys design onto the board position in the top left-hand corner of the grey box. Do not put it to close the edge, and leave some bleeding room for the Cricut, and for you to cut the sign out.

'Duplicate' the design as many times as you need to. You can fit approximately 10 signs across, and 3 signs down. If you do not want to leave any space, shrink the last row of key ring designs down, to fit it to make 4 rows of 10.

In order to edit each design's text, select each individually, hit 'Detach', and double click on the text. Do not forget to 'Attach' once you have the correct text.

You will need to 'Flatten' each of the designs so that the text, and car are cut out together.

When you have all the key ring signs laid out, select the grey backing square and delete it.

Select all the designs and 'Attach' to ensure they are printed on the same sheet of vinyl.

Stick the vinyl onto the cutting board using the brayer or cutting tool to smooth it out.

Load the cutting board into the Cricut.

In Design Space, click 'Make it'.

Use the scraping tool, or your finger to make sure the vinyl has been stuck down properly onto the tag.

Gently pull off the transfer tape.

Connect the gold link chain to the jump ring on one end, and the key ring loop to the other.

Connect the jump ring to the tag.

Chapter 13: Cricut Projects to Create with Glass

Etched Monogrammed Glass

Materials:

A glass of your choice – make sure that the spot you want to monogram is smooth

Vinyl

Cutting mat

Weeding tool or pick

Glass etching cream

Instructions:

Open Cricut Design Space and create a new project.

Select the "Image" button in the Design Panel and search for "monogram."

Choose your favorite monogram and click "Insert."

Place your vinyl on the cutting mat.

Send the design to your Cricut.

Use a weeding tool or pick to remove the monogram, leaving the vinyl around it.

Remove the vinyl from the mat.

Carefully apply the vinyl around your glass, making it as smooth as possible, particularly around the monogram.

If you have any letters with holes in your monogram, carefully reposition those cutouts in their proper place.

Following the instructions on the etching cream, apply it to your monogram.

Remove the cream and then the vinyl.

Give your glass a good wash.

Enjoy drinking out of your etched glass!

Live, Love, Laugh Glass Block

Materials:

Glass block

Frost spray paint

Clear enamel spray

Holographic vinyl

Vinyl transfer tape

Cutting mat

Weeding tool or pick

Fairy lights

Instructions:

Spray the entire glass block with frost spray paint and let it dry.

Spray the glass block with a coat of clear enamel spray and let it dry.

Open Cricut Design Space and create a new project.

Select the "Text" button in the Design Panel.

Type "Live Love Laugh" in the text box.

Use the dropdown box to select your favorite font.

Arrange the words to sit on top of each other.

Place your vinyl on the cutting mat.

Send the design to your Cricut.

Use a weeding tool or pick to remove the excess vinyl from the design.

Apply transfer tape to the design.

Remove the paper backing and apply the words to the glass block.

Smooth down the design and carefully remove the transfer tape.

Place fairy lights in the opening of the block, leaving the battery pack on the outside.

Enjoy your decorative quote!

Snowman Lantern

Materials:

Cricut Maker or Cricut Explore

Standard Grip mat

Vinyl in desired colors

Transfer tape

Scraper

Weeder

Glass etching cream

Glass faced lantern

Instructions:

Log into the *'Design Space'* application and click on the *'New Project'* button on the top right corner of the screen to view a blank canvas.

Click on the *'Projects'* icon and type in *'Snowman Lantern'* in the search bar.

Click on *'Customize'* to further edit the project to your preference or simply click on the *'Make It'* button, and load the vinyl sheet to your Cricut machine, and follow the instructions on the screen to cut your project.

Using a weeder tool, remove the negative space pieces of the design.

Use the transfer tape to apply the vinyl cuts to the glass face of the lantern.

Then use the scraper tool on top of the transfer tape to remove any bubbles and then just peel off the transfer tape.

Lastly, apply the etching cream following the instructions on its package, and rinse off to remove the vinyl.

Unicorn Wine Glass

Materials:

Stemless wine glasses

Outdoor vinyl in the color of your choice

Vinyl transfer tape

Cutting mat

Weeding tool or pick

Extra fine glitter in the color of your choice

Mod Podge

Instructions:

Open Cricut Design Space and create a new project.

Select the "Text" button in the Design Panel.

Type "It's not drinking alone if my unicorn is here."

Using the dropdown box, select your favorite font.

Adjust the positioning of the letters, rotating some to give a whimsical look.

Select the "Image" button on the Design Panel and search for "unicorn."

Select your favorite unicorn and click "Insert," then arrange your design how you want it on the glass.

Place your vinyl on the cutting mat, making sure it is smooth and making full contact.

Send the design to your Cricut.

Use a weeding tool or pick to remove the excess vinyl from the design. Use the Cricut BrightPad to help if you have one.

Apply transfer tape to the design, pressing firmly, and making sure there are no bubbles.

Remove the paper backing and apply the words to the glass where you'd like them. Leave at least a couple of inches at the bottom for the glitter.

Smooth down the design and carefully remove the transfer tape.

Coat the bottom of the glass in Mod Podge, wherever you would like glitter to be. Give the area a wavy edge.

Sprinkle glitter over the Mod Podge, working quickly before it dries.

Add another layer of Mod Podge and glitter and set it aside to dry.

Cover the glitter in a thick coat of Mod Podge.

Allow the glass to cure for at least 48 hours.

Enjoy drinking from your unicorn wine glass!

Chapter 14: Tips and Techniques for the Design Canvas Platform

A very important tip for you is that you need to keep your crafting supplies, materials, tools, and cleaning supplies out of the reach of children. Spray adhesives and rubbing alcohol can be fatal and the blades can cut little fingers and injure you and them very easily. It's a good idea to keep these items and the rest of your items away from your children so they don't get hurt. Keeping them high out of sight will help them stay away from it and make sure they don't spill it on your machine either. The same is true for weeding scraps. They are very small, and they could choke on them. This is why it is best to keep them separate on a box.

If you're cleaning your machine, do not ever clean it when it's on. Turn your machine off and unplug it before starting the process.

Do not spray any cleaner on your machine. The machine can only be cleaned with a soft cloth and very gently at that.

Another great tip is that you should look in other places besides craft stores to find supplies. While craft stores do offer high quality supplies other places offer the same quality and you might be surprised at what you can find in unlikely places. Some great examples are looking into clearance sales or thrift stores. Thrift stores are great for cotton, denim, and you may even find fabrics or vinyl in some. Sites like eBay or Etsy are some of the best places to look as well. One of the best places that people have found supplies is also the Dollar Tree. There are many different supplies that you can find there, and you could get an entire craft room worth of supplies for less than fifty dollars.

Keeping your mats clean is also going to be one of the best things that you can do for your machine and for your supplies. They can get quite costly if you keep having to replace them, so a great tip for keeping your mat clean is to use a lint roller. Make sure that you have removed all the papers before rolling away. The lint roller is really useful if you've been using glitter cardstock that sticks to the surface and is stubborn to remove. It might not take away everything at first go so give it a few tries.

Freezer paper is another great tip because it makes great stencils! You can get it for only a dollar, and you can use the stencils more than once.

Dollar Tree also has great supplies for transforming your craft room to how you want it and finding tools to keep your supplies organized as well so you can always find them. They offer baskets, which are great for putting vinyl or other fabrics in. They also offer bags or boxes with really cool designs on them that would brighten up your craft room as well. All your organizational needs will be met there.

Curling is another big problem with projects and avoiding it is very important. Remember that you should not peel the paper away from your cutting mat. What you should do instead is peel the cutting mat away from the paper before rolling your mat backwards away from the material that you're cutting. This will help avoid tearing as well. You should get a nice cut and a flat project if you do this. If you don't, you'll notice that it begins to shred, tear and it will massively curl.

Keeping your blade separated and organized is going to help too. You don't want to be replacing your supplies and tools all the time, so make sure they last as long as possible by taking good care of them. Use one blade for vinyl and another for fabric and so forth. This is going to help keep your blades stay sharp the way you need them to for much longer. Keeping the blade separate is also going to help you stay more organized. A great tip is that you can use a dot of nail polish so that you know which blade is. Simply apply a different colored dot on the top so that you're always able to determine which one is which. You can also use a permanent marker if you don't like the nail polish idea. A great example of this is a pair of scissors that is only meant to cut fabric. You wouldn't use those scissors to cut leather or another material because it would damage the scissors, right? This is the same with these blades as well. Remember to replace the cap as well so that they're not getting mixed up and so that you can always find them in the order that you need them.

When you are beginning a project, you need to make sure that your dial is actually set to the correct setting for the material that you're using. It is very easy to forget this and it's very easy to put it in the wrong setting which could damage your materials and it could damage your blades as well.

One of the biggest tips that we can offer you is loading your mat correctly. This seems like such a simple thing but both sides of the mat need to slide effectively under the rollers, or the mat will not be able to cut properly.

You should keep the plastic sheets that come with the mats. It's very important that you don't throw these away because you can protect the mats between uses and this will let your mats last longer. The longer they last, the more you can use them and the less money you have to spend.

Your vinyl also needs to be placed the right way up on the cutting mat. The heat transfer vinyl or HTV for short, is always going to need to be placed shiny side down when you're designing.

Your blade also needs to be placed correctly. If it is placed too low, it can ruin your mat and if it's placed too high it may not be able to cut all the way through and instead it will only cut part of the way. Doing a test cut here is also crucial to make sure that it's in the right spot and it can save you a lot of wasted material and hassle.

The tool set that the Cricut offers is not a necessity, but it's widely recommended to have this on hand when you're mastering your machine. It has a variety of different tools that can make your crafting easier and a lot less of a hassle.

Know which machine has what options. Each machine is different, and each machine can do different things. This is why you will need to make sure of the settings your machine has and what your machine can do that others cannot.

Keeping more supplies on hand is a good idea as well. This is especially true if you are going to be working with items like iron-on and vinyl. Most projects use vinyl and having some on hand can be a great idea so that you're not running to a craft store every week.

When your cutting mat has lost its ability to be sticky you might think that the best option for you is to purchase a new one. The truth though, at least in most cases, is that you don't actually have to do that just yet. Instead, the first thing that you should do is clean your mat and see if makes it work. The next thing you should attempt is to tape down your project to hold it in place. Do not do this over an area that needs to be cut but just over a few of the edges. A medium tack painter's tape is also good for this and it shouldn't damage your card stock when you are working with it.

If you are going to print and cut, you will need to use an inkjet printer. There is a very good reason for this. An inkjet printer works better than a laser because a laser can heat the toner and cause it not to be read. If you are using an inkjet printer then you might want to consider an inkjet subscription. This saves you a lot of money on the ink you will be using.

The deep cut blade is a great tool that you have at your disposal. If you have a deep cut blade, then you will be able to cut through thicker materials like leather and some forms of wood. It's compatible with the Explorer Air 2 and the Maker. Make sure that when you get this blade, you get the housing for it as well as this will keep it from getting damaged and keep you from hurting yourself with this blade.

If you have a project that needs to be cut on two different materials such as two different colors of card stock, you can do this at the same time and all you have to do is position the designs that you're going to be cutting in different areas of your canvas. On your app, you will then need to click the button that says attach and then position the materials in the same spot on the mat. This step can be applied to Design Space for the web and for your desktop.

Remember that the app has free weekly designs, but they are only free for that single week. If you don't use the designs during that time then you won't be able to use them after that because they will be gone.

Chapter 15: FAQ

Why can't I weed my design without it tearing?

This form of problem has two relatively common causes. The number one is that your blades are dull. The second explanation is that residues have built up on your blades. Make sure you are cleaning your blades properly and know how to sharpen them.

Is it necessary to turn all my images into SVGs?

No, if you have a JPG or PNG, you don't need to convert the images to the SVG format. If you want SVG files in your project, however, there are many free online tools that can help you with this method. Try to bear in mind that you may have less flexibility to modify the components of your image if you convert your file form to an SVG.

Where do I go to buy materials?

When it comes to buying your Cricut products, there's almost an infinite number of places you can get them. As the Cricut is such a powerful tool with the ability to cut so many fabrics, you can go into any art or fabric stores and find countless products that you can use for your latest and greatest craftsmanship.

As you keep learning more about how and what you can do with Cricut, you'll find out which materials and brands best match your needs. From there, by shopping online, you can always find what you need to get the best prices and quantities of the items you want, which will help you stretch your dollar even more.

Can I disable the grid in Cricut Design Space?

Yeah, the Interface Space lets you turn grid lines on or off. Open the "Account" tab on a Windows computer, or the Mac computer.

That is the three lines that are linked in the upper left corner. Upon clicking on this, pick Preferences. You can see the choices for the Canvas Grid, and you can pick your preferences. You can also see Keyboard shortcuts in the Settings menu. Click on the keyboard shortcut for turning off and on gridlines.

When using the iOS device Design Room, the option to turn off and on the gridlines is available at the bottom of the screen under Settings. You may need to swipe left at the bottom of the screen to see all the options.

What types of photos can I upload to iOS or Android apps via Cricut's design space?

Any pictures saved to your Apple or Android computer in the Photos or Gallery app can be uploaded! You can also upload those if you have SVG files saved.

If you are trying to upload a. PDF or. TIFF file, you should remember that these are not supported by Cricut Design Space.

Can I upload images through the Android app?

Hey! Cricut recognizes how important mobile connectivity is for its users, so this feature has been made available on all platforms, including Android, where you can access the Cricut Design Room.

What is SnapMat?

 SnapMat is an iOS-exclusive app that lets you get a virtual preview of your design. It gives you the freedom to match your designs in Design Space so that they suit seamlessly with what you put on your board. This interface allows you to position photos and text over your mat's snapshot so that you can see exactly how your layout will look in the design room.

Can I include multiple mats at one time with SnapMat?

SnapMat can only snap one mat at a time. If you choose to snap several mats, you can do so individually, and work your way through the designs. This ensures that each mat is fired correctly and that each one is performed accurately.

Can I save the snaps of my mat from the SnapMat feature?

SnapMat does not currently have a "Save" feature for the photos captured in it, so just take a screenshot in the middle of that process if you'd like to keep a snapshot of your mat. This will directly save a picture of your mat to your photo gallery.

If you are referring to the picture where you may have objects, it may be advisable to wait until you are ready to cut to take your snapshot.

How exact is SnapMat when it comes to where my cut lines will be?

The SnapMat technology is precise, and within a tiny fraction of an inch, the lines will be accurate too. If possible, it is best to give yourself as much space as you can to allow for minor variations, but you should be sure that overall, the lines are very close to where they should be.

How can I be sure that SnapMat will work with the Cricut mat I have?

SnapMat is compatible with all models of currently on sale Cricut mats. Though, if you have a mat that's a little older, or if it has black gridlines, the device may have a little more difficult time differentiating between the grid and the template. It's best to do a few tests runs with the mat you've got, if it's not a Cricut brand pad, to make sure it all runs smoothly.

Conclusion

A Cricut machine will allow you to do projects with insane exactness, since it replaces what you would routinely cut with either scissors, or an x-acto but with inconspicuous speed and quality. You can also get access to the library: by subscription, by paying per project, or you can transfer your records and work of art! It will become a creative force of wonder, that will allow you to smoothly work on any project you dream of, in record time. With the Cricut machines, you don't just make paper crafts, but also modify clothing with vinyl, carving, or stenciling. In any case, you will be able to cut textures of more than 100 different materials.

It will open up and allow you to utilize your newfound wisdom, on the cutting-edge craft project designing, and creation offered by Cricut. You are now ready to follow the detailed instructions described in this book to create your own personalized, and one-of-a-kind, craft projects that reflect your creativity, and serve as an exhibit of your self-expression. You will be able to turn even the most unlikely, and seemingly, unrealistic ideas into beautiful craft projects in no time.

If you have worked your way through the projects in this book, you are well on your way to becoming a Cricut pro. Like a recipe book, the projects, along with the ideas in this book, can be adjusted, adapted, and added to, so that you can make each one uniquely yours.

With the Cricut, you are going to find birthdays, special occasions, seasonal holidays, and even school projects to be a lot easier, as well as more personalized. Everyone loves receiving gifts, cards and so on, that have been designed especially for them.

You do not have to stop at just making gifts for family and friends; you can even sell your specially designed crafts at markets, or online.

Expressions and artworks have made some amazing progress in the previous decade, and couple of things demonstrate this reality more than the Cricut machine. As you have seen, this machine is all that you need to turn any bit of paper, any take home gift, or any placemat into the craft you had always wanted.

You have gone to the correct place. With this book, you will learn precisely what you have to know to make your own creative projects in a matter of seconds.

This guidebook has been written to help you appreciate the power of your Cricut machine in terms of the projects that can be done with it. The step-by-step approach used to describe these projects will inspire your creative mind and produce designs that are even better than the ones described in this book.

You will be able to turn even the most unlikely and seemingly unrealistic ideas into beautiful craft projects in no time. You have learned all about the free resources including images, fonts, and projects that are available through the "Cricut" library so you can save money as you learn and sharpen your craft skills.

You've just become a professional Cricut user! If you forget things quickly, have this book with you every time you want to work on your Cricut machine.

Thank you and happy crafting!

CRICUT DESIGN SPACE

A Proven Step-by-step to Master the Design Space and Get the Best Out of Your Cricut Project Ideas. 369 Design Ideas, Screenshots and Detailed Illustrations with Tips & Tricks

Introduction

Cricut is a material design and cutting system which is specifically known as a die-cutting machine. It allows you to do numerous DIY projects like cards, invitations, vinyl designs, and much more. No matter what creative idea you might have, with the help of Cricut, you can probably do it. Cricut is a die-cutting machine that resembles a printer that has cutters attached to it. It can be used for printing and cutting of various materials. Are you still wondering what a Cricut machine is? The best way to explain itis that it is a home die-cutting machine used to create paper and various crafts and arts. It is basically an excellent cutting machine known as "the perfect entry point to the exact crafting universe." In fact, it is an artisan's companion who gives you the freedom to create amazing designs for different occasions. Many people think that these machines just cut paper, but they can do so much more than just cutting paper.

The world has been transformed with that machine as its products have been able to add special visual designs to the simple paperwork that we know. The Cricut machine has several models and versions some of them include Cricut Expression, Expression 2, Cricut Imagine, Cricut Gypsy, Cricut Cake Mini, Cricut Personal Cutter, Cricut Crafts Edition and Martha Stewart and the Cricut Explore air. The tool obviously fits into any type of craft you are working on. And there is also a die cut machine which gives you that extra-precise, sharp, and smart cutting application. The process of cutting materials by hand during crafts has been reduced drastically, thanks to this wonderful machine. Moreover, you can perform multiple projects all at the same time due to the effectiveness of this device. It contains several cartridges which are always available to help you explore different forms and shapes of several designs. In addition, moving from one project to another is easily possible with the use of the Cricut machine.

Any material can be shaped into the design you want it to be. Furthermore, you can also create patterns which are already pre-installed in the software that comes with it. The design software tool comes with pre-loaded designs for instant use. You can purchase this machine from your local craft store or the online store. There are different price ranges, based on the kind of model you are using, and you can pick one according to your needs. Anything which makes your work easier and faster is a very important investment and the Cricut machine is definitely one. Due to the efficiency of this machine, we now also have it in several places we never thought it would be in previous years. We have them in offices and specific workshops. If you think that the Cricut is a home-only tool, you are quite wrong. This time-saving device allows your work to be professional, and the beautiful thing about it is that we have no limits to what it can do. I am sure that you're reading this to gain more ideas and you might want to jump into making things and doing some stuff. Yes, that is cool; however, we first need to understand some basics else we would be making serious mistakes, and the process will look very confusing.

This guide will cover - The machine and the design space software, respectively. It may seem like too much information at first, but there's no need to be worried. You'll get used to it after a short time and see how all the systems work together. This guide will help you get a concise overview of your tasks and will encourage you to come up with fresh and innovative ideas. With a little practice, it should become effortless to use this machine and the design space program. You will take a closer look at some of the core features in the second section. You will also understand individual interface attributes and how they interact.

Chapter 1: What machine should I buy

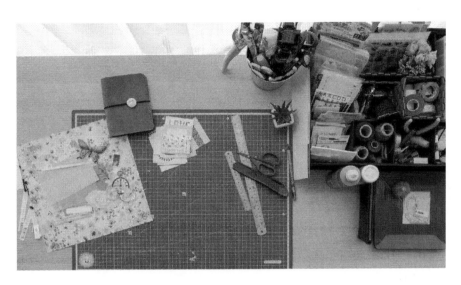

Here we will explore the machines available and help you decide the option that is best value for money for you. We will cover each of the currently available versions, what they can do, and the characteristics ideally suited to what types of crafts are outlined in this chapter.

Cricut Explore One

This is the simplest machine they sell, in terms of what's typically available from Cricut. This machine promises the ability to cut 100 of the most common materials presently available for use with your Cricut machine and is also extremely user friendly.

The Cricut Explore One is regarded by Cricut craft plotters as the no-frills beginner model and runs at a slower speed than the other available versions. The Cricut Explore One has just one component clamp within, so cutting or scoring can't be performed simultaneously, as compared to the others found in the current model line. Nevertheless, they can be performed in quick succession, one right after the other.

While this is a fantastic tool for a wide variety of crafts on 100 different materials and will get you on the right track to create beautiful crafts that are often cut from others, the cost is not as high as you would think. If you're going to use your art plotter mainly for those special occasions, then this is a fantastic tool to have on hand.

Cricut Explore Air

With all of the features of the Cricut Explore One and more capabilities, the Cricut Explore Air model comes loaded with Bluetooth functionality, has an integrated-in storage container to hold your tools in one place while you're working, so they won't roll away or get lost in the shuffle.

This model does have two on-board accessory clamps which allow for marking and cutting or scoring simultaneously. These clamps are labeled with an A and a B, so each time you load them up, you can be confident that your tools are going in the right positions.

This model is designed to handle the same 100 materials as the Cricut Explore One and runs at the same pace, so the difference in price represents individual variations and similarities! A fantastic deal and a powerhouse of a machine.

Cricut Explore Air 2

The Cricut Explore Air 2 is the current top-selling craft plotter from Cricut and is probably the best value they can give for the price. This model cuts materials at twice the speed of both the previous ones and has Bluetooth support and two adapter clamps on board.

The storage cup at the top of the unit features a smaller, shallower cut to hold your replacement blade while they aren't in use. If you want to swap to a different project between several different tips, they're all readily accessible. All cups have a smooth silicone rim, so you won't have to worry about your blades getting rusty or scratched.

It is the perfect tool for the job for someone who finds themselves using their Cricut with some frequency. You will be able to do your crafts twice as quickly, and each time, even at that pace, you will get a favorable outcome!

The Cricut Maker

The Cricut Maker is known as the flagship model of Cricut. It's the one that can do almost anything under the sun on almost any material you can bring into your machine's mat guides. The price point is the only drawback of this powerhouse model, and unless you want to make crafts to sell, this model proves to be quite expensive. Either way, you can be confident that whatever you do with this machine will always be of the highest quality. This baby is going to pay for itself in a short time if you sell your crafts.

This machine is full of exciting features for the enthusiastic crafters who want to turn up at the party with the most exquisite creations, that are ahead of their colleagues. This model really has everything.

There is no other Cricut machine with the speed of the Cricut Maker. The cuts that can be made using the precise blades that fit this machine are smoother than anything from a straight knife or other craft cutters you could ever expect. You can easily remove the tip from the housing using blade housings, add the next one, clip it back into place and start to roll your designs. Moreover, the machine will identify the loaded material, so at the start of the project, you won't have to specify the type of material. One common problem in the other models is that the project is halfway completed before the crafter discovers that the dial has been set wrongly.

The machine is, as some other models, fully Bluetooth compatible, and 10 times more powerful than any other with a specialized rotary cutter attachment that allows it to glide effortlessly through fabrics with accuracy.

Cricut Mini

These models were compatible with a Cricut device called the Gypsy, not the same as the Cricut Design Space currently in use today. Each machine has triumphed in innovating the processes of handcraft cutting.

Cricut's main goal was to amend the complexity of operating with its machinery while creating its newest line of models. Some crafter groups exchange hacks and mathematical leads to plan their machines as precisely as they want them to and this machine makes it easier than ever to operate.

The new selection of models available allows you to be as imaginative as possible in the design process so that no operations are unmanageable and take away from your creative flow.

When you own one of these machines, it needs upgrading, but you don't need to upgrade if you've done your crafting well with the one you have on hand. Cricut has always created products of superior quality, and Cricut Design Space still supports cartridges containing various thematic design elements.

Cricut Cartridge Adapter is a USB adapter that enables the import of your cartridges into Cricut design space so that all your elements are accessible in an organized place.

Design Space

Like many machines that are being placed on the shelves, this device also does come with a unique software filled with different settings and features to toggle with. All these components ensure that when you are using this instrument you end up with a beautiful, customized, and accurate product. Cricut's very own software is called "Cricut Design Space," and all of Cricut's devices come with this software, whether it is Cricut mini or Cricut Explore Air. Every Cricut owner must have this software installed in their device. The Cricut must be directly connected to the device via cable or by Bluetooth. Either way, the device needs to be close to the machine. The software is free and has a good user interface that makes it clear and easy to work with, even if you don't have any prior experience working with a similar device. Its user-friendly feature encourages creativity in an individual. The program is based on the Cloud, so even if your device is destroyed or has become inaccessible for any reason, the different design files can be safely recovered. It can be opened onto almost every device and available at any moment. A laptop, tablet or mobile can be used as well, and starting a project on one device and switching in between to another is possible. It can even be accessed offline. After the program has been installed, you need to create the designs from the beginning or use any one of thousands of templates already stored in its library. Design Space has a large, diverse collection to motivate a new crafter to start constructing and inventing. One can play around with varieties of fonts and images and new inspiring ideas. For optimum usage, a Cricut Explorer connected to a computer will be amazing. This way, all of the features are available, and the machine works without lag.

Cheat Sheets

The cheat sheets refer to the 12 functions of design space that can be used from the "Layers" panel. These features are amazing when it comes to customizing your pictures. Therefore, in this panel, you will be able to see some interesting features such as slice, Weld, connection, disconnection, Flatten, Unflatten, Visible / layer Escondido, Outline, Group, Ungroup, duplicate, and delete. So, let's go through each function and find out what you can do:

Slice - this feature is for two superimposed layers and can be divided into separate parts.

Weld - helps more layers join in a single form, eliminating any cutting lines that overlap.

To attach - You can use this feature to keep your cuts in position so that your pictures on the cutting show exactly like on the design screen. In addition, with this option, you should be able to inform the machine which image layer you wish to place the marker or text on.

Take off - it is exactly the opposite of the above function, as it can remove any bonded layer, allowing a separate cutting or removing of all other layers.

Flatten - this feature can convert any of the images on a printable form, by merging all selected layers in a single layer.

Unflatten - dividing the printable layers of an image into individual printable layers.

Outline - if you want to cut roads in a layer or to hide / Contours Show, this is the option you need to use, however, if the image has several layers, these will be grouped first.

Ungroup - this is the reverse of the group function as the function divides sets of images, or text layers, so they can be sized and moved individually on the screen design. For example, if you click Ungroup on a single layer of a text, you will be able to resize and move each letter of the text independently. This option does not influence how the images are presented in the cutting.

Double - if you want to create multiple versions of the same image, this is the option to use.

Remove - just select an item on the screen design, and it will be removed.

Score - you can also set the layer to score, but scoring a pencil is needed.

Print - With this option, you can transform your layer in a one-printable, so it can be printed and only then cut with the Cricut machine. The Flatten function mentioned above can be very useful because it can transform your multiple layers image on one to print a layer.

Remember that the Cricut Essentials iOS app does not come with Layers panel or the Edit menu, so in this case, you only need to tap.

Canvas Overview

Before you cut up your projects, the Canvas area is where all the designing and artwork happen. Here, you can organize your project, upload images or fonts.

The Cricut Design Space is similar to other design programs that most of us are using, like Adobe Creative Cloud, Photoshop, or Illustrator. And so, if you have any experience with these programs, then it won't be difficult for you to understand Design Space.

There is also the choice of getting a Cricut Access membership. With this, you can create your designs and let your creativity flow.

So, the Canvas Area is where you edit and touch up your designs before cutting them, but because there are many options that might overwhelm you, we will be taking these options one-by-one to explain their uses.

The Canvas Area is made up of the Right Panel, Left Panel, Top Panel, and Canvas Area.

Right Panel

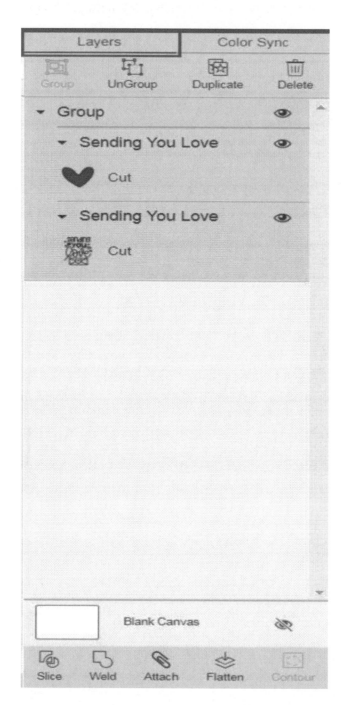

The Right Panel deals with layers, and so it can also be called the Layers Panel. Layers signify the designs that are on the canvas area. The number of layers that you use depends on the complexity of your design or the project that you're working on.

When making a birthday card, you will have texts and different decorations, and probably a picture or two. All of these are the layers of the design.

This panel allows you to create and manage layers when making a design. Every item that is on the layers panel will display the Fill or Line type that you are using.

Group, Ungroup, Duplicate, and Delete.

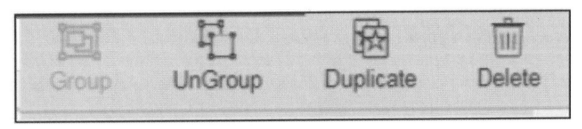

These settings allow you to move different designs around the canvas area.

Group: This allows you to group layers. When you have different layers that come together to make a complicated design, you use this option to bring them together. For example, if you're making a house, there will be different parts of that house. A standard home will have a roof, door, walls, and windows. 'Group' allows you to arrange all the layers and ensure that they stay together when you're making a design.

Ungroup: You can also separate a design of different layers, by clicking on this button. This is pretty much the opposite of 'Group'.

Duplicate: As the name implies, this option will duplicate the layers that you select on the canvas.

Delete: This option will delete any layer that you select and remove it from the canvas.

Blank Canvas

This is also a layer in the Right panel that gives you the option of changing the color of the canvas. If you're experimenting with your design, you can use this option to place it against various backgrounds.

Layer Visibility

This is represented by a little eye that is on every layer on the panel. It signifies the visibility of that layer or design. During designing, if you see that a particular segment or element doesn't look right, you can click on the eye to hide it. That way, you don't end up deleting it permanently if you decide to put it back. The hidden item can be identified with a cross mark.

Slice, Weld, Attach, Flatten and Contour

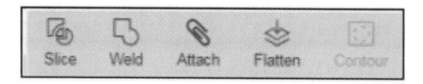

It's important to learn how to use these five tools. No matter what you're designing, they will come in handy.

Slice: This tool is meant for cutting out texts, shapes, and other elements from a whole design.

Weld: This is used for combining shapes to make a new shape. If you want to do something different with your designs, you can join two or more shapes together.

Attach: This is like a more powerful version of the Group option. It connects shapes and changes the color to match whatever background color you're using. This will remain even after cutting.

Flatten: This tool is useful when you're about to print two or more shapes. To do this, you should pick the layers that you want to print and select the Flatten option.

Contour- If you want to hide a layer of design, or just a small part, you can use this option to do so. Although, you can only do this when your design has layers that can be taken apart.

Color Sync

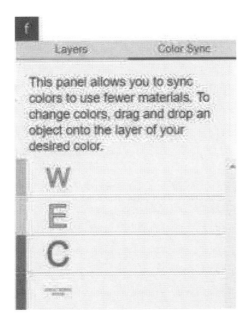

This option is meant for evening out the colors of your design and background. You can use this to change different shades of a color to just one color. It synchronizes the colors, as the name implies.

Left Panel

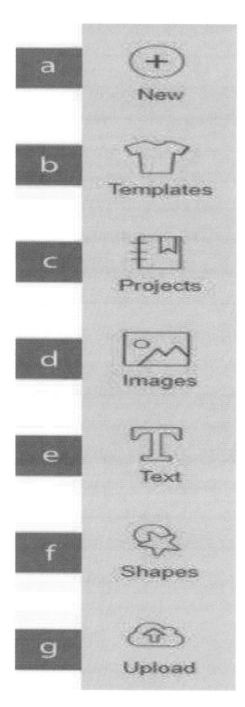

The left panel includes all the options you need for inserting. You can add shapes, texts, images, even ready-to-cut projects.

With this panel, you can add everything that you plan on cutting. The panel has seven options, and we will explore them all.

New

You select this option when you want to create a new page apart from the one that you're using to design.

It's advisable to save your designs before you move to the new page just in case you need it on another time. If not, you may lose your designs.

Templates

A template is used to give you a feel of what your design will look like when you cut it out on a particular type of fabric like a t-shirt or a bag. If you're making an iron-on design on a bag, it will show you a picture of the bag, and you can place the design on the template so you can plan how it will look in real life.

Templates are great because they give you an idea of what your design looks like when cut out. It won't cut out an actual backpack for you.

Projects

If you're ready to cut, then you should go to projects. You will pick your project, edit it, and tailor it to your taste and click on the 'Make It' option.

A large number of the projects are available to Cricut Access members, or some are available for purchase. Apart from these, a few are free.

Images

Images allow you to add a personal touch to your designs. With this option, you can insert pictures provided for you on Cricut Design Space.

Cricut even provides free images every week, although some come with Cricut Access.

Text

The text option allows you to add a text to your design or just on the canvas area. It opens a small window telling you to add text, and so you can do that and customize the font and color.

Shapes

You use this option when you want to add shapes to your canvas area. Cricut Design Space offers some shapes, namely triangle, square, pentagon, hexagon, octagon, star, and heart.

There is also the Score Line tool under the Shapes option. You can use this option to fold the shapes into different shapes, especially when you're making cards.

Upload

The last tool in the Left panel is the Upload tool, which allows you to upload your files and images apart from those Cricut provides for you.

With this, you can upload images or patterns.

Top Panel

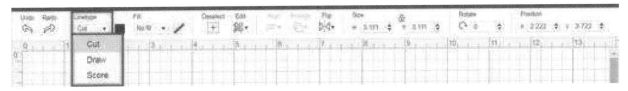

The top panel is the busiest panel. It has two different subpanels, and generally, the top panel is used for the general editing and organizing of elements and layers of design.

First Subpanel

This allows you to name your project, save it, and eventually cut it. Here, you can navigate to saving, naming, and sending your project to the Cricut machine for cutting.

Toggle Menu: This part of the subpanel allows you to manage your account and your account subscriptions. This menu also gives you the option of updating your Cricut Design Space, calibrating your machine and others.

Project Name: You can use this to name your project. Your project will be automatically called 'Untitled' until you give it a name that you can use to identify it.

My Projects: This is a library of all your projects saved on the Cricut Design Space, and so you can always refer to old projects.

Save: This option saves your project into the library. As you work, you should save in case your browser crashes.

Cricut Maker / Cricut Explore: When you're using Cricut Design Space for the first time, it asks you if you're using a Cricut Explore machine from the series or a Cricut Maker. Seeing as the Cricut Maker is a more advanced machine, it provides more benefits on Design Space than the machines in the Explore series.

Make It: After uploading your files, you click on Make It so that it can start to cut. The software will categorize your projects depending on their colors. Also, if you're planning to cut more than one project, you can use this to increase the projects that you want to cut.

Second Subpanel

This subpanel is the editing menu. It allows you to edit, organize, and arrange images and fonts on the Canvas Area.

Undo & Redo:

You can click undo when you make a mistake or create something that you don't want. And you can click on redo if you mistakenly delete something that you need.

Cut under (Line type): All your layers on the canvas area have this line type. After selecting the Make It option, the Cricut machine cuts the designs on your canvas area. Cut under allows you to change the colors of the layers and the fill too.

Draw (Line type):

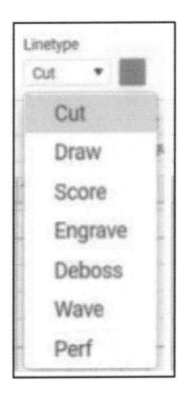

Cricut also allows you to write and draw on your designs. When you select this line type, you're given different options of different Cricut pens, and so, you can use these to draw on the canvas area.

Here, when you click on Make It, your Cricut machine will draw or write instead of cutting.

Score (Line type): This is an advanced version of the Scoring Line in the left panel. When you select this option for a layer, the layer will look scored. And so, when you click on Make It, the Cricut machine will score the materials instead of cutting them.

When you want to score, you will require a scoring stylus or scoring wheel. The scoring wheel can only work with the Cricut Maker.

Engrave, Wave, Deboss, and Perf (Line type): These four tools are brand new! They were released by Cricut recently and they can only be used by Cricut Maker users. Also, users have to have the latest version of the Design Space application. These tools allow you to have significant effects on a lot of materials.

Fill: This is mainly used for patterns and printing. You can only use this option when Cut is selected as a line type.

Print:

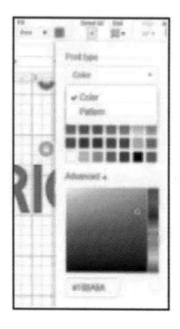

Cricut users really like this new option. It allows you to first print out your design, and then cut them out. To use the print option, when the fill option is active, you first click on Make It. And then, you send the files to your printer at home before feeding it into the Cricut for cutting.

Edit:

This icon contains three options on the drop-down menu. There is the cut option that allows you to remove an element from the canvas, the copy option which copies the same component without removing it and the paste option, which inserts the element that was cut or copied.

Select All: You can use this to highlight everything on your canvas area.

Align: There are different options under this, and it is important that you master all of them. They are:

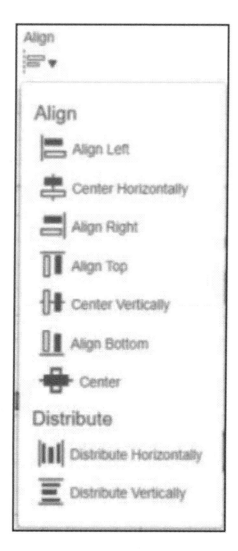

Align Left: This option ensures that all the elements are aligned to the left. The detail at the end of the left side will determine how the other details move.

Center Horizontally: This will align all the elements horizontally.

Align Right: This will align the elements to the right. As with align left, the item at the end of the left side will determine how the other items move.

Center: This aligns both the horizontally aligned and vertically aligned elements to the center.

Distribute: This allows you to create the same spacing between elements or layers.

Distribute Horizontally

Distribute Vertically

Flip:

If you want to reflect your designs as though they are looking at a mirror, you can use this option. It provides two options.

Flip Horizontal

Flip Vertical

Arrange:

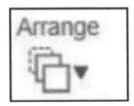

The arrange options allow you to move elements like images, texts, or designs to the front or back of others. It provides four options.

Send to Back: This will displace the selected designs or elements and take them to the back.

Move Backward: If you select an element and click on this, the elements move back once. If you have three parts, you can move one to the middle of the other two.

Move Forward: this is the opposite and it moves the element forward once.

Send to Front: This will displace the selected element and take it to the front.

Size:

This provides you with the options to adjust, increase or decrease the size of the elements or total design. Everything that you create has a scale, and you use this to modify the size. This is especially if you have a specific format that you're following.

Rotate:

The Cricut Design Space allows you to rotate the element or layer to any angle that you choose.

Position:

Seeing as the canvas area has grid lines, you can use these options to pick a particular position for the element on the X and Y axis.

Font:

For your projects, Cricut provides you with different fonts if you're using Cricut Access. If not, you can use your system's font or use the Cricut fonts for a price.

Font Size: This allows you to increase or decrease the size of your font.

Line Space: This is especially useful when you want to ensure that your texts on your design are evenly spaced or spaced according to your preference.

Letter Space: This allows you to arrange the spaces between the letters.

Style:

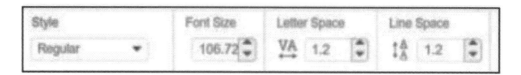

This includes Regular, which is the default setting. Bold, which makes the font thick. Italic, which tilts the font sideways. Bold Italic which combines both the Bold and Italic function.

Curve:

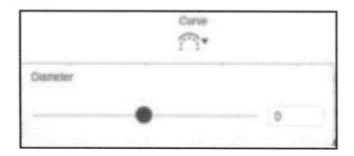

You can also design your texts by using the curve setting. You can curve your text upwards or inwards. You can also curve your texts into a circle.

Advanced:

On the top editing panel, this is the last option.

Ungroup to Letters: This allows you to disconnect each letter into single layers each.

Ungroup to Lines: This allows you to disconnect a paragraph on different lines.

Ungroup to Layers: This is a very tricky option, and it's only available on Cricut Access or if you purchase it.

Cricut Vocabulary.

With regards to the beginning stages of working with a Cricut machine and the Design Space programming, it can be overwhelming, attempting to make sense of what every one of the capacities and terms. Even though you probably can't wait to start using your awesome craft materials, and would rather skip the instructional exercises, it can be useful to acclimate yourself with all the terminology that Cricut machines use.

Align

At the point when at least 2 items are chosen on the canvas, this capacity aligns them as indicated by the determination of focus, left, right, and so forth.

Attach

The attach function has two functions. It enables you to hold images set up comparative with one another on the cutting mat and furthermore gives you a chance to attach score lines and add to images.

Arrange

Organizing a picture enables you to move it in front, behind or in the middle of other picture layers present on the canvas.

Color Sync

Color Sync board helps by merging the colors of one project so as to diminish the number of various materials or colors of materials you would have to use when heading off to the cut screen.

Contour

The Contour apparatus gives you a chance to shroud segments of a picture layer rapidly with the goal that they won't cut out.

Cut Button

The Cut key corresponds to the Cricut symbol button on one side of your keyboard. The button is pressed to begin the cut.

Cutting lines

Cut lines are the outlines of the form of the frame of each surface that will be cut when starting.

The Cut Screen a.k.a Make it Button

The screen that appears after you click the "make it" button at the top right-hand side, this screen will be available when the machine is cutting out designs.

Cutting Mat

The cutting mats are what you will adhere your material on, to stack into your Cricut machine.

Delete

Delete will permanently remove an image from the canvas.

Deselect All

Deselect all items as of now selected on the canvas.

Design Space

Cricut's cloud-based programming for designing and doing your projects.

Drawing Lines

Drawing lines or drafting lines will be the type of line used by the pen to write text or to draw an image.

Duplicate

Clone any image on the screen

Edit Bar

The editing bar that allows you to cut and reorder any item on the canvas.

Fill

Used when you want to fill an image present on the canvas.

Flatten

Flattening helps when a present vector, which has at least 2 layers, can be transformed into a printable image for the Print then Cut element.

Flipping

Flipping the image will transform it 180 degrees horizontally or vertically.

Group

Group command empowers numerous image layers or text present on the canvas to be selected and moved at once as one item so as not to influence their format.

Images or Image Library

Images that you can purchase or use for free in the Cricut Library or as complimentary gift segments of Design Space.

Layers (Panel)

Layers refer to bound together images on the canvas. Various images can be "layered" together.

Load Button

The load button is the two-fold bolt button present alongside the cut button on the machine. This will be squeezed to load and unload the cutting mat from the machine.

Material Settings

Material settings are available in Design Space or on the dial or the Explore machine. These are critical to setting the weight that the blade will use on the selected material.

SVG (a.k.a Scalable Vector Graphic)

An SVG cut document is a vector record that can be scaled to bigger or smaller and hold its goals. It is comprised of lines that include infinite specks to accomplish this flexibility.

Text or Font

Text is the means by which you can type words and redo your writing with exceptional fonts and contents within Design Space.

Undo

Undo an activity in Design Space.

Ungroup

Ungrouping allows you to move each layer of a vector on the canvas on its own.

Upload

Upload allows you to include your own vector, print or example fill images to Design Space.

Weeding

The way to remove undesirable extra vinyl from a cut design.

Weld

The welding device empowers you to consolidate 2 single shapes into one new shape for a solitary cut line. Welding is regularly used with text to create consistent cursive words.

Design Space Projects for Beginners

Custom Shirts

Custom shirts are incredibly easy. The beauty of this is, you can use the Cricut fonts or system options, and from there, you can simply print it on. Personally, I like to use the iron-on vinyl because it's easy to work with. Just take your image and upload it into Design Space. Then, go to the canvas and find the image you want. Once you've selected the image, you click on the whitespace that will be cut – remember to get the insides, too. Make sure that you choose cut image, not print from cut image, and then place it on the canvas to the size of your liking. Put the iron-on vinyl shiny side down, turn it on, and then select iron-on from the menu. Choose to cut, and make sure you mirror the image. Once done, pull off the extra vinyl to remove the vinyl between the letters. There you go! A simple shirt.

Vinyl Decals

Vinyl can also be used to make personalized items, such as water bottle decals. First, design the text – you can pretty much use whatever you want for this. From here, create a second box and make an initial, or whatever design you want. Make sure that you resize this to fit the water bottle, as well.

From here, load your vinyl, and make sure that you use transfer tape on the vinyl itself once you cut it out. Finally, when you adhere the lettering to the bottle, go from the center and then push outwards, smoothing as you go. It takes a bit of time, but there you have it – simple water bottles that children will love! This is a wonderful, simple project for those of us who aren't really that artistically inclined but want to get used to making Cricut items.

Printable Stickers

Printable stickers are the next project. This is super simple and fun for parents and kids. The Explore Air 2 machine works best.

With this one, you want the print then cut feature, since it makes it much easier. To begin, go to Design Space and download images of ice cream or whatever you want, or upload images of your own. You click on a new project, and on the left side that says images, you can choose the ones you like, and insert more of these on there.

From here, choose the image and flatten it, since this will make it into one piece rather than just a separate file for each. Resize as needed to make sure that they fit where you're putting them.

Cards!

Finally, cards are a great project idea for Cricut makers. They're simple, and you can do the entire project with cardstock.

To make this, you first want to open up Design Space, and from there, put your design in. If you like images of the beach, then use that. If you want to make Christmas cards, you can do that, too. Basically, you can design whatever you want to on this.

Now, you'll want to add the text. You can choose the font that you want to use, and from there, write out the message on the card, such as "Merry Christmas." At this point, instead of choosing to cut, you want to choose the right option – the make it option. You don't have to mirror this but check that your design fits properly on the cardstock itself. When choosing material for writing, make sure you choose the cardstock.

From there, insert your cardstock into the machine, and then, when ready, you can press go and the Cricut machine will design your card. This may take a minute, but once it's done, you'll have a wonderful card in place. It's super easy to use.

Basic Tools in Cricut Design Space

Cricut machines can also be used with a ton of tools, and most of them are pretty straightforward to use. Here are some of the best tools to consider for your machine:

Wavy tool: Helps you cut waves into your design.

Perforation tool: Helps to make perforated markings in your design.

Weeding tool: This is one of the best tools to use when working with vinyl because it helps with peeling vinyl from the backing sheets.

Scraping tool: This helps remove any tiny pieces off of the design and prevents the material from moving around.

Spatula: This is a great one because it helps with moving the design off the backing without tearing the material and can keep it free of debris.

Tweezers: These are good for pulling the tiny pieces of vinyl or other design elements from the middle without pulling the edges or tearing them.

Scissors: Cricut scissors are durable, made of stainless steel with micro-tip blades – perfect for detailed work.

Paper trimmer: This is really convenient with straight cuts, so you do not need to use scissors or a ruler. It is essential for working with vinyl.

Brayer: If you are using fabric or larger pieces of vinyl, this is actually one of the best tools to keep the material stabilized on your mat so the mat itself is not damaged.

Backup mats: This should be obvious, but if you are going to work with larger projects, the carpets do lose their stickiness after a while. This can prevent you from having to leave your project to pick up more.

Easypress Tool: This is awesome for iron-on vinyl that you do not want to iron. It also holds the vinyl much better, even if you wear it a lot, and eliminates the temperature and time guesswork you may otherwise have to do. It is a little pricey, but there are beginner options.

Brightpad: Finally, you have a Brightpad, which helps make the lines that you need to cut more visible. If you are doing more than just one cut, this is handy, since it will help with tracing, and with adapting the patterns, too.

These tools are essential, and to pick up the first few on the list, you will want to get the toolset, since it is much cheaper. But if you are going to be using your machine a lot, I highly recommend spending a little extra by picking up tools to use with it.

Chapter 2: Starting a New Project

After setting up your Cricut machine according to the instruction, there will be directions on your screen that you must follow to create your first project. You will still be using the link you found on the paper when you were setting up your machine. If you have not yet received your machine and are interested in knowing how it works, or you are looking for extra clarifications, here's what it will say.

First Step

First off, load a pen into the accessories clamp. You can pick whichever color you think will go best with the paper you have received. Next, you want to turn the knob so that the indicator is pointed to "cardstock," considering that is what you will be working with. Have you had a proper look at your mats yet? The blue mat is what you will want to use for this project. You should remove the plastic cover - keep it, don't throw it away as you will need to recover your mat when you're done to avoid dust accumulation - and lay down the paper on the mat with the top left corners of the material and the grid aligned.

Second Step

Make sure that the paper is pressed flat before you push it between the rollers firmly. The mat has to rest on the bottom roller. When it is in place, press the "Load" button to load your mat between the rollers. Press the "go" button, which will be flashing at this stage, and wait for the machine to work its magic on your project. Once everything is done, the light will flash, and you can press the "Load" button again to unload the mat. Your paper will still be sticking to the mat when you remove it.

Third Step

Be careful when removing the material from the mat. Don't be too hasty; take your time so that it doesn't tear. Pull the mat away from the cardstock instead of doing it the other way around. After completing that step, you can now fold the cardstock in half, insert the liners into the corner slots of the card, and it's done!

You have just made your first ever Cricut project in a matter of minutes from start to finish! Congratulations! What are you waiting for? Do more projects! There are a ton of templates you can play around with—practice, practice, practice.

Launching the Platform Downloading and Installing,

Cricut access (monthly and annual)

Unlimited Access to more than 400 attractive fonts.

Unlimited Access to more than 50,000 cut-ready, covet-worthy premium Cricut images.

10% discounts on every product you purchase on cricut.com. This includes machines, materials, accessories, and many more (including sale items.)

10% discounts on Premium licensed images, fonts, and ready-to-make projects. These projects are from brands such as Disney, Anna Griffin, and Simplicity.

Priority member care line (50% reduction in wait time.)

Downloading and Installing

The first stage of learning the Cricut Design Space is to know how to download and install it correctly. The steps are not so complicated, all you need is to have the basic computer skills, i.e., know your way around your PC or Desktop. Follow the steps below to get your Design Space downloaded, installed, and launched.

Go to your internet browser on your PC or Desktop, then open the following address to access Cricut design website.

Once you are on the platform, select "Download." The download should start immediately, and the display will change once it starts downloading. However, the display could be quite different

depending on the browser you are using. The screenshots being used are from Google Chrome.

Once the download has been completed, either go to your "Downloads" folder or double-click on the file that appears after the download on your browser.

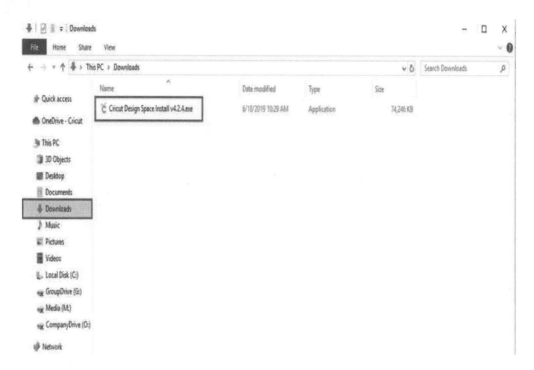

You might get a popup, asking you if you want to trust the application or not, select "Yes" and wait for the next window.

Beta v4.2.4

You should have a setup window displaying the installation progress popup shortly after.

Go ahead and input your registered ID and password on Cricut to sign in.

For most computers, a Design Space icon gets added automatically to your home screen. Right-click the icon and then select "Pin to Taskbar," or get the icon dragged to the taskbar to get the shortcut pinned for easy access.

And that's it! You're done with the installation of your Design Space. That wasn't so hard, was it? You can now proceed to launch the app when you are ready. You can also share your feedback by using the feedback tab located at the lower part of the design space menu.

Lastly, you need to ensure that your Design Space has the latest version. This will make sure you're up to date with all that Cricut offers, and you get the best results from your Cricut Machine. To find the current version of your Design Space application, follow the steps below:

Left click on the small arrow located on the Taskbar to reveal hidden icons.

Place your mouse on top of the Design Space icon (don't click.)

The Cricut Bridge version should appear.

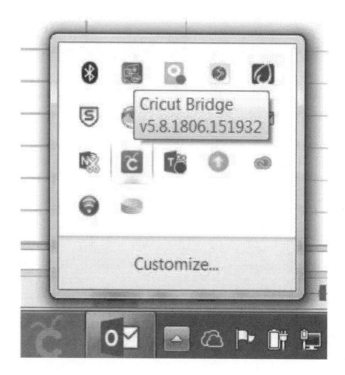

Getting Started

Now that you have your Design Space downloaded and installed, the next step is to launch the app and start making use of it. However, before we discuss that, I'll quickly give a short walkthrough on how you can set up your Cricut machine. This is for Cricut users who are new to the whole system.

Setting up your Cricut machine doesn't take too much time or stress. Although you need to be watchful while doing it, it should take you approximately an hour to finish the setup. Fortunately, you will find some tools inside the package to help you through the setup. The following are the tools you'll need to get your machine set up:

Cricut Maker

Power Cord and USB cable

Fine Point Pen

A Fine Point Blade

Rotatory Blade with Housing

FabricGrip Mat 12" by 12"

LightGrip Mat 12" by 12"

An internet-enabled computer with the basic requirements. (If you're using the Desktop platform)

Note: The computer will not come with the box.

The following are the procedures for setting up your machine:

Unbox the package, and you'll find a couple of tools placed on the machine, and the power cord should be under it all. Unwrap the machines and the supplies you find inside the box.

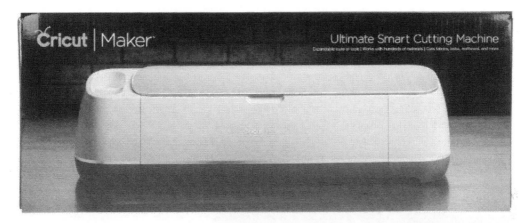

Log in with your previous ID or create a new one if you don't have it.

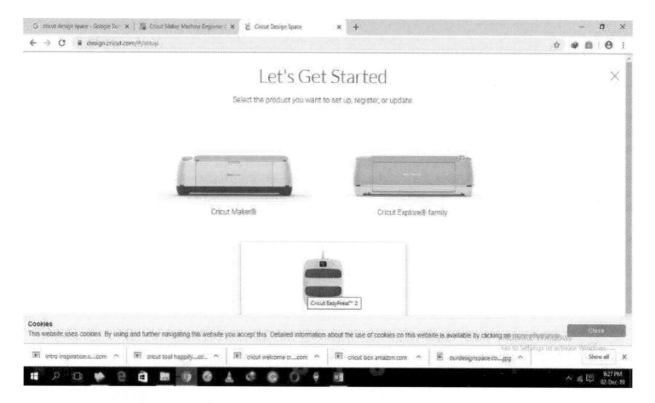

Plug all the cables in the right place, the USB cord from your machine to the computer, and the power cable to a power outlet.

And that should get your machine all set up!

Now back to our primary objective; the Cricut Design Space. Once you set up your machine and Design Space for the first time, you get a one-month free subscription to Cricut Access. Let's discuss for a while about Cricut Access.

Cricut access

Cricut Access grants you access, either monthly or yearly, to the image library of over 50,000 unlicensed images, over a thousand projects, and over 400 fonts.

There're three flexible plans available to choose from:

Cricut Access - Monthly

Cricut Access - Annual

Cricut Access - Premium

With Cricut Access, you will benefit from your subscription with:

Unlimited Access to more than 400 attractive fonts.

Unlimited Access to more than 50,000 cut-ready, covet-worthy premium Cricut images.

10% discounts on every product you purchase on cricut.com. This includes machines, materials, accessories, and many more.

10-50% discounts on licensed images, fonts, and ready-to-make projects.

Priority member care line option.

Cricut access (premium)

Unlimited Access to more than 400 attractive fonts.

Unlimited Access to more than 50,000 cut-ready, covet-worthy premium Cricut images.

10% discounts on every product you purchase on cricut.com. This includes machines, materials, accessories, and many more (including sale items.)

10% discounts on Premium licensed images, fonts, and ready-to-make projects. These projects are from brands such as Disney, Anna Griffin, and Simplicity.

About 50% discounts on licensed images, fonts, and ready-to-make projects.

Free Economy Shipping on orders worth more than $50.

Priority member care line (50% reduction in wait time.)

To purchase through Cricut.com, follow the steps below:

Proceed to sign in by inputting your Cricut username and password.

Choose your desired plan, and then proceed by adding it to your Cart.

Proceed to checkout your order and complete the purchase.

Once you have successfully submitted your order, your new Cricut Access Plan should activate immediately.

To purchase on the Design Space (Windows or Mac,) consider following the procedures below:

Sign in by inputting your Cricut username and password on the Design Space.

Click the menu icon on the Design Space, then click on "Cricut Access."

Go through the available plans and choose the appropriate option.

Photo credit: help.cricut.com

Enter your Credit Card details (or just review it if you've made a purchase before), and then click "Continue."

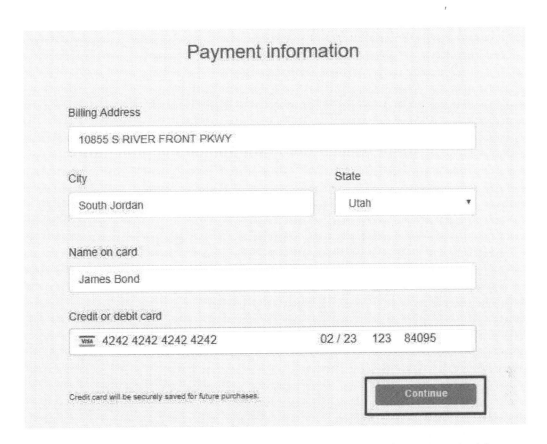

Payment information

Billing Address

10855 S RIVER FRONT PKWY

City

South Jordan

State

Utah ▾

Name on card

James Bond

Credit or debit card

VISA 4242 4242 4242 4242   02 / 23   123   84095

Credit card will be securely saved for future purchases.

Continue

When your payment information has been saved, enter your password to proceed with your purchase, and then click on "Authorize."

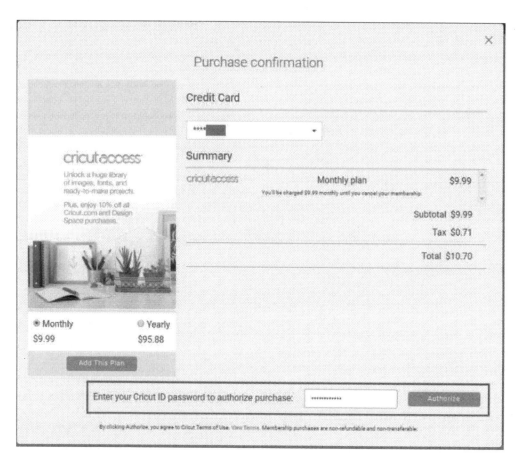

Once you have successfully authorized your purchase, your new Cricut Access Plan should activate immediately and should be available in every Design Space platform.

Design Space Environment

Before we conclude this introductory chapter, it's necessary to introduce you to the Design Space environment. It is usual for a new user of Cricut Design Space to get easily confused on their first session. We'll take an overview of the general things you see when you first sign in.

We'll be discussing majorly on the Design Space menu contents. The menu serves as a way of navigating through primary screens in the Design Space such as "Home" and "Canvas." From the menu list, you can likewise get to every other feature of Design Space such as Settings, Help, Print then cut calibration, Link Cartridges, Account Details, and Manage Custom Materials.

Home

The "Home" button, when clicked, will always take the user to the Home screen. And at the Home screen, you can go through the numerous curated project lists. You can also get swift access to previous projects or start new ones. Your project won't be removed when you navigate through the Home screen until you decide to start a new one by adding it to the canvas.

Machine Reset Basic Object Editing.

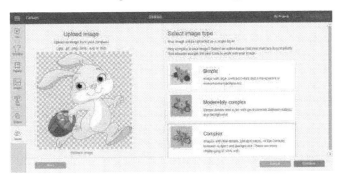

First, you will need to browse the image on your computer and upload it using the "Upload" command. After that, you will want to choose, from the three image options, the "Complex" type.

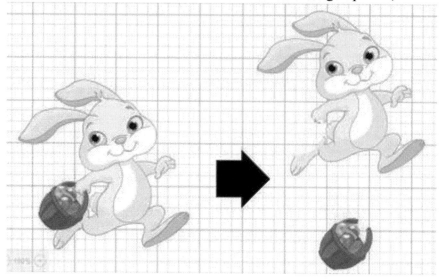

Once you have done all that just select "Continue".

In the next part, you will be taken to a window with various editing options. You will have the option Undo/Redo any action or Zoom in/Zoom out from the image (1). On the left side you will have the most important tools for this job: "Select & erase", "Erase" and "Crop" (2). In this example, we will be using all three of these tools so you can get the full set of information from this technique. First, we will separate the basket from the rabbit and after that, we will separate the rabbit from the basket.

If necessary zoom out to be able to view the entire picture.

If you want to separate a small part of a larger picture, use the "Crop" tool to isolate the targeted area. In this case, we need only the basket so most of the image can be cropped out.

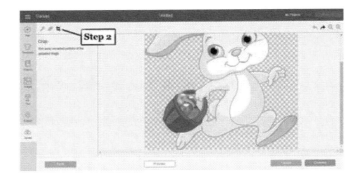

Step 3: Once the rest of the image is cropped we need to remove any part of the remaining picture that we don't want. To do that we can use the "Select & erase" tool.

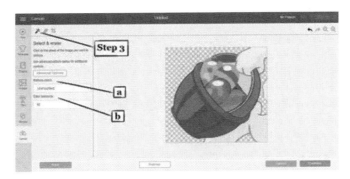

By selecting "Advanced Options" you can directly remove the color by using the "Reduce colors" tab (a). You can also increase the "Color tolerance" (b) which allows you to clear large portions more easily with the "select" method.

To remove the fine lines and small details we can use the "Erase" tool.

Tip: Depending on your image you can increase or decrease the size of the eraser by moving the slider left or right.

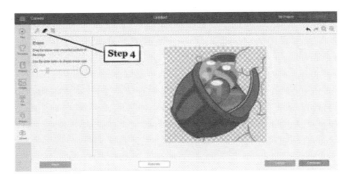

Click "Continue" button.

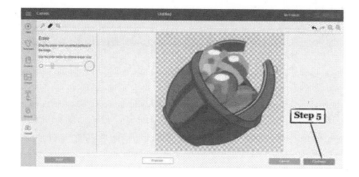

Select the type of image that you want to save and click "Save". Here you can choose between a "Print then cut image" or "Cut image".

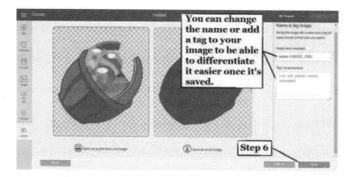

Once we have our first part separated (the basket) we can move on to the rabbit. To do that we need to upload the image again and repeat the process.

Follow the same steps as before but now remove the basket using the "Select & erase" and the "Erase" tool again.

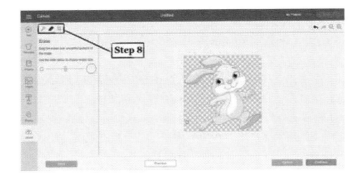

Once the image is saved we can add our separated pictures on our canvas. To do that you have first to select each image and then use the "Insert Images" button.

Result: Each image is now considered its own layer and can be resized, moved, and edited to your liking.

How to Browse and Search for Cartridges,

While making a project, you may decide to utilize structures from cartridges (image sets). Images inside cartridges for the most part have a comparative design feel which can help your task to feel increasingly durable.

To review distinctive cartridge choices, start by getting to the Cricut Image Library. Click "Addition Images" from the left menu of the design screen.

Another window will open containing the Image Library. Select the Cartridges tab on the upper left of the screen to search in sequential order a list of more than 400 cartridges.

The view will change to incorporate a list of all Cricut cartridges, every one of which is listed by an even tile.

Tip: Purchasing a whole cartridge can be a huge cost saver over buying singular images.

To show every one of the images found inside a cartridge, click "View All Images".

The view changes to show all of the images inside the cartridge. Here you can look and browse inside this particular cartridge. The text in the hunt bar demonstrates that you are looking through just inside this cartridge.

To look for a particular image in the cartridge, type the term in the inquiry bar and select the amplifying glass.

The outcomes show the images inside the cartridge that have been labeled with your hunt term. When images are chosen, click "Addition Images" to add them to the design screen.

Tip: View all images from the cartridge once more, by tapping the "X" in the inquiry field. Come back to search all cartridges, by tapping on the Cartridges list.

You will now be able to move and estimate images to envision what they'll look like on your task.

Searching for Cartridge with Filters

Designs are produced from components saved on capsules. Each cartridge includes a computer keyboard overlay and education booklet. The plastic computer keyboard overlay suggests key collections for this chance only. Nevertheless, lately Provo craft has published a "universal overlay" which can be used with cartridges released after August 1, 2013. The objective of the universal overlay would be to simplify the practice of clipping by simply needing to learn 1 keyboard overlay rather than being required to find out the overlay for every individual cartridge. Designs could be cut on a PC using all the Cricut design studio applications, on a USB attached gypsy device, or could be directly inputted onto the Cricut device employing the computer keyboard overlay. There are two forms of cartridges, font, and shape. Each cartridge has many different creative attributes which could allow for countless distinct cuts from only 1 cartridge.

Advanced Tips and Tricks Working with Text Adding

Many people forget that the pen is still in their machine after finishing a project and that can be a big no-no. The reason for this is because if the lid is not on it, it will dry out and the pens can get very expensive. So be sure to put the pen cap back on and make sure it is all the way on.

Keeping some supplies on demand is a good idea as well, particularly if you're going to be working with vinyl and cardstock. Since most projects use vinyl, you could have some of that on hand along with a pack of cardstock and things of that nature.

When your mat loses its stickiness, you may think that you have to buy a new one. You do not, however, at least in most cases, because there are tips you can use here too. Clean your mat and see if that works and then tape your project down to hold it in place. Not over an area that needs to be cut but just over a few edges. A tack paint that is medium tape is good for this and shouldn't damage the cardstock.

A trick for installing fonts into your computer, you may need to sign out of the app and then back in before your new font will show up. If this does not work, then be sure to restart your computer.

If you have a project that cuts on two different materials (such as a pink cardstock and a purple cardstock), you can do this at the same time by positioning the designs you will be cutting in different areas of the canvas on your app. Click Attach, then position the materials in the same spot on the map. This tip can be applied to Design Space for desktop and web.

If you use all of these tips, you will be able to use your machine to your heart's content and make any project. You will also be able to save money so that you're not spending a fortune on supplies every time you run out. Utilize these to your benefit and enjoy being able to use your machine with better knowledge.

Text Edit Bar Overview.

The edit bar remains grayed out until an image, shape, template, or text is placed on the canvas. It is located directly beneath the header bar, but directly on top of the canvas.

The options on the edit bar are determined by the selected object on the canvas:

Templates — When you use a template, the edit bar will tell you if you can adjust the template. These are predetermined by the system and you will need to make your selection based on what the template has been designed with. The edit bar will list the changes that you can make; for instance, a T-Shirt template gives the option of 'Type', 'Size', and 'Color'.

Common options — There are some common options that both text and images us on the edit bar. These are options are:

Undo — This will undo the latest edit, addition, or deletion.

Redo — This will redo something that has recently been undone.

Linetype — This option tells the Cricut to use a blade to 'Cut', 'Draw' with a pen, or use the Scoring stylus or wheel to create a scoreline. You can 'Deboss' with the debossing tip, 'Engrave' with the engraving tool, and change a line to perforated which is 'Perf' or wavy 'Wave'. These are add-on tools to use with the Cricut.

Linetype Swatch — This is the little box next to the 'Linetype'. When you click on the box, it will bring up a color swatch. This will change the color of the object selected on the screen.

Fill — The 'Fill' option is used for cutting or printing. This option tells Design Space where to send the project to first. It is used for print and cut projects.

Arrange — The 'Arrange' function changes the order of how objects appear on the screen when they are layered on top of each other. There is a stacking order to objects when they are layered on the screen. 'Send to Back' sends the selected object to the bottom of the layer stack. 'Move Backwards' moves the selected object one layer back. 'Send to Front' sends the selected object to the top of the layer. 'Move Forward' sends the selected object one layer forward.

Flip — This option is used to flip the image horizontally or vertically to create a shadow image or mirrored image.

Size — You can change the size of selected objects on the screen by selecting them and dragging them with the mouse. This option allows you to size the selected object or entire text box more accurately if you need an exact size. You can set the width and height of an unlocked object. Locked objects will set to scale.

Rotate — This option rotates the selected object by the degree you set in the box.

Position — You can move selected objects around the screen by selecting them and dragging them with the mouse. For more accurate positioning, you can set the x-axis and y-axis position in these boxes.

Editing Text — The edit bar changes slightly when you are editing text. There are a few additions to the common options listed above:

Font — There are different types of fonts to choose from. Some are free and some can be purchased. The system will also pick up the system fonts you have installed on the device that you are working on.

Style — This option allows you to change the style of the font to Bold, Italic, Underline, Bold and Underline, Regular, or Writing.

Line Space — This option sets the line spacing between lines of type.

Alignment — This option is used to set the text alignment to center, left, or right.

Curve — Curve lets you curve the selected text up or down.

Advanced — Allows you to ungroup a word to individual letters so that you can move or size individual letters in a word, line, or layer.

How to Select Font

If you have ever worked with the Image Edit Tool before, then you will be familiar with the Text Edit tool in Cricut Design Space. It is because the two tools are similar in their mode of operation in rotating, sizing, and positioning of text. The similarity of the tools will excite you because it makes the job simpler when editing the text and locating the right font. With this, you can personalize projects easily.

How to Edit Fonts

The Edit bar in Cricut Design Space, grants you access to edit the features of particular images or text. These features include Linetype, Size, Rotate, Fill, Position and Mirror. In the Text layers, there are additional options, including Line Spacing, font styles and letter spacing. So how do you edit the font? Here, I will show you.

Select the text object you want to edit on the Canvas, or you can insert text from the design panel, or select a text layer from the Layers Panel. Once it is selected, the Text Edit Bar will pop up directly below Standard Edit Bar. Note that the Standard Edit Bar will be hidden when you are not interacting with the text.

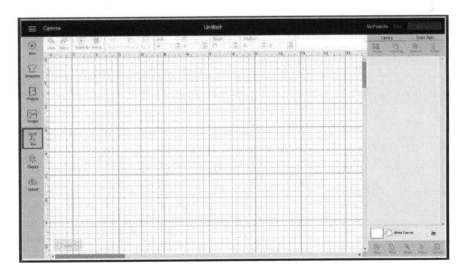

When the Text Edit Bar pops up, you can begin to manipulate the font using the options described below.

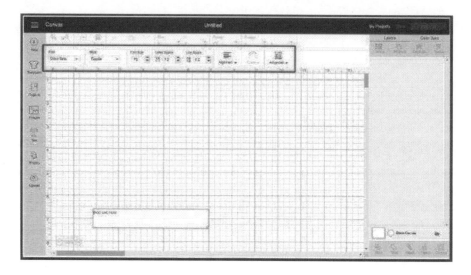

Text Sizing.

Navigate to the left-hand side of the Canvas and select the Text tool. When the Text tool is selected, the font list will open if you are using iOS/Android or the Text bar and text box will pop up for users with Windows/Mac.

Select the desired font size and the font type you intend to use and then input your text. If you intend to start on a new line of text on the same textbox, use the 'Return' key after the prior line of text. Do not freak out if you did not choose the font setting before typing the text, with Cricut Design Space, and it is possible to type the text before selecting the font on a Windows/Mac computer.

Click or tap on any area outside the text box to close it.

To edit the text is pretty simple. Double click on the text to display available options.

The Edit bar is found at the top of the Canvas for Windows/Mac users and the bottom of the Canvas for iOS/Android users.

Chapter 3: Intermediate and Advanced Level Projects

Pumpkin Pillows

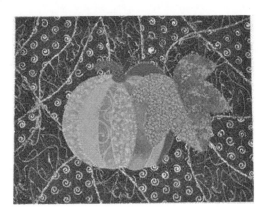

Materials:

Burlap pad spread

Printable heat transfer

Material paper (whenever required for your image)

Iron

Printer and ink

Pumpkin record of your choice

Steps

Download the pumpkin records that you want to use to your PC as a jpg document. Utilize the transfer button in configuration space to import. For the blue pumpkin particularly, make certain to pick the unpredictable picture type. The other two imported fine with the reasonably unpredictable setting.

When you add to the canvas, you can see that it is a print. At that point cut by the layer's menu on the correct hand side. Resize to whatever size you require for your pumpkin pad. You should remember the size of your heat transfer. The Cricut will likewise print an outskirt around the picture so as to see it on the machine. It will have to be adjusted if the picture is too huge to even consider fitting with the fringe.

Press start and wait until it ready and you can cut it. Ensure that the material size is right for your before you begin to heat transfer.

Cowhide Notebook

Materials:

Cricut Maker

Blade

Scoring Wheel

Cricut Metallic Leather

Foil Poster board

White cardstock (12×24 sheets offer better material usage)

Regular Iron-on in white

Material Paper

Specialty blade

Needle

String

Scissors

Weeding apparatuses (optional)

Cricut EasyPress

Simple Press tangle

Speedy dry glue

Cricut Cut File

Steps

Calfskin spread – cuts incredible with the blade sharp edge. Make certain to move the star wheels right to one side before cutting.

Iron-on applique – make sure to reflect your picture before cutting. Cut with your fine point cutting edge and remove extra bits with your weeding instruments.

White card stock – cut nine pieces that are scored down the middle. The 12×24 size papers offer better material use here. The single scoring wheel works extraordinary for ordinary card stock. The machine will score your material first, at that point stop and request the cutting sharp edge.

Foil card stock – the scoring wheel is an absolute necessity for this sort of material! Utilize the twofold wheel to guarantee an incredible overlap line with no breaking. You can change the scoring wheel from single to twofold effectively with the Quick-Swap Drive Housing.

Utilize the Easy Press for best performance.

Put the weeded bit of iron-on straight forwardly on the calfskin with the transporter sheet and keep everything joined.

Spread the whole thing with material paper to secure your surface.

Follow the guidelines of Cricut Easy Press rules for time and temperature.

Remove the transporter sheet while still warm.

At that point, utilize a speedy dry section to put the foil banner board within your scratch pad as demonstrated. Line up the folds with the little cuts in the cowhide.

Simply pull up on the circle you made in the calfskin and afterward get it through the rectangular opening. Include a pen and this is one charming DIY cowhide diary!

Makes for a beautifully customized gift.

Wood Coasters

Materials

Basswood 1/16″ thick

Cricut Maker

Blade sharp edge

Covering tape

Specialty paint

Wood stick

Enviro-Tex Lite-Pour-On High Gloss Finish

Castin'Craft Opaque Pigment in your preferred shades

Mix sticks

Estimating cups

Blending cups

Cricut cut document

Instructions:

Cut the basswood with the Cricut Maker and the blade sharp edge. There are a couple of things to remember when utilizing your blade sharp edge to cut wood.

Make certain to use your solid grasp tangle and tape the wood down around all edges with veiling tape.

Cut with the fitting basswood setting and watch your machine cautiously. Part of the way through the cut, begin checking the slice to check whether it is finished. Remove the material from your machine once the pieces are carved right through.

This starfish configuration functions admirably with the blade cutting edge yet extremely perplexing plans won't cut well.

Name and Kiss Glitter Tumbler

Material

Pink and red glitter vinyl

Green StandardGrip mat

Strong grip transfer tape (comes with the glitter vinyl)

Cricut Fine-Point Blade

Weeding tool

Scraping tool

Pair of scissors for cutting the material to size

A tumbler, your choice of size and color

Directions:

Start a new project in Design Space.

Select 'Templates' and search 'Drinking Glasses.'

Select the template.

Customize the template to match the height and width of your tumbler. You can change the color if you need to.

Select 'Shapes' from the left-hand menu.

Choose 'Circle,' unlock it, and resize it to w = 2.457" and h = 1.628". It should look oblong, like a lemon.

Make the oblong shape pink.

Move it to the middle of the tumbler template and position it to fit perfectly.

Click 'Text' from the left-hand menu, choose a nice font, and type the name to personalize the tumbler.

Move the text into the middle of the pink oblong shape and squash it to fit.

Select the oblong shape and text, right-click, and select 'Attach.'

Click 'Image' from the left-hand menu, and search for lips. For a free option, #MF727550 is good for this project.

Rotate the lips until they are straight.

Move the pink oblong shape out of the way and move the lips to fit in the same position as the pink oblong shape. The oblong shape will stick onto one side of the tumbler while the lips will go on the opposite side.

Change the color of the lips to red.

Save the project.

Click 'Make it' and you see two boards on the left-hand side panel. One will be in red, the other one in pink.

If you look at the board for the first picture, you will see how much vinyl you will need to cut up. Use the lines on the cutting board to help you cut the perfect size vinyl for both the red and pink section of the cut.

Stick the first color (1) onto the cutting board and load it into the Cricut.

Press continue, and select the material type. For the Cricut Maker, there is a setting for glitter vinyl; for other Cricut machines, follow the instructions inside the pack.

Make sure the Cricut dial is set to custom.

Make sure the fine-point blade is in the holder.

When the Cricut is ready to cut, press 'Go.'

Unload the first cut from the Cricut.

Load the second (2) paper and follow steps 20 to 24.

Use the weeding tool to clean up the lips, the oblong shape, and the text.

Cut two pieces of strong transfer paper the size of each of the decals.

Working with glitter vinyl is tricky, and you have to be extra careful when pulling off the backing paper.

The best way to get the backing paper off is to put the design on a flat surface. The transfer paper must be against the surface and then carefully pull off the backing paper.

Position the lips in the middle of the tumbler, and stick it on using the scraping tool to ensure it has stuck correctly.

Pull off the transfer paper. This part should not be as hard as the glitter vinyl is very sticky.

Repeat steps 30 to 31 for the name in the oblong shape Burlaps

Materials:

Burlap (a genuinely tight weave works best)

Shabby Glue

Pouncer brush

Wax paper

Cricut Maker

Cricut Strong Grip move tape

Cricut green tangle

Earthenware pot (roughly 3 creeps in distance across at the top)

Styrofoam ball

Greenery

Craft glue and paste firearm

Cricut delicious document

Steps:

Start with a 12 x 12 square of burlap and lay it on to ensure your work surface. Blend the paste creamer in with water. At that point use a pouncer brush to apply this blend all over your burlap.

Allow it to dry. This might take a long time. At that point simply strip your hardened burlap from the wax paper sheet. Presently we need to get this solid material to adhere to a Cricut tangle. Apply solid grasp move tape to the rear of your burlap. At that point place the non-clingy side of your exchange tape down onto your tangle. Press it down truly well. You can even utilize a brayer or moving pin here.

Felt Banners

Materials:

Dowel slice to 5.5″

Felt

Heated glue

Yarn

Steps:

Plug in your heated glue firearm to get it warmed up, at that point cut your felt utilizing the turning sharp edge and texture tangle. Strip away the additional felt.

Strip off the flag. Spot the dowel on top, and crease over the top edge to see where the dowel should be set.

Include a line of craft glue.

Carefully overlay the top over. On the off chance that you have a low-temp stick firearm, or thick felt, you may have the option to squeeze it down with your fingers… yet to be protected you could utilize a pencil or the rest of the dowel so you don't burn your fingers.

Coffee Sleeves

Materials:

Felt (I used the Cricut felt sheets)

Iron on Vinyl (I used the sparkle vinyl in silver)

Cricut Cutting Machine

Weeding instruments (optional)

Cricut Easy-Press (optional)

Velcro

Texture paste or sewing machine

Cut document

Steps:

Start by cutting your pieces. Cut the words from sparkle iron on vinyl utilizing your fine point cutting edge. Make sure to reflect the cuts on the iron on vinyl and spot its glossy side down on your tangle. Cut the sleeve itself from felt. On the off chance that you need to mark your cutting two of the sleeves one after another, you might need to change the situation inside Design Space to capitalize on your material. It needs to cut every sleeve from one sheet of felt.

Start by featuring your first tangle with a sleeve. At that point click on the sleeve itself.

Next snap the second tangle that has a sleeve. Snap the sleeve itself and snap the three dabs. At that point pick "move to another tangle".

Pick the tangle with the principal sleeve.

Presently you simply need to turn it and move the position, so it isn't covering the first. You would now be able to cut two sleeves from one sheet of felt.

Remove all material from your vinyl pattern including the focuses of your letters.

Earrings for Women

Materials:

Fake calfskin

Cricut machine (any of them will work the fake calfskin)

Adornments discoveries (snares and bounce rings)

Adornments forceps (two sets are needed when working with hop rings)

Sharp article to punch gaps

Cut record

Step:

Start by downloading a free SVG record and transferring it to your Cricut machine. If you are having issues with the process look back at previous instructions. Then resize the document accordingly before cutting. To cut the false calfskin, place the material face down on the tangle.

At that point place your cuts in Cricut Design Space and pick fake cowhide as your material. Cut the calfskin with your machine.

When the cut is finished, remove the tangle from the machine and strip back the extra material to uncover your cut hoops.

Then remove the studs themselves from the tangle. Remember that pieces cut from the internal parts of the studs may make adorable hoops themselves so don't dispose of anything until you are use you have utilized the entirety of the pieces you need.

To gather the hoops, use your weeding instrument to puncture the highest point of every single one.

At that point use your gem pincers to open up the circle in the opening or to expand the bounce ring contingent upon how you are making your hoop.

Pet Name Collars

Materials

Heat transfer vinyl

Cricut EasyPress (or iron)

Green StandardGrip mat

Cricut Fine-Point Blade

Weeding tool

Scraper tool

Directions:

Start a new project in Design Space.

Measure the color to get the length and width.

Choose 'Square' from the 'Shapes' menu on the left-hand side menu.

Set the square's color to grey.

Unlock the shape and set the dimensions accordingly.

Choose a picture of either a dog or a cat (depending on the pet).

Choose a collar and size it to be able to fit onto the shape.

You will want to use the image a few times across the collar.

It is a black cat hissing.

Size it down and make 5 copies of it.

Select the fifth cat and flip it horizontally so it is facing the other cat images.

Make 3 copies of the flipped cat picture.

Select the 'Heart' shape from the 'Shapes' menu from the left-hand side menu.

Unlock it and size it to the same scale as the cat to fit onto the collar.

Change the color of the heart to red.

Make 6 duplicates of the heart.

Select 'Text,' choose a font, make the color red, and type in the pet's name.

Position the name in the center of the collar (the square).

Place the cat facing left at one end and a cat facing right at the opposite end of the collar.

Place a heart next to the cat on either end of the collar.

Place another cat after the heart, then another heart, etc.

Do this pattern for both sides of the collar ending by the name.

Select and remove the grey square.

Hold down the <Ctrl> key on the keyboard and select each of the cats.

Right-click and select attach.

Do the same for the hearts and include the name in the selection.

Click 'Make it.'

The cutting screen will show two cutting mats, each with a different color.

You will notice that the cats and the hearts with the writing are spaced correctly as you laid them out.

Choose 'Mirror' as it is heat transfer so it needs to be mirrored to iron the image onto the collar.

Cut the corresponding vinyl color a few inches larger than the grey square was.

Stick the cut vinyl to the green cutting mat and load it into the Cricut machine.

Make sure the fine-point blade is loaded.

Click 'Continue,' choose the correct material, and ensure the dial is on custom.

Click 'Go' when the Cricut is ready to cut.

Once it has finished cutting, remove the design from the Cricut.

Stick the next color vinyl sheet (cut to the correct size) onto the green cutting mat.

Load it into the Cricut.

Check that all the settings and materials are correct.

Do not forget to 'Mirror' the image.

When the Cricut is ready to cut, press 'Go.'

When the cutting is done, use the weeding tool to clean up the designs.

Start off with the cat transfer design.

Position it facedown on the collar.

Place a cloth over the transfer paper.

Use a pre-heated Cricut EasyPress or iron to push down, heating the vinyl onto the collar.

After 30 seconds, use the brayer tool or scraping tool to go over the design.

When the transfer has cooled down, peel the backing paper off.

Repeat steps 44 to 48.

When you are done, you will have a personalized pet collar that any animal lover would love as a gift.

Gift Bags Toppers

Materials:

Card stock (white, red, and earthy colored)

Dry glue

Twine for labels

Gap punch for labels

Cricut machine

Cricut pens (optional)

Blessing sacks

Instructions:

Transfer the SVG document to your Cricut and cut the entirety of your segments. You should resize to fit the blessing pack you are working with. Overlap the medical attendant cap and specialist pack topper into equal parts.

Utilize glue to add the red cross to your pieces. Use extra glue or even staples to connect the pack toppers to the highest point of your blessing sacks. Then add glue to add the cap and adhere to the highest point of your blessing labels. For the labels, you will likewise need to punch a hole and add some twine to attach them onto your blessings.

In this way, top off those blessing packs or make a present for someone special. This is a great gift for people to show them how you feel and wish them well during difficult times.

Back Packs

Materials:

Rucksack

Cricut machine

Cricut cut document

Mosaic iron-on

Mickey work iron-on

Simple Press Mini

Weeding instruments

Iron-on defensive sheet

Simple Press tangle

Instructions:

Start by cutting your structure with your Cricut machine. You can cut either the Star Wars plan or the Mickey Mouse heads or think of an alternate design that is all your own. Make sure to put your material face down on the tangle and mirror the cut. At that point load the material with the tangle into your Cricut machine.

If it's not too much trouble note that ANY of the Cricut machines will make this venture. At that point cut your plan from iron-on. Remove the entirety of the extra iron-on around your structure. The twofold liner of the mosaic iron-on is somewhat special.

Weeding apparatuses make weeding somewhat simpler, yet they are not required. You will need to weed around the outside of any letters. You should be left with just what you need to be moved to your rucksack.

The work iron-on that has the Mickey heads weeds in a similar way as Everyday iron-on. Simply remove the extra material by pulling it up.

At that point you can add your design to the rucksacks. Start by adding the Easy-Press tangle to within the surface if conceivable. At that point press the material for a couple of moments to remove any wrinkles and any dampness.

Make certain to check the Cricut Heat Guide for the time and temperature to use with your iron-on. At that point include your plan set up and begin squeezing. Make certain to keep the Easy-Press Mini moving while at the same time squeezing.

Press for the full time and allow it to cool. Remove the bearer sheet from your iron-on. On account of the mosaic, the primary liner may fall off and detach from the second.

Simply remove the second liner after you expel the first. In the event that any of the squares begin to pull up, simply press again then attempt to slowly remove.

3D Butterfly Wall Art

Materials

Cricut holographic sparkle unicorn removable vinyl in pink, teal, and silver

Cricut essentials removable vinyl in gold and wine

Cricut glitter cardstock in wine, gold, silver, lavender, pink, and blue

Cricut glitter tape in pink

Green StandardGrip mat

Cricut Fine-Point Blade

Weeding tool

Scraping tool or brayer tool

Pair of scissors for cutting the material to size

Glue dots or 2-way tape for sticking cardstock to the wall

Tape measure

Pencil

Rubbing alcohol

Directions:

Open a new project in Design Space.

Select 'Images' from the menu on the left-hand side.

Choose a picture of a butterfly; this project uses #M28D239 as an example.

Unlock the butterfly and change the dimensions to 24" wide and 24" long.

This makes the butterfly 2' by 2.'

The butterfly wings will be in three different colors with the tail of each wing extending out with the glitter tape.

The smaller 3D butterflies will fly out from the glitter tape.

To slice the butterfly, you will need to use a technique called contouring.

Duplicate the butterfly and move the duplicated image off to one side out of the way.

Select the original butterfly image.

On the bottom right-hand menu where you find the Slice, Weld, Attach, and Flatten options, you will see the Contour option.

Select the 'Contour' option.

A box will appear on the screen with the butterfly image in the main pane and images in the right-hand panel.

You can zoom the butterfly to 50% in order to see what you are doing if it appears too large in the viewing frame.

To do this, you will find the zoom bar in the main panel at the bottom left-hand corner.

You are going to select various pieces of the butterfly's wing to hide, so you only have the body and bottom wings leftover. It will all make sense once you have done it.

Using the images in the right-hand panel, select the shapes in the boxes in the right-hand panel that match up with the shapes in the top wings.

As you click on a shape in the right-hand panel, it will grey out in the viewing window.

If you accidentally select one of the bottom wings or the abdomen, simply click on the shape again and it will reappear.

Once you have finished greying out the top wings, select the 2 antennae as well.

You will also want to select the 2 long wing tailpieces at the bottom of the butterfly.

There are two small pieces that are in the middle of the abdomen and just above the bottom wings that you will want to keep.

Click the 'X' in the top right-hand corner of the 'Hide Contour' box.

The butterfly will now appear without the top wings, antennae, and wing tails on the grid.

Change the color to light blue and move the image to one side.

Move the duplicated full butterfly to the workspace.

Select the full butterfly and repeat steps 11 to 23. Get rid of the abdomen, bottom wings, and tail as well as those two little pieces halfway down the body.

Leave only the top wings and antennae.

When you are done contouring the top part of the butterfly, change the color to armadillo.

If you put your two shapes together, they will line up perfectly.

You will now be able to cut them in two different colors.

Save the project.

Use the silver holographic vinyl for the antennae and the top wings.

Use the teal holographic vinyl for the abdomen and bottom wings.

Measure the space on the wall, marking it off with the pencil.

Wipe down the surface with a clean cloth and the rubbing alcohol. You can use any product to clean the surface that has an instant dry and leaves no residue.

Once the images for the butterfly have been cut, use transfer tape cut to size to transfer the images onto the wall starting with the bottom wings and abdomen.

You are not going to want to have the vinyl transfer over the bottom part.

Before you apply the transfer tape to the top wings, cut around the bottom section where the abdomen will go. Leave a gap so that the vinyl does not layer over the bottom part.

Cut the transfer tape into the same shape, then transfer the wings onto the wall lining them up with the body and bottom wings.

Cut two ½" wide by 3" long glitter ribbon pieces and give them a swallowtail cut at the one end.

Cut off the inside part of the swallowtail, leaving the tape to taper off to a single point.

You may want to reinforce the tape's stickiness by giving it a few glue dots.

Apply 1 ribbon over each of the butterfly's tail wings, leaving only the top funnel bit leading from the wing in vinyl.

Open a new project in Design Space.

Select 'Images' from the menu on the left-hand side.

Choose the same picture of a butterfly—#M28D239.

Unlock the butterfly and change the dimensions to 3.15" wide and 2.33" long.

From the top menu, set the 'Linetype' to 'Cut.'

Leave the color as it is.

Save the project.

Click 'Make it'

You can fit 12 butterflies on a sheet of 12" by 12" cardstock.

You can make 72 butterflies with the 6 different glitter cardstock colors.

Set the 'Project copies' to 72 and click 'Apply.'

This selection will load 6 cutting boards with 12 butterflies per board.

Select each board and lay the butterflies out with enough room between, above, and below them.

Use the glitter cardstock and load a different color card each time you are ready to cut the next sheet.

As the sheets are done, remove the excess cardstock, weed the butterflies, and bend them in half to get an open wing effect.

Place two glue dots on each butterfly and tape them from the glitter ribbon to flow down and up around the sides of the bigger butterfly.

Open a new project in Design Space.

Select 'Text' from the menu on the left-hand side.

Type "Live Be," unlock the text and set the size to fit.

Choose the font you like for the wall decal. This project uses 'A Perfect Day' font as an example.

Set the font size you want depending on how tall and wide you want the font to be on the wall.

Change the text color to gold (to be cut on the gold removable vinyl).

Duplicate the font.

Change the text to "Life Free."

Change the text color to dark red (to be cut on the wine removable vinyl).

The slogan will be "Live Life Be Free." "Live" and "Be" will be printed in gold, while "Life" and "Free" will be printed in wine.

Click 'Make it.'

Use the removable vinyl to cut the letters.

When the letters have been cut and weeded, transfer them onto the wall using transfer tape into the position you desire.

Chapter 4: Tips and Tricks for beginners

There are so many tricks that can help you use your Cricut machine better and faster to ensure that you are getting the most out of it.

Look in other places besides craft stores to find supplies. Some great examples are sites like eBay or look into clearance sales. One of the best places that people have found to be a great place for supplies is the Dollar Tree. You can find vinyl, fabric, or boards to use.

Another tip that ties into the Dollar Tree is that you can find supplies for transforming your craft room into how you want it and finding tools to keep your supplies organized.

Keeping your mats clean is also going to be a great way to make them last longer so you do not have to replace them as often and waste your money. A great tip for keeping those mats clean is to use your lint roller. Make sure that you have removed all the little papers and roll away. The lint roller trick is especially beneficial if you have been cutting glitter cardstock. Since this does not remove everything, you should be aware of that, but it will get rid of most things.

Freezer paper makes great stencils, and you can get it for only a dollar!

Keeping your blades separate and organized will help too. Having separate blades for vinyl or fabric will help the blades stay sharp and the way you need them to longer. Keeping the blades separate is also going to help you be more organized. If you want, you can use a permanent marker on each of the blades so that you know what blade is for what particular material you want to cut with them. It is like owning a pair of fabric scissors. You would not use fabric scissors to cut paper, so instead, keep your blades sharp by keeping them separate. You can make a small mark which blades are for what material. If you do not want to use the marker on them, you can make a chart. Just remember to replace the cap so that they are not getting mixed up.

You can also spray paint your vinyl if you need a color and you do not have it just make sure that it is Rust oleum metallics spray. Make sure that the vinyl is uncut and that you dry it before you cut it.

Make sure that you do a trial run of your materials that you are going to use for your project first. This is going to help ensure that you have the proper cutting techniques, and you have the proper settings in place. This also ensures that you are not wasting materials, time, or money.

Besides Cricut pens, there are a variety of other options that work for Explore machines. They include American Crafts, Recollection, Sharpies, or even Crayola.

You can also use your own system fonts in your projects. You can go to sites that offer fonts to find a lot of amazing ones for free and then you can use them for your machine.

If you have a smaller or more intricate design you can use a weeding box. This is especially helpful if your cutting multiple designs on one mat.

Make sure that your dial is set to the correct setting for the materials. It is very easy to forget that this is on the wrong setting and then the cut can be wrong.

Load your mat correctly. Both sides of the mat need to be able to slide under the rollers or the mat will not cut in the correct manner.

When you can no longer make a smooth cut or an effective cut, you need new blades. Be careful when replacing them because you can cut yourself pretty badly.

You can clean your cutting mats with baby wipes as well. They need to be water based and using them to keep your mats clean can help them stay sticky longer. Make sure that these baby wipes have no fragrance. If they are not water based, they will damage the mat and you will not be able to use it again.

Keep the plastic sheets that come with your mats so you can protect the mats between uses. This helps your mats last longer so that you can use them repeatedly.

If you are not sure about the correct cut setting, run a small test cut first. This is especially true if you have a larger project. Doing this is going to make sure that you are not wasting expensive materials that you want and need. It will also make sure you understand what cuts can do to materials.

Your vinyl needs to be placed the right way up on the cutting mat. The heat transfer vinyl should always be placed shiny side down.

Many card projects require that you have a stylus. If the machine you bought is part of a bundle it can have the stylus inside it already, but some may not. This is something to ask the person at the store when you are buying one because the stylus can really help.

Make sure that you do a practice project before a real one as well because this will let you get adjusted to your machine and make sure that you do not waste materials on your first project. When you buy your machine, there should be a practice project already in place.

Make sure that your blade is placed correctly. If it is placed too high, it may only cut part of the way through, but if it is down to low, it will ruin your mat. A test cut will make sure it is in the right spot therefore could save you a lot of frustration.

The Design Canvas Platform

The following are ways you can work smarter on the design canvas platform:

Making use of Cartridge for searching similar images: Most times, the numerous results of images from the search bar in the image library can overwhelm a Cricut user. Whenever you search for an image, too many dissimilar results pop up. It, most of the time, makes it difficult to single out one favorite image out of these results. And sometimes, when a favorite image is found, there are many similar images. To stop this from happening again, ensure that you make use of the cartridge of the image you're searching for. The easiest and fastest means of accessing a cartridge of an image is by clicking the small information (i) icon that is located at the bottom right of the image on the Design Space image library. By doing that, the image's details will be revealed. A green link will also appear, giving you access to every image of equal similarity. Knowing this will enable you to start matching or coordinating images, which is more effective than the results from the search bar.

Cutting, Drawing, or Scoring Lines: In the past, Cricut users had to search for designs that had specific attributes for drawing and scoring a line (instead of cutting.) Not anymore, those days are behind all Cricut users. With the latest upgrade that has been made by Cricut on the Design Space, a user can comfortably change lines from cutting to drawing to scoring by merely making use of the easy-to-use "Line type" menu positioned at the topmost toolbar.

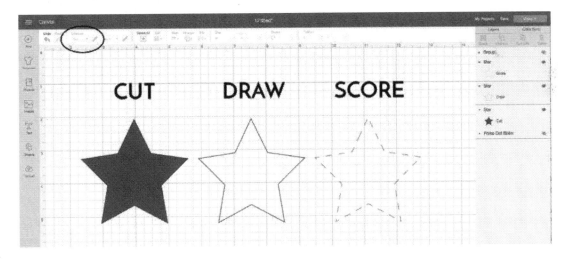

Color Management: If you can maximize the use of the "Color Synchronization" tool, you can significantly save much time working on different projects. This will likely ensure that you are using colors that match across various designs. A lot of times, when you work on a lot of designs on the Design canvas simultaneously, you may end up with several shades of similar colors. Instead of choosing all the single layers autonomously to recolor, go to the "Color Sync" tool positioned on the tool panel on the right side. The colors you will find on this panel are the ones that are presently in use. Notwithstanding, you can also drag active layers that are currently on the design by using your mouse and dropping it in a new color that hasn't been used on the design. If you desire to maintain the use of matching colors throughout your project designs, or you wish to have some layers with the same color in order to cut more efficiently, making use of the "Color Sync" is the fastest and most comfortable means of doing it.

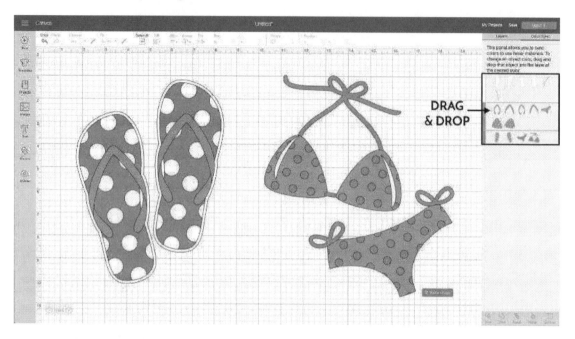

Applying the Hide Tool: A lot of users find themselves crowding the Canvas area with too many redundant images while they work on their projects. And they end up cutting all the elements on the Canvas area when the time comes to cut out their projects. There're likewise sometimes when you will wish or have to cut out some portions of the design you're working on. Instead of getting these unnecessary images deleted off your canvas screen, you can just hide them by clicking the little eye icon positioned by the right side of the layers panel beside the image. You should note that any image you hide won't be permanently disconnected from the Canvas. However, it will not be added with the rest of the images when moving your project for cutting. You may also toggle the Hide icon on/off. This will make it easier to cut the parts needed only, and also keep an organized and clean Design canvas at the same time, without getting the images you still want to work on mixed up.

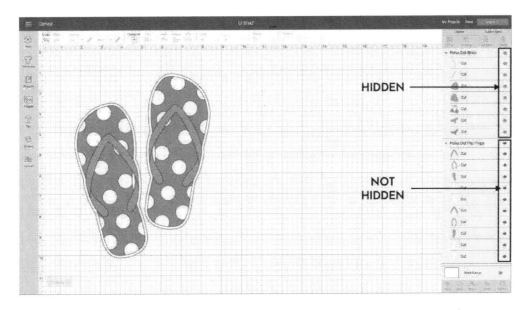

Adjust Image Patterns: The Fill tool located at the topmost toolbar allows you to modify the way you fill images. Picking a single layer from the panel, colors can be switched, or the image interior can be given a different pattern.

Utilizing Keyboard Shortcuts: Almost every computer program has keyboard shortcuts. Microsoft, Adobe, CorelDraw, and so on, they all have keyboard shortcuts. And just like them, the Design Space has keyboard shortcuts too. There are shortcuts for virtually every command you can think of: shortcuts for Copy, Cut, Paste, Duplicate, Undo, Delete, and many more. These functions are at the corner of every image, positioned at the topmost toolbar by the right side of the Layers panel. A lot of time can be saved by using as many shortcuts as possible. You can even make use of the functional keyboard shortcuts that work on different computer software out there. Most of these keyboard shortcuts are common; you can make use of "Ctrl + C" for copying, "Ctrl + X" for cutting, "Ctrl + V" for pasting, "Ctrl + Z" to undo mistakes, etc.

The Cut Screen Platform,

A lot of Cricut users tend to think they won't be able to go further with their project editing once they send it for cutting after designing. They believe the editing ends immediately after clicking on the "Make It" button. But there're still so many actions and editing that a user can carry out on the "Cut Screen" platform. And if done wisely, you will be able to save a lot of time and spare some materials.

By making these adjustments, you won't only be able to make your work more perfect than the default settings would make it, you will also have your cut exactly how you desire it. Your project looks better with these adjustments, especially when you're working on a scrap or an oddly shaped material. Just make sure that your Cut screen gridlines are fit into the gridlines of your mat to ensure that your design fits the material correctly wherever it is placed.

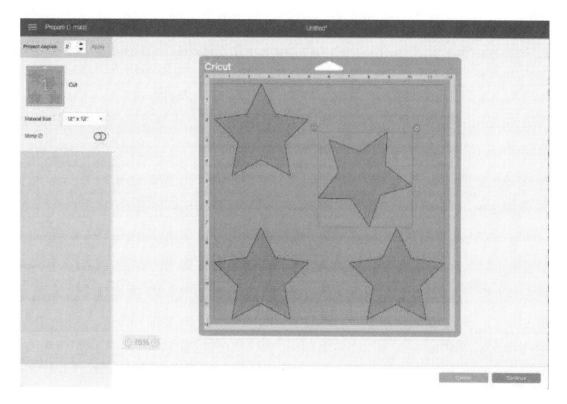

Photo credit- thehomesihavemade.com

Moving Images from a Mat to Another: Although your images can be moved around just a single mat, you can likewise move the images from a mat to another without having to go back to the Design canvas to change colors. This can be done by clicking the three tiny dots positioned at the uppermost left side corner of that image you're currently working on. Once you've done that, select the Move to Another Mat option. Then you will be allowed to choose the mat you want that image to be on. You'll easily notice the change.

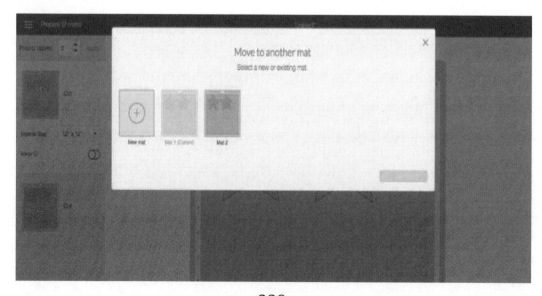

This feature can be used anytime to conserve materials. If you're skillful enough, you can arrange all your images to fit into a single mat. This is also a perfect way of quickly changing the colors on designs without having to exit the Cut screen to manually modify the color of the designs.

Re-cut or Skip Mats: This feature will really prove useful to you if you just know how to use it on the Cut screen. After sending your designs for cutting, the remaining processes don't require much attention. As long as your Cricut machine is fed with the correct paper color and size just exactly as the Cut screen illustrates it, you shouldn't worry about the results; your project should come out precisely the way you designed it. Nonetheless, you may find yourself wanting to re-cut a particular mat after cutting it the first time or wishing to skip the mat that is next in line. The good news is that can be done easily without you needing to exit the Cut screen.

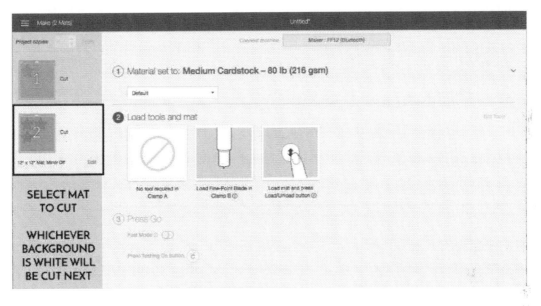

However, you need to do this before you load your mat into the machine. You're free to select a particular mat you wish to cut manually by merely clicking or selecting the mat by the left-hand side of the Cut screen. The mat you handpicked will be skipped automatically by the cutting machine.

Saving Commonly Used Materials: Many Cricut users feel stunned when they learn about this particular feature after using the Cricut software for a long time. They realize how much they'd missed! You're certainly missing so much if you're not making use of the Custom materials option. A lot of people, especially those people making use of the Explore Air 2 series, do not make use of this feature unintentionally because their Cricut machine is set to Vinyl, Iron-in, Cardstock, etc. Only people that use the Cricut Maker machine can notice the "Custom materials" function within the Design Space easily since there is no available option to choose the material you are cutting.

Photo credit- cricut.com

You don't have to go through the stress of scrolling through more than a hundred custom materials so as to find the common Cardstock, Vinyl, and Iron-on Vinyl settings over and over again. You can just add each one of these to the Favorite box. It shouldn't take you more than a few minutes to scroll through the Materials menu and locate the materials that you make use of regularly. Just click on the star positioned under the Materials menu, and then proceed to select "Favorites" instead of "Popular" on that same menu. Once you've done that, all that will be left is just a menu showing all the materials you mostly cut. That is way easier and more comfortable, right?

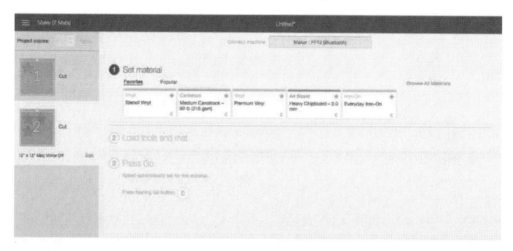

Connecting Two or More Cricut Machines Simultaneously: Even though a typical Cricut user doesn't often make use of more than a single Cricut machine, it's possible to connect more than one machine to your Design Space account at the same time. You can do this by either using Bluetooth when using a wireless machine model or using a USB with your PC. Moreover, you shouldn't worry about getting your machines and your designs mixed up during the cutting session. The number of Cricut machines you connect to your Design Space doesn't matter. The first step you'll take when you reach the Cut screen is to select which machine you want to use to cut your design. You will find this function in a drop-down menu located at the top. With this step, Cricut ensures that its users can stay assured that they're using the intended machine for their project all the time.

Easily Adjusting Cut Pressure: Even though it looks fantastic to have the capability of modifying your materials' settings, sometimes all that is required is an extra or lesser pressure to allow your Cricut machine to efficiently cut through the material you set. If you want to adjust the cut pressure, once you've selected your material of choice on the Cut screen, adjust the pressure by using the drop-down menu provided at the top. You can choose to decrease, increase, or make use of the default pressure. Using this technique, you can effortlessly and swiftly change your cutting depth without having to rummage around the custom settings of your material.

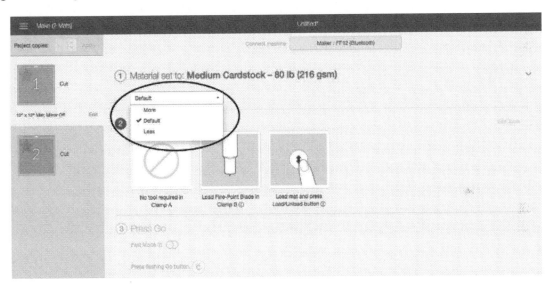

Mirror Setting: There're times when Cricut users have to do their design cutting in reverse, particularly when they are working with projects with Iron-on. This process of reversing is known as "Mirror." Although your designs can always be flipped on your Canvas screen horizontally, there is also an option provided to mirror designs while using the Cut screen.

This setting doesn't only enable you to mirror the images or mats you want to flip; it also allows you to create and adjust your designs without having to flip them on the Canvas screen. It gets easier to view and customize your designs on the mat.

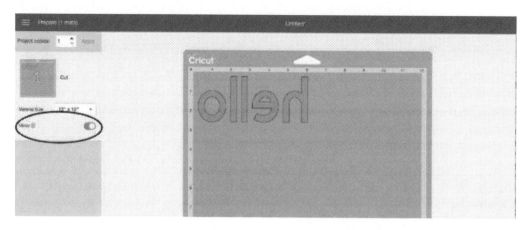

Filling Your Mat by Adjusting Project Copies: A lot of Cricut users don't get to use this cool Auto-fill function, either by unawareness or unavailability. This function can only be accessed on Cricut machine models that are old. Using the old machine models, a single star can be put on your Canvas, and you can select your paper size manually, and then select "Auto-fill" without stress. Once you click on "Auto-fill," your Cricut machine will fill up the paper with stars automatically, fitting in as many stars as your paper can comfortably take. Even though you will not find this function in the most recent Design Space, there is an easy way of doing almost the same thing the function does in newer machines.

All the tips and techniques that have been given so far should be carefully studied. Some of them may look subtle, but you shouldn't overlook them if you don't want to end up wasting your time or materials. Many full-time Cricut users are always on the hunt for information on how they can save time and materials while on the Design Apace. The information is in your hand right now, what you do with it is now your decision.

Using Advanced Design Space Tools

There are many Design Space tools that will look mysterious to a beginner or new user. Some will almost seem meaningless and redundant. However, these tools are not useless or worthless; you just don't know how to make use of them yet. The following are some of the advanced tools on the Design Space.

How to Make Use of The Flatten Tool

Pick the layers that you want to flatten by clicking on "Select All," or by pressing and holding the "Ctrl" key on the keyboard while clicking on the layers.

When you've selected all the layers you want, click on "Flatten" positioned at the lower right corner.

Once you've done that, your image becomes flattened. All you will see on the Layers panel is one layer with a text that says, "Flatten."

The Color Sync Tool

Like the Flatten tool, the Color Sync tool also has more than one function for Design Space users who know their way around it. Below are some of its functions:

The Color Sync tool can be used to recolor shapes, layers, etc.

It can be used to match the colors of all layers on the Canvas.

It is very useful for consolidating material colors.

It saves a user so much time and materials.

This feature wasn't available in the old version of the Design Space. But now that it is available in the new version, why not learn how to use it properly? This tool makes it much more comfortable to synchronize colors in a project so a user can cut them all on a single material. All you have to do is open the "Color Sync" panel located at the right side of the screen, and then start dragging and dropping all the shapes respectively into the selected layer you wish for it to synchronize to. If you desire to cut every star in chartreuse, for example, then just drag every other star to that same layer at the "Color Sync" panel. It feels so much easier to do this, and knowing they are all going to have the same color with no extra work.

Sketching on the design space

One of the coolest facts about using the Cricut Explore model is that users can also upload images they've drawn themselves! There are two techniques of doing this, one is by making use of Illustrator, and the other is by making use of the Design Space. And since we're discussing about the Design Space, I'll only mention how to do so on the latter. This is the process:

You first need to have the intended image on your computer by importing it. So, if you've hand-drawn what you want on a piece of paper or your tablet, the next step is to scan it to your computer, take a photo of it with your mobile device and send it to your computer, or save and send it to the computer through your tablet. Whichever way you want to do it, ensure you save it as a PNG or JPEG file.

Convert the sketch using the Design Space by first uploading the image, making use of the "Upload" tab by the left side.

You will be requested to choose the image type; you should select the option that fits your image background. Proceed by clicking "Continue" and let your image be saved as a Cut image, and then click "Save." You will notice that your image is now a Cut file.

Chapter 5: Selling and Make Money

Make and Sell Leather Bracelets

Bracelets are fashionable items, especially leather bracelets. The Cricut machine can easily cut real or faux leather giving you less work to do. You can cut, make, and sell leather bracelets, considering the materials needed are just snaps, with your Cricut machine, leather, without a lot of money or trouble.

If you are interested in selling this craft, you can also create room for preordering, where a buyer can order for a particular design to be created by the designer.

Sell Iron-On Vinyl

This is another money-making opportunity that the Cricut machine provides. You make a design with the iron-on vinyl and sell it to people. The iron-on vinyl can be in the form of text or design. It can also be made for each season or celebration, be it Valentine, Halloween, Christmas, or Easter. Buyers may also create custom orders for what they want.

Sell Stickers

This idea is targeted at kids. You can make money by designing educative and entertaining stickers for toddlers and other age groups. Stickers of the alphabet or maps of a locale can be made. Stickers are also used in decorating places like the wardrobe or closets.

Make and Sell Party Decorations and Buntings

There is always a celebration in our day-to-day lives as human beings. It can be a milestone celebration or simply a fun-seeking escapade. Party decorations made with the Cricut machine can be sold at these occasions.

Window decals

Everyone has a peculiar image, an object we are practically obsessed with. Getting a vinyl window decal of one's favorite image will go a long way in giving your decor a boost. Making and selling window decals is quite easy and profitable.

Make and sell canvas wall art

Customized wall art would generate quick and easy money. Get inspirational sayings or designs and make them into wall art for sale.

Design and sell onesies

Onesies or bodysuit are generally cute already and can be even better with amazing artwork. Onesies for babies can be made with a lot of cute sayings or quotes in addition to the standard "Daddy loves you" or "Momma's baby."

Become a Cricut affiliate

This includes being paid to make tutorials video by the Cricut company. These videos are uploaded to the internet for the netizen to make use of. To become a Cricut affiliate, you need to have a strong internet presence. You must also have a tangible number of followers on your social media accounts.

Post tutorial videos on your vlog

This has nothing to do with being an affiliate; rather, you create a blog for videos and upload tutorial videos and get paid through the generated traffic.

Use of social media

You can make any of the crafts you find or create and post pictures of them online, announcing to those on your list that it is for sale. This works better because whoever is buying gets to see the picture of whatever he is getting before ordering it. Personalized crafts should also be included in your order of business.

Design and sell T-shirts

T-shirts are always in vogue. Most especially for college students, a designed tee would be a great fashion item. Get creative with your sayings and quotes and create a t-shirt business in no time.

Design and sell hoodies

Hoodies are great for cold seasons. Unique and custom-made hoodies are a great way to make some money with your Cricut machine.

Design and sell leather neck piece

A leather pendant can be designed for a necklace and sold out to interested buyers. An all leather neck piece can also be made and sold.

Design and sell banners

Banners can be made for celebration, festive periods, camping, parties, religious activities, or sporting activities. You can focus on all of them or certain holidays in particular if that is what you are passionate about.

Design and sell window clings

Window clings with the design of the seasons can be made and sold. Other designs or images can also be used for creating window clings.

Design and sell stencils

Stencils can be created and sold for those that want to hand-paint a post or sign. It would also generate a nice amount of money.

Design and sell safari animal stickers

Stickers of safari animals are attractive items. They will be particularly great for animal lovers and children.

Design and sell labeling stickers

Labeling stickers can be made for labeling things in the house. Things in the kitchen, pantry, playroom, classroom, and other places can be labeled with labeling stickers.

Design and sell Christmas ornaments

Christmas is a period people celebrate and decorate their workplace, house, and religious settings, among others.

Design and sell doormats

Beautiful doormats can be made with the machine and sold to customers. It can be designed with either text or images. Customized doormats can also be sold.

Design and sell kitchen towels

Towels used in the kitchen can be designed and sold at affordable prices. The towels can be designed with text or images of delicacies.

There are countless things you can make with Cricut. Likewise, there are countless things you can make, which are marketable. Independent entrepreneurship is easier than it's ever been thanks to the internet and web platforms that make selling your products a breeze.

Chapter 6: FAQ

Where can I find images to use for my project?

One of the great things with Cricut is that you can upload files from any source so long as you have the legal rights to use this image, as the space for Cricut Design and the ability to house so many different file types is fantastic. If you do sell your designs it is incredibly important to use copyright free images or purchase the images you include in your designs.

Do I need to buy all my Cricut fonts?

Cricut Design Space can use fonts installed on your computer when you browse for your fonts. The fonts can be purchased or used for downloading via the Cricut Design Space with little to no problems. Across the Web, too, there is a range of resources for this.

Nevertheless, if you use a font, make sure you have a license to use the font for the reasons you want to use it! Fonts have copyrights, just like images, and can be limited to what you can do with them.

Why does my blade cut my support sheet?

It could be due to inappropriate seating on the blade in the package, so move the package back, bring the blade into it again, load it up again and try again. It could also be because the content dial is not adjusted correctly. You can plunge the needle right through the whole material and the back if you cut anything very slim but have the dial set to cardstock.

Why don't my pictures appear right on my mat?

Once you press "Print it," it is likely that your print version doesn't look like anything in Design Space. When this happens, go back to Design Space, highlight all your photos, click "Team," then click "Attach," and all your project cutting needs will be kept right wherever they are.

Which Cricut machines are compatible with Design Space?

All the motorized cutting machines they have on the market are compatible. It includes the Cricut Explore, Cricut Explore Air, Cricut Explore Air 2, and the Cricut Maker. With the current version of Design Space, you can use all of these tools to build countless projects for each style.

How do I use Design Space on My Chromebook?

Cricut's Design Space is unfortunately not currently designed for Chromebook OS compatibility. It is because the need for the application to download the plugin is a significant obstacle to the operating system, but that doesn't mean that there will be no compatibility in the near future.

Can I use the Design Space on more than one device?

Sure, all designs, components, fonts, transactions, and photos are accessible via any internet-connected device and your account credentials, thanks to the web-based and club-based features of Cricut. You can start a design during the day and then wrap it up once you're back in your crafting space from any device.

How many times can I use an image purchased in the Design Space?

Any design asset or feature you purchase from the design space will be yours to use as much as you like when you have an active Cricut Design Space account. Feel free to cut as many designs as you want from your purchased images.

Can I deactivate or switch the Design Space grid?

Indeed, you can switch grid lines from the design room. Open the Accord menu (three lines stacked at the top left) and select Settings on a Windows / Mac device. The Canvas Grid choices are available, and you can select your preference. You can also see shortcuts in the settings menu. Select the keyboard shortcut to turn off and on grid lines.

How do I convert to metric units?

To switch to centimeters from inches on a laptop or desktop, open the Account menu, you'll see three stacked lines in the upper left corner, then select Settings. You'll see the options to select inches or centimeters.

What exactly is SnapMat?

SnapMat is an iOS-exclusive feature that lets you get a virtual preview of what you are making. This gives you the ability to align your designs in Design Space so that they fit perfectly with what you put on your mat. This functionality allows you to place images and text over your mat's snapshot so that you can see exactly how your layout should be in the design space.

What are the benefits of using SnapMat?

SnapMat gives you the certainty that when you send your design to cut through your Cricut, your images will be placed in. It will show you where your pictures are to be drawn, how cuts are made, and how the text lines up. With SnapMat, you can tell your Cricut to cut a specific piece of a pattern that you've stuck on your mat, write in specific stationery areas, gift tags, envelopes, or cards, and you can get the most out of your scraps and spare materials left from past projects.

Can I include multiple SnapMat mats at one time?

SnapMat can snap one mat at a time. If you want to snap multiple mats, you can do so individually, and work that way through your designs. This ensures that each mat is shot correctly and that each one is done accurately.

What's Cricut Design Space Offline Mode?

This feature is available exclusively through the iOS platform. This feature allows you to download your items for later use in an offline environment. This is ideal if you plan to work on your designs for a prolonged period of time in a space that doesn't have an active internet connection. You can still work on your designs during that time, without worrying about losing those creative thoughts.

What is available for offline download?

You can download any element or asset that you own, or you have purchased rights through Cricut Design Space for offline use. This includes images you uploaded from other devices, images, or assets that you obtained through an active membership in Cricut Access. It is up to you to pick what assets you want to make available for offline use.

How do I save projects that allow me to use them offline?

This step can only be accomplished with an active internet connection, so be sure to download before going offline. Open a project that you want to save for use offline and select the option "Save As." Select the option "Save to this iPad / iPhone," and this will allow you to use the project without any connection at a later time.

How do I save Offline changes to my projects?

If you are going to work on a project in offline mode, tap "Save," and the file you saved to your device will be updated automatically without having to reselect the option "Save to this iPad / iPhone" if there is no internet connection.

Can I download images for subsequent offline use?

You may download images to your device for later, offline use, while you have an active internet connection. To do so, open the "Images" screen, select an image, and tap "Download." When this is done, the image label will indicate, and the image will be available immediately, irrespective of an available internet connection.

Conclusion

The detailed book with instructions and step-by-step guidance including pictures is written in an easy to understand language so you can have this book with you as you work to design your projects using the "Design Space" application, cut them using the "Cricut" cutting machine and then use the "Cricut Easy Press" for professional-looking projects. The 60+ project ideas covered in this book are only a tiny fraction of what you can do with your "Cricut" devices. It would be wise to sharpen your crafting skills by exploring and playing with the "Design Space" application in your spare time before you start creating some of the more advanced level projects.

Design Space makes Cricut a user-friendly die-cutter, and I can't stress enough how much you'll get out of the machine as you learn each process. If you're a newbie, as I said before, start slowly so you don't become overwhelmed and abandon your machine without giving it a chance.

Whether you adore fonts, shapes, or animation characters, you'll have the ability to locate a cartridge that can fit your taste. But when choosing a cartridge out of Cricut, the very first thing which you will need to consider is how far your budget will probably be. The selection of costs of these capsules can appear as low as just a bit below fifty dollars and may soar alongside a hundred bucks. If you're the kind of person that enjoys a lot of colors, you can stick with the basic silhouette cartridges and just take advantage of different colored papers to perform your cutouts. If you would rather create using words, then look out for the scrapbook designs, you might even use the ribbon cartridges.

Some people are huge fans of our certified character collections. You'll have the ability to use cutouts of your favorite cartoon characters from Disney and other animated movies. For many adults who have kids in the house, this is going to be a superb chance to bond with your kids and educate them on how to be artistic and creative.

Beyond being easy to understand, this book is a guide that you can always come back to whenever you need it or whenever you seem to be forgetting something important about Cricut. Keep the tips and tricks provided close by as a reference guide so you aren't searching all over to find the answers to your questions.

You will be able to turn even the most unlikely and seemingly unrealistic ideas into beautiful craft projects in no time. You have learned all about the free resources including images, fonts, and projects that are available through the "Cricut" library so you can save money as you learn and sharpen your craft skills.

Cricut always gives their users a lot of options to choose from, so, try as much as possible to carry out extensive research about their products, materials, and subscriptions.

Thank you

CRICUT EXPLORE AIR 2

The 7 Most Effective Strategies to Craft Out Original Cricut Project Ideas. A Complete Practical DIY Guide to Master Your Cricut Explore Air 2 and Cricut Design Space

Introduction

What Is Cricut?

Cricut is a die-cutting machine. It is more like a printer with a cutter attached to it. It can be used to print and cut different materials including heavyweight and lightweight materials. In fact, it is a craftsman's companion that gives you the freedom to create amazing designs for different occasions.

The Cricut machine also has large collections of designed images in its library that will make your work super simple. What you need as a beginner is to get access to one or more images, place the desired material to be cut onto the sticky mat, and get the Cricut machine to cut it for you.

The materials it can cut include paper, vinyl, craft foam, faux leather, fabric, sticker paper, and more.

Overview

Many people have heard of the Cricut machine and it's been making a big splash in the crafting world because of everything that you can do with it. You might be surprised that you would be able to work with this machine with a lot of different materials and it can be a really fun way to make some great items.

When Cricut machines first came out you needed cartridges to be able to cut out your letters and the shapes that you want to use for your items but now, you don't need cartridges at all! Now everything is done digitally because everyone understands that we have great technology at our feet, and we should use it to our advantage.

Most Cricut machines will work over Bluetooth or Wi-Fi, which means that you can design with your iPad or iPhone. You can also use Cricut from your computer. This makes designing your passions easier than ever, with complete versatility that will help you be able to do whatever you want. There are a variety of creative options available to you.

There are four types of Cricut machines that are the most popular and they are the Cricut Maker, the Cricut Explore Air, the Cricut Explore One, and the Cricut Explore Air 2. It can be hard to choose between them, but you should know that every Cricut machine does have things in common including what they come with.

All machines come with the following items:

- Practice project materials

- A power adapter

- A cutting machine

- Access to free projects that are ready to make

- A cutting mat that is twelve inches by twelve inches

- A USB cable

- A free trial membership to access Cricut

- A guide for making setup easy

- A fine-point premium blade and housing for the blade

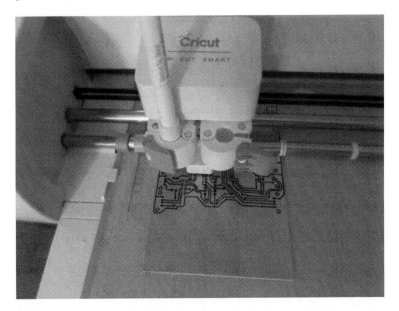

Another thing that you should know is that certain models come with additional items as well as a specialized writing pen, different blades, and even wheels.

A Cricut machine is a cutting machine. Specifically, what is known as a die-cutting machine. You can use it for paper crafting along with other crafting supplies as well. It's a machine that boasts that it is great for crafting with precision. Many people think that these machines just cut paper, but they cut so much more than that.

So now that you know what the machine is, we will tell you what it does and why it's so amazing. So, let's get started. When using your computer or smartphone, whichever form you decide to use for this, it connects to your machine, and then it will send whatever design you choose to your cutting machine. The design will indicate what it needs, for example, it might need a pen or other tool for scoring and cutting.

Every machine will have its own software that is a part of their brand. It will be free to use and to download onto your machine. Cricut even has an app you can use. The app is user-friendly, and you are able to upload images and create designs. You can make your designs from scratch or purchase the designs from others. You can also upload images and purchase designs from the application and modify them into your custom designs.

The app is extremely easy to use, and the software is very simple while being user-friendly as well. It gives you the freedom to have creativity with your projects. What you make in this will tell your machine where it needs to score or write. It also tells us where to cut as well.

If there is just one step, then the machine can do a full design. However, if there are multiple steps, then your machine will convey this to you through the device that you have connected to it. It will tell you if you have additional steps as well.

The Maker model comes in three colors while the Explore series comes in many more, though there are other differences between them as well. The first in the Explore series is the basic machine in their lineup which is beneficial as it is always the cheapest. Depending on what you want your machine to do, they can cost over $300. Explore Air 2 is their newest model. As such, it has more features and has the highest price of the machines.

The Maker is alone in its category and is said to have more versatility than the others and is the only one with an adaptive tool system for you to take advantage of. It's unique also in the fact that you have a toolset that can get you more materials than before. It even has technology that controls the direction of your blade as well as the pressure with a rolling action. This means it is going to be able to work with your material a lot better.

Now the basics are covered, and you know what a Cricut does as well. Now you're probably wondering what kinds of projects or designs you might be able to make with it. We'll be talking about that later on in the book as there are literally hundreds of different ways you could use your Cricut. The pens also help with designs. A machine like this uses different ones for different purposes and projects and they are great for having your machine do exactly what you want.

A machine like this isn't necessarily a printer, though it can be said that it comes close. If you use the print then cut option it will let you have any design to your project, and it will take it from there for you to be able to use it properly. If you want to think about this easily it would be a little like making stickers.

It also cuts more than paper. These machines are not just for die-hard scrapbookers anymore. It cuts so much more than that. As such, this book will include a master list of everything that will work with your machine, and how to gain the most benefit from it.

How to Set Up Your Cricut Machine for Windows/Mac and iOS/Android

The Explore Air 2 is compatible with smart devices such as tablets, smartphones, and PCs. This is a very helpful feature. For example, you can create a design while in transit and click print when you get home.

Now that you have purchased the Cricut Explore Air 2 machine, are you confused about how to set it up?

Follow these easy steps to set up your Explore Air 2:

For iOS/Android

After you must have plugged your machine in, switch it on and pair your device with the Cricut machine via Bluetooth.

Download and install Design Space.

Launch the app, then sign in or create a new Cricut ID.

Tap menu and select "machine setup" and "app overview."

Select new machine set up.

Follow on-screen instructions to complete the setup.

To set up the Cricut Explore machine, here are some of the steps to follow:

Plug in the machine, then power on.

Enter your browser and go to:

DesignCricut.Com/Setup.

Follow the instructions on the screen to sign up or create your Cricut ID and press submit.

Download and install the design or software. You will be asked to make your first project and with that you will know that your setup is complete.

You will need to set up your machine with your personal computer and perform your first project on the Cricut.

It is recommended to know the exact spot to place your machine before proceeding to set up the machine. It is recommended that you put your machine near your computer or where you will be using another connected device such as a tablet.

Even though your Cricut cutter can operate wirelessly without connecting directly to your computer, it is ideal for you to be near your machine for easy access to load and unload mats as well as pressing the necessary buttons.

You should also consider which perfect surface to place your machine on — a flat surface ten inches from the machine will be a great choice to guide against your unload mats falling on the floor or hanging awkwardly.

You will need a range of ten inches of space above the top of your machine. This space creates room to open the lid of the machine and easily put things like the pen into the Cricut machine.

The following steps will show you how to set up your machine correctly:

- Plug in your machine to the power source with the power adaptor and switch it on.

- Connect your Cricut Explore machine to the computer using the USB cable.

- Open the web browser on your computer and go to the Cricut website. Log in if you already have a Cricut account, but if you are new, go ahead and set up a Cricut account on the website.

- After creating your account, you are now ready to set up your Cricut machine by connecting to the design portal on the Cricut website.

- Click on the download icon to download the latest plugin software.

After implementing the above process, the below steps will guide you through the completion of the installation process for both Mac and PC.

Installation Setup for Mac

- After downloading the software, click and open the finder tool in the Mac toolbar.

- The next step is to locate the downloaded folder on your computer and double-click the Cricut Design Space file you already downloaded.

- The terms and conditions will come up. Review and agree to them.

- Drag the Cricut plugin into the internet plugin folder.

- After this, click the authenticate icon.

- After you have authenticated the internet plugins, close Cricut Design Space and download the windows frame to return to your Mac browser.

- Restart your browser and return to the Cricut website to continue with the setup process.

- Click on the "Detect Machine" icon and click continue when your Cricut machine has been detected.

- If you do not want to subscribe to the software, check the box to enable your trial subscription and tap continue.

- After this, you will receive a thank you note denoting that your Cricut Explore Air 2 is all set up for your first cutting project.

Hint: To take full advantage of the free trial subscription, do make sure you check the open trial box before you click continue. This page comes up for both the Mac and PC installation process.

Also, your free trial subscription allows you to access the Cricut image library of over 30,000 images and 300 fonts without a credit card or any other requirements.

Installation for PC

- After downloading the plugin software to your PC, close your browser.

- Tap the start menu and click to open the documents folder.

- Select the downloads and double click the Cricut Design Space file to open the setup of the file.

- Then click continue when the setup is on.

- Review the terms and conditions and click the accept button.

- Follow the instructions to install the software.

- When you have successfully installed the Cricut Design Space software, click the finish button.

- Next, tap on the "Detect Machine" icon. When your machine has been detected, tap "continue."

- Check the box to access the free trial subscription, then click continue.

- You will also get a thank you card to ascertain that your Cricut Machine is set up and that you are ready to carry out your first cut.

How to Cut Heavyweight and Lightweight Materials

Before delving into this project, I would like to explain a few important tips for this project that will help you accomplish the task accurately. Go over them as much as you can to fully understand each of these tips. It will definitely help you.

a. Do not eject the mat when you pause the machine to clean or replace a blunt rotary blade. If you remove the mat, it will be difficult to get the correct alignment of the cut and finish your project with accuracy. So, what you can do is pause the machine, remove the rotary blade, clean or replace the rotary blade, put it back in, and hit the Cricut button to continue. You will have to do all these things without ejecting the mat because if you do eject the mat, you will terminate your project and will have to start all over.

b. Before you unload your material from the machine, make sure that you check your project and that the cut has been done all the way. If the cut is not all the way, you can restart the cut all over as long as you did not eject or move the mat.

c. The Design Space will also notify you of the progress of the cut: how many passes to complete your project, and the amount of time remaining to finish your project. This is amazing as it will help you see the progress of your work any time you check on it. This is especially helpful if you have other tasks that need taking care of.

The materials required for this project includes the Cricut machine (Maker or Expression), 3" x 24" basswood, painter's tape, and a rotary blade.

The first thing, as usual, is to design your text to be cut on Cricut Design Space.

There is no room for assumptions here because it will save you time and as well as money. But if you already know that and you have your design ready, it is time to get to the task at hand.

1. You have the design in your Cricut design space, so click Continue.

2. Select the type of material by clicking on 'Browse All Materials.'

3. Type in "basswood" in the materials and choose the type of basswood, preferably 1/16 basswood.

4. Click Done. Ensure that you follow the instructions on the cutting window by moving the star wheel to the right of the machine. I believe that you still remember why this is important. Then the materials should be secured to the Strong Grip mat using tape. Of course, the material should be no more than 11" wide.

5. Insert the rotary blade into the accessory clamp. By the way, the machine will give a warning if the blade is not inserted.

6. Now, you load the mat into the machine by pressing on the Load/Unload button.

7. The machine will start cutting when you press the flashing Cricut button. It will make an entire pass of the image the machine is going to cut before cutting the full image. Of course, this will take time because of the thickness of the cut. Therefore, you can do other pressing tasks at hand.

8. Unload the mat by pressing the Load/Unload button which will be blinking when the task is complete.

9. Remove the tape and your material from the mat.

10. Use the weeding tool to remove your design from the whole material gently.

Working on this project would have stirred your creative mind on many ideas you can accomplish following this approach. Release your creativity and get to work. I am really excited, and I hope you are too.

How to Design with the Cricut Machine

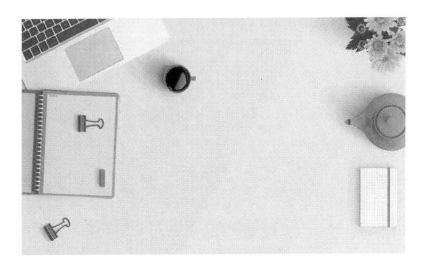

Working with Fonts in the Design Space

Cricut Design Space permits the use of fonts downloaded from third party sites. That means if you don't want to use the custom fonts in the Cricut Design Space, you can download the fonts on your Windows/Mac system through chrome browser. The process of installing fonts from third-party sites will be explained later in this subheading.

Using a font in Cricut Design Space isn't as difficult as it seems if you know how to use it. The following steps will explain in detail how to use a font in a Cricut Design Space:

After you have installed your font, restart your Cricut Design Space to refresh all the fonts, including your new font.

In the work area of your Cricut Design Space, click the "Text" icon to start writing your text.

Add your text. Ensure the text is highlighted.

Click on "Font".

From the drop-down on the taskbar, select, "System Fonts". All your fonts in the system will load at once. This may take a few seconds.

Select your preferred font.

The selected or highlighted text will be displayed in the new font.

That's it. Your text is now in your new font.

If Cricut doesn't have your desired font, follow these steps below:

- First of all, download a font. If you are using a Windows or Mac system, use a Google Chrome browser to download because it works very well with Cricut Design Space.

- Ensure you know the exact location of the folder where your font is downloaded. Click to open the downloaded font. You may need to extract the font using extraction software if there is a need to.

- Double click on the font file. Once you have done this, a tab will open for installation. Click install.

Congratulations, your font is installed in your Cricut Design Space. Remember to always refresh Design Space to show your installed font.

How to Add Text to Cricut Design Space

1. For users of Windows, navigate to the left-hand side of the Canvas and select the Text tool. For iOS or Android users, the Text tool is at the bottom-left of the screen.

2. Select the font size and the font type you wish to use and then type your text in the text box. Do not freak out if you did not choose the font parameters before typing the text. With Cricut Design Space, you can type the text before selecting the font on Windows/Mac computer.

3. Click or tap on any space outside the text box to close it.

How to Edit Text in Cricut Design Space

To edit the text is super simple. Double click on the text to show the available options. Select the action you wish from the list of options displayed including font style, type, size, letter, and line spacing.

How to Edit Fonts

1. Select the text you wish to edit on the Canvas, or you can insert text from the design panel, or select a text layer from the Layers Panel.

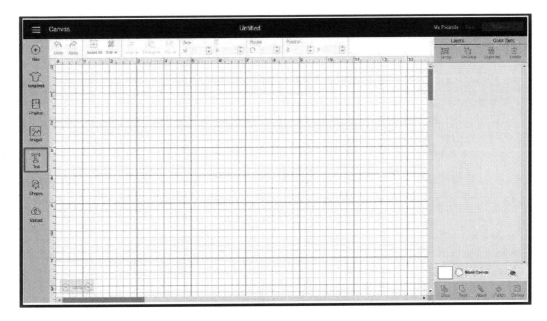

2. When the Text Edit Bar pops up, you can start changing the font using the available options. These options include Font, Font Drop-Down, Font Filter, Style, Font Size, Line Space, Alignment, and more.

How to Write Using System Fonts

A simple way to write with fonts using the Cricut pen and Cricut Explore Air machine is to change the line type of your text from 'Cut' to 'Write'. Next is to choose the font type you wish to use and select the "writing style" of your choice. Note that the fonts used in the writing style are similar to the text written by hand but the Cricut machine will write it as if it is tracing the outside of the letters. I believe you know how to use fonts now and what the final form of the fonts will look like. Now I want to discuss the different types of fonts.

Adding Fonts

A lot of folks have the misconception that they need to add fonts to Design Space. The truth here is that you don't need to do that. To get your desired fonts, you will have to download them to your PC and then install them. The downloaded fonts will only be available on the system to which you downloaded and installed it on and not on any other system in which you log into your Design Space account.

Go with the following steps to download and install fonts to the Design Space on your PC:

Get a site where you can download the fonts from. Here are some of the sites that you can make use of: esty.com, fontsquirrel.com, fontspace.com, creativemarket.com, datfont.com. Note that some of the fonts are free, while others are not. If your finished product is going to be sold, you should obtain the license or get commercially free fonts. On any of the sites that you choose to get your font from, you can browse through the catalog available there to pick the one that best suits your current project. Click on download when you have decided on the font you want to go with. It will download straight to your PC.

Search for the downloaded file on your PC, or better still, go straight to the Downloads Folder, it will most likely be there. The data comes in a zipped folder; unzip it (right-click on your mouse or the touchpad and select the unzip option) to get access to the fonts.

When you are in the folder, tap twice in quick succession on the .ttf file. A prompt will come up initiating the installation of the fonts. Tap on confirm to begin the process.

Open your Design Space and open a fresh page, and from there, click on the text tool. Enter a sentence or a word and then move onto the font selection option. You can tap on the system option to have a look at all the fonts that are installed on your PC, or you can simply enter the name of the font that you want.

Despite the large library of custom images that the Cricut Design Space has, there are files that you may want to cut yourself that may not be available in the system. Since Cricut Design Space supports DIY designs, you can design your own files and upload them to Design Space for cutting. You can either use Adobe Illustrator or Photoshop to create your own designs.

How to Use Images in Cricut Design Space

How to Cut One Image out of Another Image

It is possible to remove a part of an image to form another image using the Slice tool in Design Space, and it's super easy too. Use these steps to remove an image out of another image:

1. Position the two images to overlap each other.

2. Select the two images.

3. Click on "Slice". This button is at the bottom of the Layers Panel for computer users, in the Actions' menu at the bottom of the screen for Android and iOS users.

4. Separate the layers to review your new shapes.

5. Edit or delete the images separately.

6. Go to Layer and slice your image till you get your desired design.

How to Upload Images on Cricut Design Space on Windows/Mac and iOS Devices

Uploading your images to Design Space is a walk in the park once you get a grip on the basic concepts. As stated earlier, there are two significant categories of image files that can be uploaded to the Design Space.

Vector Images: .dxf and .svg files. They are uploaded in more than one layer in such a way that you can edit varying independent parts on the platform.

Basic Images: .png, .jp, .gif and .bmp are uploaded in the form of a single-layered image. This implies that what you see in the preview of the image before printing and cutting is exactly what you will get after the whole process is completed.

After your image is ready, which you might have bought on the Cricut platform or designed yourself, the time is now here to upload it. The next logical step to take is to open the Design Space.

Tap on the 'Browse Files" tab and search for the relevant file from your PC.

If the file is a vector image, a preview will come up after the upload is complete. At this point, you can rename the image and save it from this point.

On the other hand, if the file is a basic image, you can carry out any of the following functions: - Select the type of vision; this serves to determine the complexity of the picture. If the image that has been uploaded does not contain too much information, you can pick the Simple Image option, and if the details in the image are more complex, you can select the Moderately Complex or Complex Image Options.

- Tap on the Continue icon.

- Select and Erase; here, you can carry out the editing process on your basic image. This involves erasing and cropping out the unneeded parts by making use of the available tools. When you are satisfied with the result, tap on the continue button.

- Name and Tag; in this section, you can give your image a name and also decide if it will be a cut image or a print and cut image.

- Save. You will then be taken back to the upload image screen.

The image is now prepared and ready to be cut or printed.

To Upload and Use Images

Open the Cricut Design Space environment and click, "Upload Image" from the left-hand menu.

Browse through the list of uploaded files and select the image.

Select, "Insert Image".

Select the type of image.

Another tab will open, select the part of the image you want to cut, and the part you do not want to.

Choose whether your image is a regular image or a print-then-cut image.

The file will appear in your work area on the screen. Sometimes, the imported data does not come in the correct dimensions, so you might have to edit. The "edit" menu is on the right of the screen.

Select, "Go" in the top right of the screen and cut your design.

How to Use Cricut Design on iOS

The Cricut Design Space App on iOS is easy to use, just like the software program on Windows/Mac. You can have access to your images, cut projects, and do a lot of things on the app. The Design Space App for iPad and iPhones are practically the same. The difference is the vast space that the iPad has, which is not available on the iPhone. On iPhones, the icons and some menus will appear together or clustered in one box. On the iPad however, you will see the lists clearly and separated in a large file in the panel.

If you have no experience using the Cricut Design Space on your iPhone or iPad, the following steps will explain better.

First of all, you need to download and install the app on your iOS device. Next, you sign-in.

You will be taken to the home section of the app. You will see various options like "Cut Project", "Create a New Project", etc. at the top panel. You will also see the Profile Picture option, at the top panel.

If you wish to get started on creating designs before cutting, go to the canvas area. You will be able to access a variety of options such as tap, pinch zoom, double-tap, and other hand gestures.

At the bottom of the screen, 12 menus will allow you to adjust your project. Examples of such lists are Image, Text, Shapes, Upload, Edit, Settings, etc. Every menu in the Cricut Design Space is designed to perform one function to the other in the canvas area.

There are thousands of images and cartridges you can find in the Cricut Design Space. You can also find pictures you uploaded to your computer. To have access to some cartridges, you need to make a separate subscription, known as Cricut Access.

When you want to type on the canvas area, click, "Text". Then, choose the font and then type.

There is the option to add shapes. There are nine shapes you can choose from: Triangle, Square, Pentagon, Hexagon, Star, Octagon, etc.

There is also an "Action" menu. Here, you will find options like Group, Attach, Slice, Weld, Flatten, Duplicate, etc. Grouping a project will organize the project better and incorporate the layers in one place. Attach is similar to Group. Let us say you want to attach shapes. When you select it, your inserted shapes will have the same color.

Welding enables you to combine two shapes into one.

Just like the name, the slice tool is used for cutting shapes, texts, and pictures.

Let us talk about another menu in the Design Space. The edit menu enables you to carry out modifications to your project. It allows you to organize and align all the elements in your canvas or work area. In the edit menu, you will find options like Font, Style, Alignment, Linetype and Fill, etc. The functions will be explained below.

The use of fonts on the Cricut Design Space on iOS devices is similar to that of Windows/Mac.

The "Style" option is pretty simple. Once you have picked your preferred font, you have the option of setting your text as Regular, Bold, Italic, etc.

With the "Alignment" option, you can align your text to the left, right, or center.

Selecting the "Linetype" menu will give you access to options like cut, draw, score, engrave, perf, wave, and deboss.

The "Fill" option is used specifically for printing. It is activated once you have activated the "cut" option in the line type.

The Contour Feature in Cricut Design Space

With this feature, you can successfully hide parts of an image, thereby making it possible to add more features to your images.

Making use of the Contour feature in hiding part of an image can also be used when you do not want to cut out any part of the image. Take, for instance; you have a rainbow rose flower that has different colors with varying layers, and based on the design you have in mind, you do not want the red color to show. Hiding the red color might make the flower turn out not how a flower should as an important part of the flower would be lost. To get around this, a contour is used.

To get started, the different layers of the flowers are ungrouped, sequentially.

After you have done that, you then pick the layer of interest, which is the red petals. Choose the red flowers, tap on Contour in the bottom right corner. All the cut lines available for the part highlighted will be seen. Click on the highlighted sections and hide the areas. Tap on the close screen icon on the sub-screen on which you are currently working.

You can carry out the same procedure for multiple parts of the flower. And just like that, you have added the contour and hidden the red petals without distorting the real image of the flower.

Maintenance of the Cricut Machine

Maintenance and Care of Cricut Cutting Machines

All Cricut cutting machines fold away with protective face plates. You should always make sure that these are closed when the cutting machine is not in use.

The EasyPress machines will need a protective bag to be stored in which is a good investment to prolong the life of these presses. You should look at buying storage bags for the cutting machines as well for a bit of extra protection and to be able to move them without damaging them.

<u>Changing Cutting Machine Blades</u>

At times, the cutting blades will become blunt, especially with continuous use. There are replacement blades that can be purchased in order to maintain clear precision cuts.

These blades are sold separately from the blade housing compartments and are not difficult to change. Although care should always be taken as the blades may be blunt for cutting, they will still be considered sharp and can cut through skin.

For Cricut cutting machine blades that use blade housings like the *Bonded-Fabric blade* and the *Fine Point blade*:

Press down on the dop of the blade housing cap.

355

Pull out the blade (be careful as it can still cut).

Hold the housing with the blade side up.

Slide the new blade into position until it clicks.

Cricut cutting machine blades that use the *gear housing* (housing with the gold gear on top) utilize blades like the *Rotary blade* or the *Scoring blade*:

These blades like the scoring blade and the rotary blade are a little more difficult and require a bit more assembly.

The new blades come with a blade kit:

The kit comes with an empty cap that contains the new blade and washer.

The kit also comes with a small screwdriver.

Each blade comes with a protective cap. Place the protective cap over the blade housing.

You will note that the small screw at the bottom of the blade is accessible through the protective cap.

Use the small screwdriver to unscrew this little screw and put the little screw to one side.

Pull the cap with the bottom blade off of the drive blade housing.

Place the blade housing into the new protective cap that contains the new blade and washer.

Push the cap on tight and make sure that the screw holes line up.

Using the little screw that you took out of the old blade, screw it into the new blade using the little screwdriver until it is securely in position.

Caring for Cricut Cutting Blades

If you want to extend the life of your Cricut cutting machine blades, you will need to take care of them.

Always make sure that you only use the blades for the materials that they are compatible with. This list can be found in Chapter 1 of this book or on the Cricut website. Trying to use the blades on materials that are too tough for them is going to blunt if not break the blade.

Most blades come with a protective cap. When these blades are not in use, store them in a safe place with their protective covers firmly in place.

Make sure that you store them in a place that is free of dust and grime. The best place is in the Cricut's own storage drawer, as these close away and protect the blades from dust and grime.

To sharpen the blades, you can use a piece of crumpled up aluminum foil and poke holes in it with the blade for two to three minutes. But this is not ideal, and a blunt blade should be replaced to maintain the cutting machine's precision cutting ability.

Cleaning and Maintaining the Cutting Mat(s)

The Cricut cutting mats are sticky to keep materials being cut firmly anchored to the mat during cutting. These mats can become clogged with particles, especially mats that are used with the new Knife Blade that works with the Cricut Maker.

To clean the mats:

Never try to scrape any leftover material from the mat. This can damage the mat and will remove its stickiness.

Scraping materials from the mat may also embed them deeper into the mat.

Remove any leftover materials with a tweezer or weeding tool.

To remove dust or extra stubborn materials you can wash the mat:

Place the mat flat in a sink.

Use only lukewarm water on the mat.

Only use plastic-bristled scrubbing brushes to gently scrub the mat.

Rinse the mat with lukewarm water.

Leave it to completely dry lying flat and draining on the sink.

When the mat is dry, the stickiness should return.

Keep mats stored in clean and dry areas where there is little dust. Any dust or particles can cause damage to the mat and projects.

To keep them safe and sticky, use a piece of protective sheeting to keep them covered when they are not in use.

It is best to store mats in a craft box or tote bag used to store other craft materials.

Only use materials designed for the mat in order to prolong the life of the cutting mat.

Only use the mat with blades that it is compatible with or you will damage the cutting mat and possibly the cutting blade.

Cleaning the Cricut Cutting Machine

The Cricut machine is going to get dirty as it cuts paper, cardboard, vinyl, and is exposed to everyday dust. The machine is not difficult to clean either; all you need is a soft cloth and some glass cleaner spray.

Here are some cleaning tips:

Never use anything that is corrosive or can damage the machine to clean it. Stay away from acetone (nail polish remover), strong cleaners that contain harsh ingredients such as bleach, or strong countertop cleaners.

Always make sure that the machine is turned off and unplugged before attempting to clean it.

If there is grease buildup on the rollers or dirt on any of the feeder bars or roller wheels, use a cotton puff with some window cleaner on it.

Caring for the Machine, Accessories, and Tools

The best way to care for the machines, accessories, and tools for the Cricut machines is to keep them safely stored away when they are not in use.

Most of the accessories and tools can fit into the Cricut's storages drawers (for the machines that have storage compartments, that is). For the machines that do not, it is advisable to buy one of Cricut's amazing storage totes.

Keep the tools clean by wiping them off before they are stored and after being used. You can even run them under lukewarm water, pat them dry, and let them drain before you store them.

Caring for the Cut Smart Carriage in the Cricut Cutting Machine

The little carriage that houses the cutting blades and accessories is called the Cut Smart Carriage. From time to time, you may notice it getting a little stuck or not moving freely. This may mean that there is a little dust or goo on it or it may need a little bit of grease.

Here are some tips on cleaning and greasing the Cut Smart Carriage:

Make sure that the cutting machine is turned off and unplugged from the wall before you attempt to clean the carriage.

To get the carriage to move to the side to clean it, simply push it to the side. Do not force it, be gentle.

Use a piece of tissue to clean the length of it and remove grease or grime.

Get the lubricant for the machine from Cricut or a Cricut dealer.

Move the little carriage to the middle of the carriage bar.

Using a cotton puff, some of the lubricant onto the tip of the cotton puff.

You will need to swab a light coating of the lubricant on both sides of the carriage.

Once you have applied the lubricant, gently move the carriage from side to side.

Wipe off any excess lubricant with tissue paper.

Parts, Spares, and Services

Find your nearest Cricut supplier or dealer to learn about any maintenance or repair that may have to be done on the machine. If your machine is still under warranty, it is best to get service from your local dealer instead of trying to tinker with it yourself.

Cricut offers parts and spares for nearly all of its current and older machines. These can be conveniently purchased online at their craft shop or at your local Cricut dealer. They include blade spares, roller, tools, and so on.

FAQ About the Cricut Explore Air

Troubleshooting Your Cricut Explore Air Machine

If your Explore Machine stops working or pauses when you are in the middle of your work, you don't have to worry. Here are some steps in troubleshooting issues.

Is your power button blinking red? If you notice this when you first power the machine or when you are trying to update a framework, that means you have to contact the care center for assistance.

Is the power button light flashing red when trying to load your cutting mat? Then an error might have occurred when saving a corrupted project and that means you will need to recreate the project.

Your Blade Is Not Detected

STEP 1: Make sure that the tool is properly installed and that the tool matches with the tool recommended by the Design Space. If you don't have access to the recommended tool, return to the project preview screen after which you click on the edit tool to choose a different tool. If the problem persists, then proceed to step 2.

STEP 2: Gently remove the tool again from the clamp and carefully clean the tool sensor with a light cloth. After cleaning, install it back and press the "GO" button.

Your Machine is Being Unusually Noisy

If the sound of your machine is louder than normal, then check if it is engaged in fast mode for writing or cutting. If checked and it is engaged in fast mode, then you have to contact your care center or proceed to step 2.

STEP 2: Check to ensure that you are making use of the power cord that the machine came with. If you are making use of a different cord, the voltage coming into the Cricut machine may be wrong and may be the cause of the grinding noise. But if you are using the power cord the machine came with and still the machine is making the noise, then proceed to step 3.

STEP 3: Check if the pressure setting you are using is too high and if so, try reducing the pressure setting for the material you are trying to cut.

But if you have tried all these things and it is still not working, please contact the machine care center.

Your Machine is Tearing Your Material

These are some steps to take if your Cricut machine is tearing your material:

STEP 1: Check if the smart is set on the correct setting and check if you have selected the correct material in the design space.

STEP 2: Try to verify the size and quality of the image you have cut. If you are cutting an image that is of very high quality, try cutting one free from duplicity.

STEP 3: Try making use of a new blade and mat.

STEP 4: After all these steps have been completed and the problem still persists, please try contacting assistance care.

Your Fabrics Always Get Caught Under the Rollers

If you are experiencing this problem with your fabrics, check if the fabrics are placed outside the tenacious area of your mat by allowing it to pass under the rubber roller bar. If that happens the fabrics can be gripped by the rubber rollers. It is recommended that you cut down a size that will fit the mat but will not extend outside the tenacious area. The recommended and standard sizes for the tenacious area on the fabrics grip mat is 12x24 and 12x12, respectively.

How to Clean Your Explore Machine

Machines might collect dust, paper, or other particles. Cleaning your machine is very easy to do using the following steps and tips:

- Always make sure your machine is first of all disconnected before cleaning it.

- You can make use of cleaner sprayed on a soft, clean cloth to clean the machine.

- Make sure you clean the electricity panel section with a dry, soft, clean cloth or cotton; or you can simply wipe.

How to Load Your Paper

When you are using the Cricut Explore Air 2, it is recommended that your paper should be within the 3x3 range as this will help in getting an optimum result for cardstock. However, the Cricut Explore Air 2 is capable of cutting larger paper of 6x12 inches

Cricut Explore Air 2 Tips

How to Install Your Cutting Mat

Place the mat into your Cricut machine slowly, make sure that the arrow point towards your device

Click on "load paper" to hold the cutting mat firmly. This will help the loading of the mat into your Cricut Explore machine. If you notice any issues with the loading, then click on "unload" and try processing it again

How to Remove Your Cut from the Cutting Mat

Slowly remove the cut from your cutting mat. Use the Cricut tool or a craft knife to pull the image or cut. If you are facing any form of difficulty, clean off any paper scrapings remaining on the cutting mat.

How to Replace Your Cutting Blade

Firstly, remove the cutting blade assembly. After that, release the cutting blade. Slowly remove the blade from the magnet and hold it with care.

To insert a new blade, free the blade release and slowly insert your new blade shaft into the bottom hole of the cutting blade assembly, then reinsert the cutting blade assembly into your Cricut machine.

How to Apply Grease

Some tips and steps on how to apply grease to your Cricut machine:

- First, turn off the machine.

- Then push the smart carriage slowly to the left.

- Wipe around the entire bar of the cut smart carriage bar with a tissue or clean cloth.

- Push the cut smart carriage slowly to the right.

- Move the cut smart gently to the center of the machine.

- Squeeze a small amount of grease at the end of the cotton swab.

- Apply a little grease on both sides of the cut smart.

- Move gently the cut smart carriage to the left side and also to the right to distribute the grease around.

- Wipe off the grease at the end of the bar.

Review of the Best Cricut Machine for Beginners

Cricut has different models of die-cutting machines and for a beginner, you may be confused about the type that is best for you in the course of crafting. Look no further as I have you covered. I have reviewed four machines (Cricut Maker, Cricut Explore Air 2, Cricut Explore Air, and Cricut Explore One) to give insight into their strengths and weaknesses while making up your mind to which one of them you will work with.

The type of Cricut machine you may wish to get depends on the type of project you want to use it for. All Cricut machines have certain things in common including cut, right, and score, 12" wide cutting area size. They can also cut a variety of materials, as well as the Design Space software and the Print Then Cut feature. What makes them stand them out is the differences between them as will be discussed:

1. Double/Single Tool Holder: the main tool holder is what you see when you open the lid of the Cricut machine, designed to move back and forth on the carriage. A double tool holder allows you to write and cut in one step while a single tool holder will do the same function as separate steps. Among the four mentioned Cricut machines, only Cricut Explore One has a single tool holder while the rest has a double tool holder.

2. Adaptive Tool System: this is a recent addition to the Cricut machine and available only to Cricut Maker. The adaptive tool system delivers more power to the cutting force (4 kg), which is ten times more than the nearest version to it. It uses a steering system to control the direction of the blade, adjusts the pressure of the blade automatically with each cut pass, and uses a new set of tools and accessories for diverse cuts.

3. Fast Cutting Mode: this mode is used to write and cut materials twice as fast, especially when producing large quantities of materials. This feature is common to Cricut Maker and Explore Air 2.

4. Cutting with Bluetooth: this feature is common to the Cricut Maker, Explore Air 2, and Explore Air. You can use it to cut your material without using a cable.

5. All models of Cricut machines have a slot for cartridge and can be linked to your Design Space account to have access to your cartridge graphics. Newer models like the Cricut Maker come with a digital Design Space library instead of the physical cartridge and if you need to connect a physical cartridge with it, you will need to buy a separate cartridge adapter.

Cricut Explore Air Project Ideas

How to Make a Customized Graphic T-Shirt

<u>Materials</u>

- The Cricut machine

- Vinyl for the letters

- Your Cricut toolkit

<u>Instructions</u>

Start by choosing the image you want to use. This can be done in Photoshop or you can place your text directly into Design Space.

Next, open Cricut Design Space. Choose the canvas that you wish to use by clicking the Canvas icon on the dashboard, which is located on the left-hand side. Select the canvas that you will be using for your vinyl letters on. This can be anything within the categories they offer.

Then, select the size of the shirt for the canvas. This is located on the right-hand side of the options.

Now, click Upload to upload your image, which is located on the left-hand side. Select the image you are using by browsing the list of images in your file library. Then, select the type of image that you have picked. For most projects, especially iron-on ones, you will select the Simple Cut option.

Click on the white space that you want to be removed by cutting it out. Remember to cut the insides of every letter.

Next, be very diligent and press Cut Image instead of Print first. You do not want to simply print the image, you want to cut it as well.

Place the image on your chosen canvas and adjust the sizing of the image.

Place your iron-on image with the vinyl side facing down on the mat. Then turn the dial to the setting Iron-on.

Next, you will want to click the Mirror Image setting for the image, prior to hitting Go.

Once you have cut the image, you should remove the excess vinyl from the edges around the lettering or image. Then, use the tool for weeding, to weed out the inner pieces of the letters.

Now you will be placing the vinyl on the shirt.

Now, the fun part begins. You will get to iron the image onto the shirt. Using the cotton setting, you will need to use the hottest setting that you can get your iron to. There should not be any steam.

You want to warm the shirt by placing the iron on the shirt portion that will hold the image. This should be warmed up for 5 seconds.

Next, lay the vinyl out exactly where you want it to be placed. Place a pressing cloth over the top of the plastic. This will prevent the plastic on the shirt from melting.

Place your iron onto the pressing cloth for around 0 seconds. Flip the shirt; place the pressing cloth and iron on the back side of the vinyl.

Flip your shirt back over and begin to peel off the sticky part of the vinyl that you had overlaid on the shirt. This will separate the vinyl from the plastic backing. This should be done while the plastic and vinyl are hot. If you are having trouble removing the vinyl from the plastic backing, then place the iron back on the part that is being difficult. Then proceed to pull up and it should come off nicely.

This should remove the plastic from the vinyl, which is now on the shirt. Place the pressing cloth on top of the vinyl once again and heat it to ensure that the vinyl is good and stuck.

How to Make Stickers with Cricut

Materials

- Cricut Explore Air

- Printable sticker paper by Cricut

Instructions

Log in to your Cricut Design Space account.

In the Cricut Design Space, you will need to click on Starting a New Project. Then, select the image that you would love to use for your stickers. You can use the search bar on the right-hand side at the top to locate the image that you want to use.

Next, click on the image and click Insert Image so that the image is selected.

Click on each one of the files that are in the image file and click the Flatten button at the lower-right part of the screen. This will turn the individual pieces into one whole piece. This prevents the cut file from being individual pieces for the image.

Now, you want to resize the image, so that it is the size that you wish it to be. This can be any size from within the recommended space for the size of the canvas.

If you want duplicates of the image for sticker sheets, you should Select All, then edit the image, and then click Copy. This will allow you to copy the whole row that you have selected. Once you have copied, you can then edit and paste the multiple images to make a sheet. This is the easiest way to copy and paste the image over and over again.

366

At this time, you are ready to start printing your stickers. Click the Save button on the left-hand side of the screen to save the project, and choose the option Save as Print and then Cut Image. Once done, you can click the green button that says Make It. This will be located to the right of the screen.

Verify that everything is how it needs to be and click Continue. This will give you a prompt to print the image onto your paper. Make sure you have used the sticker paper for the stickers; otherwise, it will not work.

Print out the image with your printer. If the Cricut sticker paper is too thick for your printer, using a thinner sticker paper is fine.

After the design is printed, adjust the Smart Set dial to the appropriate setting. Place the paper onto the cutting mat and load it into the Cricut machine by pushing against the rollers. Press your Load and Unload button that is flashing.

Press Go, and this will begin to cut your stickers. Since the stickers are small and intricate, you will need to be patient.

A tip for getting a good cut is to not touch the mat. Once the first cut is done, repress the flashing button to re-cut the stickers on the same lines that were previously cut.

How to Make DIY Paper Succulent with Your Cricut

This pretty little project can be made to fit into any container you already have and can instantly add a little punch to your mantelpiece, table setting, or display. Make as many or as few of these different succulents as you want.

Materials

- Cardstock in teals and pinks.

- Ink pads in different coordinating colors of teal and pink.

- Sponges or dabbers for the ink.

- Hot glue gun.

- Foam to fill your container.

Instructions

In Design Space, look for the design file for succulents. If you want to create the design yourself, create one large petal-shaped flower and then copy it about six times. Scale each copy down to a smaller size. If you need to, remove a petal or two to make it appear more proportional. For the spiral and pointed succulent, make a spiral with three rings. The center of the ring should be a circle on the end. Add pointed triangles to the outside of the spiral lines.

Once you have your designs ready, send your file to cut on your different colored card stock. Remove your pieces and place corresponding flower pieces together on a covered work surface. Using your sponges or dabbers, add a touch of ink to the outer edges of each petal shape or on the tips of the spikes of the spiral. You can keep the colors matching or contrast with a pink tip on a teal succulent and vice versa.

Gently curl the edges of the petals up on the ends to make them more three-dimensional.

Using your hot glue gun, glue the layers of the succulents together and roll the pointed succulents and glue them together as well.

Place the floral foam inside your container, about a half-inch from the top. You can place your succulents on the foam or glue them down in the place where you like the arrangement. Once all your succulents are placed, consider covering the exposed foam with paper grass or shredded paper. You can glue this covering down if you like but it typically looks best when it is loose.

How to Make Personalized Paper Bookmarks Using Your Cricut Machine

Materials

- Cricut machine

- Printable sticker paper

- Inkjet printer

Instructions

Log in to the Cricut design spaces.

Start a new project and click on the Images on the screen's left side. Select the image(s) you want.

Click on the Text icon and input your text.

Select the font of your desire from the available font package.

Highlight the documents and change the color by using the available colors on the color tray.

Click on the Print option to change the file from a cut file to a print file.

Click on the Ungroup icon to adjust the spacing of the text.

370

After adjusting the spacing, highlight all, and use the Group icon to make them one whole piece again.

Click on the Shape icon and insert a shape.

Change the shape's color using the color tray.

Highlight the text and use the Align drop-down box.

Make use of the Move to the Front icon to move the text to the front.

Highlight the design and click on Group.

Highlight the whole image and use the Flatten button to solidify the design as one whole piece.

Resize the design to the appropriate size you need. You realize this by clicking on the model then dragging the right side of the box to the extent you desire.

Click Save at the top left to save your project. Save it to be a Print and Cut image, after which you click the Make It button at the right hand of the screen.

Examine the end result and click Continue if it is what you expected. This will lead you to print the design onto the paper.

Adjust the dial on the Cricut machine to the required settings.

Place the sticker paper on the cutting mat.

In the machine, load the cutting mat and push it against the rollers.

In order to cut the sticker, press the Load / Unload button and then the Go button.

Your planning sticker is ready.

How to Make a Frosty Wreath

Frosty wreaths are beautiful crafts for wall decals and door decorations for festivals like Christmas. You can use them for gifts, sell them, and even use them for home decor.

<u>Materials</u>

- Cricut Explore machine
- Fabric grip and strong grip mats
- Cricut felt
- Knife blade
- Rotary blade accessories
- Vine wreath
- Glue
- Masking tape
- Chipboard
- Fabric brayer

Instructions

Allow the chipboard to acclimatize to its environment for about 24 hours to avoid bending, or warping.

Smooth the chipboard on the strong grip mat using a brayer to adhere properly.

Use masking tape to secure the edges of the chipboard to the strong grip mat

Push the star wheels on the machine to the side, so they do not run on the chipboard leaving traces behind.

The knife blade can only cut designs less than 10.5" and larger than 0.75." Anything more than that will destroy your blade.

Pause the Cricut Explore machine frequently to check the progress by lifting the edge of the chipboard.

To save your strong grip mat from wear, use a knife tool to cut the remaining when the Cricut machine has almost cut through your design.

Now time for the project. I expect that you know how to design the text for the chipboard in the Design Space, so I will not go there again.

When you are done with the text design and you have selected the chipboard from the list of materials on the Design Space, load the chipboard on top of the strong grip mat into your Cricut Explore machine.

Press the flashing Cricut button to load and cut your design. Remember to pause frequently to check the progress and remove any loose chipboard piece, especially in the snowflakes. This is helpful to avoid stuck pieces that can damage the rotary blade. When it is almost cut through, unload the mat, and use the knife tool to cut the remaining chipboard to save your mat from wear.

Load the second chipboard piece for the snowflakes and follow step 2 to remove the piece stuck, and knife blade to finish the segments of the snowflakes, not cut through.

Use any color of your choice to paint the snowflakes, depending on how you want the final appearance of the project to look like.

For the felt snowflakes, set the material to 'Felt' and use the same method for the chipboard to prepare the felt on the mat, this time using the fabric grip mat. Please be careful with the dimension of the felt snowflakes, so that you do not experience challenges cutting and removing them from the fabric grip mat. Also, scrape them gently from the mat, as the cut material can break easily.

Use the glue to attach them together on the 8" vine wreath to taste and enjoy your beautifully designed and crafted frosty wreath.

Vinyl

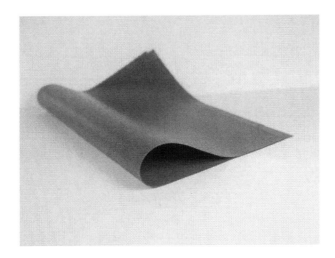

Heat Transfer Vinyl (Better Known as HTV)

This is a common and easy-to-apply method, especially for those starting from scratch. After cutting the piece of vinyl out, you use your iron to apply the vinyl to a fabric surface. It holds up through the washing machine and looks very professional. You can customize your favorite clothing. There are a variety of brands, but the most often recommended is Scissor EasyWeed. Easy to use, it comes in a variety of styles and colors and it holds up through the washing machine, it looks perfect. It is ideal for socks, T-shirts, stuffed animals, canvas tote bags, costumes, or anything with fabric.

Printable Vinyl

Printable Vinyl comes both in Heat Transfer and Adhesive types. All you need to have with this particular material is a normal inkjet printer, and the design can be printed out on your vinyl.

Take pieces of vinyl of different colors, cut them, and put them all on your Cricut Mat. Then to make it easier to take a picture of it, I suggest laying your mat on the floor. Then from your Cricut App, click categories, then Projects in the Cloud, then select the project you are going to cut and click customize. Finally, replace and then make it.

Next, click on Snap Mat. You can place the camera over the floor on your mat, wait for the box to turn green, hold it for a few seconds, and then take the picture.

Once the picture pops up, select use, and then select continue. You can start your creation with multiple colors on one mat. You can create images and text and swipe from one color to another.

When you have your image or text over one color and you select it, the selected one will come up with a spin and 3 dots, if you click on the 3 dots you can then select move to another map. Once you have your images and text positioned on each one of your colored mats where you want to click continue. It will show that you have vinyl selected and you can go to your Cricut to cut your creation out.

As a novice, your journey to finding the ideal vinyl cutting machine should focus on a gadget with demonstrated execution, notwithstanding long-haul strength. Different variables will help you in your examination of vinyl cutters.

We can sort the vinyl cutters into two primary classes: individual and business models. What do you intend to use your new vinyl cutter for? If you intend to deal with complex structures and signs in large numbers, then you should search for a business model. For specialist or at-home use, you'll need a customized machine. This model usually comes in a more convenient size, and superbly handles smaller jobs. They are additionally more affordable and easier to use, which makes them perfect for apprentices.

Various models additionally work on different engines, with the two principle choices being the servo and mechanical motors. The advanced servo works easily and gives more exact increases in cutting head and drive motor (improving the general machine precision). Since physical riggings drive the mechanical stepper, it will, in general, be loud during activity. It additionally shows restricted precision when used to cut little pictures. Therefore, I prescribe you to go for the servo motor if possible.

Material compatibility is something most amateurs will overlook when looking for a vinyl shaper. Check what kinds of materials and textures the machine you wish to purchase can cut, aside from vinyl. Search for one that professes to cut plenty of materials. Don't simply accept their claims, however. Check past client reviews on whether it slices through the materials it claims.

Ensure the machine you intend to put resources into accompanies a less intricate activity system and is anything but difficult to use to make accurate cuts. Make sure to peruse different reviews about usability. Check that it is natural to do basic errands like supplanting the cartridges with pens for printing and stacking papers into the machine. It's likewise fitting to affirm that the machine you need to purchase works with the most widely recognized sorts of papers, such as vinyl, magnet paper, leather, and glue paper.

A few machines even include software that makes your work a lot simpler and allows individuals to accomplish progressively specialized crafts. They additionally present you with a library of free structures that you can use for snappy activities or as a learner. The different variables that add to the usability of a cutting machine includes programmed settings and a remote capacity.

Vinyl cutting machines frequently glitch. That is a reality that most experienced clients will concede to. In that respect, getting a model that accompanies a client guarantee is a significant thought. Other than guaranteeing you the nature of the machine, a guarantee goes about as your safety net. It implies you'll understand what to do if your machine quits working, such as requesting a substitution or having the proprietor specialists repair the issue.

Notwithstanding how straightforward or propelled a vinyl shaper you're searching for is, it must fall inside your financial limit. Similarly, as with the various items out there, these machines will fluctuate as far as cost goes. The models that come at a greater expense will, in general, be of a higher caliber.

Best Vinyl Cutter Picks

1. USCutter Vinyl Cutter MH 34 in. Bundle

This machine is commonly viewed as one of the most flexible devices ever made. It accompanies vinyl shaper PNC1000 drivers, which enables it to work with VinylMaster Cut just as the various mainstream software, such as Cuts-A-Lot, SignBlazer, Flexi, and SignCut Productivity Pro. This shaper additionally includes two completely flexible squeeze rollers that permit you to cut a wide scope of materials.

The incredibly easy-to-use machine is as extraordinary for specialists as it is for private companies searching for the best value plotter accessible. It can, without much of a stretch, handle all your straightforward tasks. What's more, it doesn't expect you to have any related knowledge before working on it.

With a limit of approximately 31" of cutting width and 8' maximum cutting width, you can have confidence that it'll be able to deal with the entirety of your occupations. Extra helpful things included in this bundle include exchange tapes, vinyl rolls, attractive spaces, a squeegee, a blade, and a graph for easy beginnings. Most importantly, it presents you with lifetime phone support, so you'll know what to do when your machine glitches.

Features:

- 34" MH shaper with VinylMaster Cut

- Predominant metal roller double roller framework

- Roland good sharp edge

- Extra things: vinyl rollers move tapes, a squeegee, attractive spaces, a blade

- Lifetime phone support

2. Cricut Explore Air 2 Vinyl Cutter Machine

I suggest anybody searching for an individual vinyl cutter purchase the Cricut Explore Air 2 Machine. It comes uniquely intended to assist you with taking care of all your activities with a definitive speed and exactness. Likely the coolest part about this machine is the way that it permits you to transfer your structures for free. On the other hand, you can browse various (up to 3,000 pre-made) projects, on the off chance that you don't have your pictures or just have a constrained stockpile. You can devise your structures and transfer them using a computer or cell phone.

Something different that makes this machine most loved by all specialists is that it permits you to make your designs on more than 100 unique materials, going from the slenderest vellum to the thickest leather materials. Since this machine accompanies a two-fold device holder, you'll enjoy up to 2x quicker slicing and composing speed compared to other models.

Features:

- Impeccable individual DIY cutting machine

- Tremendous library of pre-made structures

- Cuts more than 100 materials

- Installed Bluetooth, remote cutting

- German carbide premium cutting edge

- Savvy set dial guarantees simple material settings

3. Cameo with Electronic Vinyl Cutting Machine Starter Kit Bundle

To be completely forthright, it wasn't justified, despite any potential benefits. All the present cutters are the same. They use similar software, have a similar size, and work at a similar precision and speed.

So, what makes the Cameo II stand apart from the remainder of the cutting tools? The ability to begin your printing venture straight out of the box is a blissful euphoria for some DIY creators. It's extremely simple to learn and utilize. If you have a tad of structuring information and add some creativity to it, you're ready.

This Cameo accompanies a starter unit, vouchers for downloading structures on Silhouette's website, and one month's worth of free membership to their download store. It's a plug-and-play machine, much the same as your printer. The vinyl shaper can slice material up to 10' wide and 12" in length. Supplant the sharp edge with a pen, and this machine will outline your structure as opposed to cutting.

378

It includes a vinyl trimmer edge, 51 selective Cuttable plans, a dark cutting edge, a cutting mat, premium exchange paper, and more. It's too great of a deal to pass up.

Features:

- The Cameo II starter unit comes prepared with all that you have to get moving

- Simple to learn, regardless of whether you have had structuring information

- Good software that supports both Mac and Windows

- Vinyl cutting sharp edges are replaceable

4. Brother CM350 ScanNCut 2 Home and Hobby Vinyl Cutter Machine

The Brother CM350 ScanNCut 2 Home and Hobby Cutting Machine also rank among the top spots with other great vinyl cutters available today. The main thing that caused me to notice this model is its built-in 300 DPI scanner, which permits you to make your cuts effectively. As it were, you can examine simply anything, including cherished family photographs, carefully assembled drawings, home layouts, and so forth, and go through them to accompany exceptionally detailed cut shapes and frameworks that fit your particular project.

We likewise appreciated the reality that this machine comes structured as a stand-alone model. In any case, it additionally gives you the option of connecting it remotely to your computer. Other incredible highlights right now include a super-huge LCD touchscreen display, 600+ included structures, and the capacity to plan SVG information documents.

Features:

- 4.85" LCD touchscreen display

- 300 DPI scanner

- PC compatibility; wireless network display

- 600+ structures and 7 integrated fonts

- ScanNCutCanvas cloud

- A web-based application that allows the client to manage PDFs

Working with the Design Space App

What Is the Cricut Design Space

Investing in a Cricut is fruitless if you don't know how to master the Design Space, because to cut any project, you will always make use of this software. In my own opinion, Cricut Design Space is an excellent tool for beginners. If you don't have experience with any design programs such as Photoshop or Illustrator, you'll find it overwhelming in the beginning, but it's pretty simple. There's nothing to fear, you just need to get the hang of it.

On the other side, if you have expertise with any of Adobe's Creative Cloud applications or Inkscape, you'll see this program's a breeze. It's primarily to touch up your projects and produce minimal designs with shapes and fonts.

By logging into your Cricut Design Space account and starting or editing a new project, you'll do everything from a window called CANVAS. Cricut Design Space's Canvas Area is where you do all your edits before actually starting to cut your projects.

Downloading/Installing

Do you know where to get the Cricut Design Space? Well, if you are on a desktop or Personal Computer, navigate to https://design.cricut.com. If you are using an iOS device such as an iPhone or iPad, find your way to your App Store and input "Cricut Design Space" on the search space.

If your smartphone runs on Android OS, enter the Play Store and use the same search term. Remember that downloading or installing this is completely free of charge. Also, bear in mind that you will be needing a Cricut ID to sign in. This you can also get for free, even if you do not have a Cricut. Simply follow the prompts provided.

Once you have entered your email and gotten your ID, you will at once be taken into the main domain of the Cricut Design Space, the place where all of the magic happens. A quick tip: bookmark this page to your web toolbar so you can find it easily whenever you want to.

The Canvas you will be shown after similar to a painter's whiteboard is the big space where all your designs and progress will reflect this space has a full grid by default to allow you to see everything about a single work without having to pinch-zoom and unpinch. Nevertheless, you can choose the appearance and measurements of the grid.

Changing the Display

Most people would want to, first of all, change the display pattern to a partial grid. Some others would even like to choose no grid at all which means there will be no background. You can do this by clicking on the blank space that appears between the zeros. You will find this option at the top left corner of your rulers.

If you are using an app version, whether Android or iOS, to remove the gridlines, select the Settings option in the bottom toolbar then toggle Grids. A lot of people do this especially when they want to take an accurate and come out well screen munch of something, without having to deal with the grid sticking out its seemingly ugly head in the background also.

All projects, skills, and preferences are respectively not created equal, and that is why the Cricut Design Space has made it possible for you to change the measurement of your grid. If you are using the desktop version, navigate to the hamburger (three lines) menu which you will find in the top left corner.

There, you will see the Settings option, select it, and then choose from inches and centimeters as you please. On the mobile version of the space, click on the Settings option that you will find in the bottom toolbar, then toggle on Metric Units on or off. When you do this, whether on a computer or a smartphone, it will surely look and sound cool, enough for a quick smirk.

Smart Guides and Shortcuts

Quick one: Smart Guides are a feature of the Android and iOS app version of the product. They are designed to help you when you want to position things concerning other things. But that could not turn out or position the way you want it to. If you want to turn this off on the app version, go to Settings at the bottom areas of the toolbar and toggle the Smart Guides off.

Meanwhile, there's something about the desktop version of Cricut Design Space that makes it somewhat cool. It has some keyboard shortcuts that will come in handy. If you want to see them at any point of use, tap on the question mark key on your keyboard and hold shift. Shortcuts that will prove useful to you include the show hide menu, toggle grid, and select all options

Other shortcuts also allow you to save and "save project as", undo this is something you will be thankful for redo, cut, copy, and paste. What's more, bring forward, send back, bring to front, send to back, and of course, delete.

If you are the kind of technophile who's more used to the keyboard than clicking on a mouse, you will find these shortcuts super useful.

How to Position Items on the Cricut Canvas

Not to discourage anyone, but it can take you several months of using the Cricut Design Space almost every day before you will find this useful, and probably a little more time before you can get used to it.

Well, this little nugget informs you on how to move and rotate your items on the mat preview. This is done to position your cuts and pen write when you want or feel the need to.

You know when you are working on a project and just want to flip things up fast? This feature lets you do so quickly and effortlessly well, almost (insert smirk emoticon here).

This comes significantly handy when you want to use up scraps and just spread them all over your canvas. If you are working on an addressed envelope, for instance, you can use this tool so that your letters reflect on the "write" side of the envelope. You may also want to reposition do so by tapping and dragging an item on your canvas to a new location. Simple enough, isn't it?

On the desktop version, move the objects to another mat and conceal them. Just click on the three dots; they are not hard to find since they are virtually in your face. So, now you know how to best position those items to make your design easier; now, on to the next on our list.

Do You Want to Sync Your Colors?

Even the newbie designer knows the essence and impact of colors. In Cricut Design Space, you need to make sure your colors are happy and in harmony, just like every other artwork.

If you have ever worked on a design that had up to five different shades of pink that all needed to be cut out on separate pieces of paper or vinyl, you would understand what we are talking about. If not, you will understand soon too.

Well, in case you do not know or probably forgot how it feels, it can be very frustrating. It becomes ironic when you develop a red face that matches terribly with the moment.

Thanks to the syncing color feature, you can get all these shades and tint to match one another. Use the Color Sync option in the desktop version by simply clicking on "Color Sync" which appears at the top of the panel on the right side.

When you do this, Cricut Design Space will show you all the colors being used in your project, and then you will be able to manage them in the best possible way.

For Android and iOS users, tap on the Sync icon in the lower toolbar to have access to the same set of options. Color syncing makes your work look more unified and professional, by the way.

Showing Others What You Are Working On

At some point in time, you would want others to have a sneak peek at your design in Cricut. If you have followed design freaks and enthusiasts, you would want to show them what you have been able to whip up, probably to tell you what you should add and remove.

Well, sharing is very possible, as long as the canvas on which you are currently working does not contain any uploaded files such as SVG files. Also, make sure that you have not disabled the "Public" option.

If all these things are in place, then absolutely nothing is stopping you from sharing your design, except, of course, you change your mind.

First, make sure you have saved the project. Navigate the Cricut Design Space to your Saved Projects location. Find the project you want and click on the Share option.

This will automatically provide you with a link you can send to people you want to see the project. It is just like the conventional Infogram share option everyone is using nowadays. You can share your design with others only on the desktop and iOS versions.

We are still waiting for the developers to include the same option in the Android app version of the design. But before that, sharing is easy, and I am sure Android's child will be too.

Getting to Know Design Space

If you're new to Cricut or have little experience using one, it can be quite intimidating. I've had friends tell me they can't figure out how to use theirs, or they feel they aren't getting the full benefits of the machine.

That's what led me to write this book and clear up the confusion. Yes, Cricut can be daunting, especially for the newbie or inexperienced.

I'm sure you're anxious to start your first project, and understandably so. You've seen all the amazing things it can do, and ideas are swirling in your mind. Cards, gifts, home decorations... you can't wait!

But wait! You want to prevent disasters and, yes, they can happen, so let's start from the beginning.

The Cricut Design Space is cutting software that has a canvas area where you'll do your design work, such as uploading images. It also provides a plethora of fonts.

Before you do anything, you'll need to go to the Cricut website and set up an account. This will provide you with a homepage that will be unique to you. Signup is simple and free. You'll need to create an access ID and password.

Once you've set up your account, you'll want to go to your page, which is broken down into six areas: canvas, design panel, edit and text edit bar, layer panel, and color sync panel.

The design panel allows you to start a new project, complete a project, add images, and upload your own images. There is also an edit bar so you can undo an action and redo it if necessary.

The toolbar at the top gives you plenty of options to layout your work by aligning it, size, rotate, etc. You'll find almost all the same tools as you would in a Microsoft Word® toolbar.

These are user-friendly and self-explanatory, so you shouldn't have any problem learning them.

Next, we'll look at some important words and terms to know.

Cheat Sheets

There are many cheat sheets available on the internet and you simply need to type "Design Space cheat sheets" into the search bar. You'll have many options to explore that will help you with any of the six areas mentioned above.

The cheat sheets are filled with tips and tricks from getting you up and running to doing complex projects.

The cheat sheets are free from most sites, and Pinterest has many to choose from. You can also purchase them on Etsy. They aren't expensive, but chances are you can find what you're looking for at no cost. It's just a matter of searching through the hundreds or thousands available online.

How to Use the Cricut Design Space

If you, as of now, have your hands on a Cricut machine, here's a brisk stroll through how it functions.

Plugin and Open the Machine

Fit in the power connector into your machine and afterward into an outlet. If you have a Cricut explore one (or just any Cricut machine that does not make use of Bluetooth) or you need to connect with your computer or work area through USB, you will also need to connect your USB cord.

Press the catch on the left side named "Open" to open up the machine.

Turn the machine on.

Press the power button on the right side of the machine to turn the machine on.

Log in to Cricut Design Space.

Cricut Design Space is the cloud-based application that you use for designing works and communications with your Cricut machine. In case you're fresh out of the new plastic client, you should utilize the New Machine Setup.

In case you're a current client, and you are utilizing Bluetooth, you ought to likewise connect with your Cricut now.

Choose a Make It Now venture to make, adapt or design your project.

When you log in to Cricut Design Space, you can scan for Make It Now ventures, search for motivation before planning your venture, pick one of your current tasks, or structure another undertaking.

When your venture is prepared, click "Make It" to tell your machine.

Choose the Smart Set Dial

Pivot your dial with the goal that the speck on the weight setting dial is confronting the material you intend to cut, compose, or score. If your material isn't recorded, pick "Custom" and select the material starting from the drop menu in Design Space.

Load Your Cutting Mat

Place your material on the cutting mat. Make certain to press the glimmering load button in the wake of situating your mat in the aides on the machine, so it stacks appropriately.

Press the Cricut to Fasten and Release the Machine to Work!

When you press "Go" in Design Space, the Cricut Button on your machine will begin blazing. Press it to begin your venture.

The Cricut will get down to business. Configuration Space will inform you on the off chance that you have to change pens, sharp blades, or mats for your undertaking.

Remove and Appreciate

At the point when your task has got done with cutting, composing, as well as scoring, you will be informed through Design Space and glimmering lights on the machine to dump your cutting mat. Go through a similar blazing and down bolt button you used to stack the mat to empty it. Take your venture off the mat, and you're prepared to appreciate and use it.

Coincidentally, if picking your first venture appears to be excessively overpowering, simply recollect that your Cricut will accompany supplies and directions for a first project.

There is also the Cricut Online Help Center (which features an entire area for new machines) and the toll-free hotline to assist you with the journey if you stall out.

How to Realize and Edit Cricut Project Ideas

On the off chance that you feel lost, it would be ideal that you do a quick brush up using the other parts of this book.

Saving, accessing, and editing projects are very simple activities in Cricut Design Space.

Saving, Accessing, and Editing Projects in Cricut Design Space While Using a Desktop

Let us begin from the earliest starting point: saving a job in Cricut Design Space using a desktop.

Cricut Design Space does not offer you the luxury of AutoSaving your ventures, consequently.

Now and again, tasks can take some time, and if you don't save your activity as you work on it, your significant time and valuable work will go to waste if Design Space Crashes.

Several people have lost numerous prior minutes working their exercise and not saving. In the end, they had to start over. Along these lines, if you don't mind, save as you work. Save changes on your ventures like clockwork or something close to that.

At the point when you start on a fresh out of the plastic new canvas, the Save option (situated on the upper right-hand corner of the window) is turned gray out, yet once you include a picture, it will enact.

To save your task, place the principal thing (picture, content, shapes, and so on.) you will use on your canvas.

At the point when you click on save, a little window will spring up, requesting that you name your task. On the off chance that you are just utilizing Cricut Images or textual styles, you will have the alternative to share your venture on Facebook or Pinterest.

Be that as it may, on the off chance that you utilize your pictures, "The public" choice won't show up. Try not to stress; however, you can even now share the things you have created from the "My projects" window.

Note: When you share ventures, you should acknowledge Cricut's Terms and Conditions; so, ensure you concur with them.

In the wake of naming your undertaking, click on Save. A blue pennant will show up over the window, advising you that your undertaking is saved.

Now, you can begin changing your plan by including content, evolving hues.

Simply make sure to save your venture each three to five minutes; trust me, you would prefer not to sit around idly if the program crashes.

If sooner or later, you need to make another venture, ensure your undertaking is saved.

No stress, however.

If for reasons unknown despite everything you have unsaved changes, Design Space will bring an admonition.

Try not to trifle with this notice; on the off chance that you click on "Replace" and not "Save," you will lose your difficult work.

Opening a Project in Cricut Design Using a Desktop

To open a venture you've just made, you have to have a clean and fresh out of the new plastic canvas.

You can discover your structures in two distinct ways.

The first and quickest one is by tapping on the "My Projects" quick link situated on the right-hand corner of the window.

The subsequent path is accessed by tapping on the Projects option on the left board of the canvas, going to the dropdown menu, and selecting "My Projects." Check out the various options in the dropdown menu to discover ready cut activities.

From the "My Projects" view, you can alter, erase, modify, and cut your as of now made ventures.

There are better places you can tap on a specific task; if you click on the "share" option, you will be provoked to include a depiction, photographs, and so forth. Also, if you click on the three dots (at the bottom-right of each undertaking), you will have the option to erase it.

Making Money with Cricut: 50+ Business Ideas You Can Make with Your Cricut

It will be helpful if you can be making a part-time income from what you like doing. You can be having fun with your design and yet be making money from it. There are many people already making money from their designs. You can turn this into a great business that will give you so much money within a month and will take care of all your family expenses. So, if you have Cricut at home and you are not maximizing the use, and you have time, then this section should be of great help to you.

50+ Business Ideas You Can Make with Your Cricut and Sell

- Wall art canvas

- Leather bracelet

- Frosty wreath

- Iron-on T-shirt

- Customized tools

- Customized cutting board

- Customized kitchen towels

- Customized lanyards

- Doormats

- Rustic signs

- Coffee mugs

- Holiday bucket

- Customized plates

- Pillows case

- Bedsheets

- Paper succulent

- Planner stickers

- Sports cuff

- Key chains

- Wooden signs

- Monogrammed ornament

- Blankets

- Laptop cases

- Monogrammed pillows

- Car stickers

- Home decals

- Christmas greeting cards

- Interior designs

- Pet tags

- Cake tops

- Scrapbook pages

- Gift boxes

- Addressed envelopes

- Felt coasters

- Customized tote bags

- Flower bouquets

- Monogrammed water bottle

- Model decals

- Paper pennants

- Metallic tags

- Paper peonies

- Santa sacks

- Christmas advent calendar

- Paper heart box

- Paper tulips

- Magnolia blossom

- Gift card holder

- Paper flower lanterns

- Paper purse

- Paper poppers

- Halloween buddies

- Paper fiery house and more

How to Turn Your Designs into Money

So many people have asked the question, "How do I make money using my Cricut?" or "Should I buy a Cricut, is the market too full? Can I still make money? How do I start?" Sometimes it is hard to give a satisfactory answer to all these questions because some of the people using Cricut do not want to tell you how to make money from this craft. They do not want to share their secrets. But this book is here to give you all the inside information you need to know if you want to make money with Cricut.

When a lot of people are starting out, and they are venturing into a craft. Maybe they have a Cricut or another vinyl cutting machine, or perhaps they do not have one, and they want to get one. They have all these questions about how to get started, and it is overwhelming at first. It can be confusing and complicated and then sometimes you will reach out to those that have one, and they do not want to share their secrets, they are afraid that you might become their competitor. But the truth is that everyone can succeed if you will build each other up there is room for us all to succeed. So, let us start with the first question.

Let us now see how we can make money from all the knowledge we have gotten. Someone rightly says, if you cannot make money from the knowledge you have gotten or if you have the knowledge and it is not useful to you in any way, then the knowledge is useless to you and society. In order not for this knowledge to be useless to you, I will show you how to make money from it. This is not to say if you are not making money from your design, the knowledge is useless if you use it only for your family and friends. If you use this only for your family and friends, the knowledge is still useful.

Several of us are on Facebook, we go to marketplaces, you may have visited Etsy, and you've seen so many shops selling signs, selling shirts, selling one thing or the other, you're like, can I still make money with craft? The simple answer to the question, Yes, you can, and it is not that hard. With everyone specializing in the area he or she knows how to do better, the market can never be saturated. Take, for instance, someone might major only in the making of T-shirts, while another on making cups, other on woodwork design, and many more. The truth is that you will not find many people that are good in one particular area. So, the market can never get filled.

Now you are ready, and you have gotten your Cricut, and you are wondering, "Where do I start?" The easiest place to start is literally by making things for your friends and family. There are so many things that you can make for your friends that they will appreciate and pay you for. Examples of some of them are stickers, design their name on their T-shirts, writing the motivational word on their T-shirts. You can brainstorm on some things you think your friends would like and start designing it for them. You can also make a design for your children and your spouse. When you are done with those designs, paste them on Facebook; you might get people that would want you to do the same design for them. This is the easiest way to start without investing so much money, and no one is buying it from you.

Selling the Craft You Have Made with Cricut

There are a lot of things we have pointed out already that you can start doing and selling to your friends and neighbors. You don't have to convince your friends to buy many of those things because I know they will like it if you make personal designs for them. So, what you have to do is to find out what your friends like and make such a design for them. For example, if you have a friend that likes football and has a team, you can design the logo of the team as a sticker for such a friend and write something good about the team for him or her too. You might also have a friend that sees clothes and likes what he or she does. You can make a lovely design with his business name for him or her. Also, you can make a sticker of his logo for him or her to put on every dress he makes.

Another way you can make money with your design is to look for people that would want you to iron-on their clothes for them. There are a lot of people out there looking for someone that would design their clothes for them. Look for the people that sell in boutiques and sell your designs to them. This is how this is done. You can offer to do a free design for someone that sells plenty of plane T-shirts for him or her to see what you do. If he or she likes what you have done for him, you can then charge the person how much you would like to receive for designing each piece of clothing for such a person. So, look for local sellers around you that you think might need your design.

Another very easy way you can make money with this is through selling to groups. You can walk up to a group of people that wear a uniform and have a group name and ask to do a design for their group. This is easy to get because each person in the group would like to be identified as a member of the group and would like to pay you for your work. Examples of some of these groups are clubs, choirs, associations of friends, etc. The best way to go about this is to offer to do a free design for the leader of the group first. The idea behind this is that, if you can convince the leader of the group with your design, you can easily sell your work to every member of the group. Secondly, the group members will be seeing the design of the leader and would be asking where he did the design. Some will even suggest to him that why 'don't the group do the design for everyone. Then he will be forced to ask you to do the design for every member of the team. Get the leader interested, and you will penetrate the group easily.

Another great way you can sell your design is online. You can create a website and sell whatever you design through the website, or you can sell through an e-commerce site like Amazon. Almost everyone is online these days, so, you won't find it challenging to sell your designs if they are excellent and attractive.

How to Save Money While Using Your Cricut Explore Machine for Business

For beginners, this is the part that gives them the most headaches, especially when your pocket is not friendly to accommodate your supplies for project and craft. So, I want to help you suggest ways you can make the most use of your Cricut Explore machine for business and get your supplies at the cheapest prices. You do not have to be fleeced of your hard-earned money any longer.

The first thing is to read the instructions on how to use your Cricut Explore machine properly. It is not for fun that manufacturers place instruction guides for their products. It is meant to help you get the most out of your machine. Follow the instructions carefully and you will save yourself some extra cash that would have been used for repairs and new purchases outrightly.

You will replace your cutting mat, depending on the usage, from time to time. Try to make use of the 12" x 24" mat because the long mats save you a lot of money. You can turn to the other side when the adhesive strength of the first side begins to diminish. Instead of buying another one, just flip it over and continue with your next project.

The blades can drain your pocket when you do not make the most use of it. I do not need to tell you about the importance of a sharp blade when cutting. If you must save money, take proper care of your blades, organize them, and never misuse the blade to cut inappropriate materials. Anything contrary to that means you will be replacing your blade often which is money draining from your pocket.

For your vinyl products, I suggest you use Expressions Vinyl which is cheaper than the other vinyl materials and even gives the same feel to your project.

Best Piece of Vinyl to Use for Your Projects: Business and Personal

There are different vinyl manufacturers churning out different products for craft, different colors, textures, and options. Be careful what piece of vinyl material you use for your project so that you do not ruin your project. Know the different types if you must work with the vinyl material or use the recommended one for your project.

Adhesive Vinyl

This is the most common vinyl material on the market. You will come across it regularly sometimes in your starter kit with your machine. It comes attached to a carrier sheet coated with silicone and you can easily pull the vinyl off. Use transfer tape to transfer it to its final place on your project, that is, after it has been cut and weeded.

There are two types of adhesive vinyl materials: removable and permanent. Removable adhesive vinyl is the regular Cricut vinyl material mostly used for indoors, temporal outdoor events, or placed on any surface that will not touch regularly or in need of a wash (wall decal). If I will suggest, I will go for Oracal 631. On the other hand, permanent adhesive vinyl is waterproof and lasts longer than temporal adhesive vinyl. They are usually rated to last six years or more. Its application is in DIY projects that need washing regularly like tumblers, shot glasses, exterior walls, car decals, and more.

Heat Transfer Vinyl

This is the type used for fabrics. It is designed to bond to the fabric when heat and pressure are applied to it. There are a number of features that can help you determine the best quality of heat transfer vinyl material: color, finish, ease of weeding, price, durability, and cut reliability. Unlike adhesive vinyl, heat transfer vinyl does not require transfer tape. I will suggest Siser EasyWeed Heat Transfer Vinyl as the best of the rest.

Cling Vinyl

This is a type of vinyl material with no adhesive attached to it but uses static electricity to attach to smooth surfaces like windowpanes and removable decorations on mirrors. It can be removed and reused again on dry and clean surfaces. I will suggest Grafix Cling Vinyl Film to you.

FAQ

Why can't I weed the design off my backing sheet without it tearing?

The two most common reasons for this issue can easily be remedied. The first reason is a dull blade. Having a dull blade in your Cricut machine can cause snagging or imprecise cuts that can lead to difficulty with pulling the design away from the blank material. There are ways to sharpen your Cricut blades, and Cricut offers very cost-effective blade replacements for purchase on their official website, as well as in retail establishments nationally. The second most common reason for this is the buildup of adhesive or craft material residues on your blade, causing imprecise cuts that can lead to tearing. Remember to stay patient when weeding your designs!

Do I need to convert all my design elements into SVGs?

In short, no. You do not need to convert any of your design files to SVGs in order to use them in Cricut Design Space. If your images are JPG or PNG, they will work just fine in Cricut Design Space. If you would like to convert them, there are several online resources that you can use to help you to do so. Do keep in mind that the SVG file type is slightly more prohibitive in the capabilities that Cricut Design Space has to manipulate them, but they can be better suited to other purposes.

Where is the best place for me to buy materials to use with my Cricut?

Buying materials for your Cricut is one of the least restrictive parts of the whole process. There is nearly an unlimited number of things that you can use with your Cricut to make stunning crafts and, as such, the places in which to get them are similarly unlimited. Crafting and fabric stores will sell ideal materials in droves, and crafting stores are all over the country.

As you continue to gain familiarity with how Cricut works, what you can do with it, what projects are available, you will be more able to find the things that you can use to create dynamic and beautiful projects. As you shop around, you will get better at finding the best materials for the best possible price. In short, just about anywhere!

Is it necessary for me to have a printer to use my Cricut?

It is not required that you have a printer in order to use your Cricut machine. The materials you can buy have colors, patterns, and prints you can choose from in order to give your project the style that you wish for it to have.

In cases when you have found materials that have printable surfaces, you can make use of Cricut's print then cut feature to line up the items you've printed in such a way that they can be cut out and used in your design. Adding the element of a printer to your Cricut crafting is something that can be done (or not done) completely at your discretion.

Is there more than one place for me to get images to use with Cricut Design Space?

This is one of the many beautiful things about crafting with the Cricut system and Cricut Design Space. Any images you can find and save to your computer are images you can import and use in Cricut Design Space. So long as you have the proper licensing to use the image for projects and distribution, and so long as the files are in the proper formats, there aren't any limitations on what you can implement into your design or how you can manipulate them so they fit the vision for your design.

Do all of my fonts have to be purchased through Cricut Design Space?

There are hundreds of fonts available to the average Cricut user and there are hundreds more that you can buy for your designs. However, these are *not* the only fonts you're limited to using. If you can find a website that offers fonts that fit your style better, you can buy or download them, install them on your computer, and then those fonts will be available for you to choose under the "System Fonts" heading in the fonts dropdown menu.

A word of caution, however, if you are looking to use a font for a project, take a look at the licensing information for it. Fonts that are marked "100% Free" on other websites will generally allow you to use that font on reproductions and things that you sell, while others will require a more involved license fee or subscription.

Why does the Cricut blade keep cutting through the carrier or backing sheet of my material?

This is often due to a project being run through your Cricut on an inappropriate material setting on the dial on the top of your Cricut Explore machine. This dial tells the Cricut how much pressure to exert on the blade, so if you set it for a thicker material than the one you're currently using, you will find that the blade will cut a little bit more deeply than perhaps you would like it to.

Additionally, this could be due to the blade being improperly seated in its housing. Pop open the Cricut accessory clamp, open the housing, and ensure that the blade is not sticking out too far. Once you've checked it, load it back into the Cricut and try again!

My images aren't showing up correctly on the preview screen of my mat, why is this?

It is possible to find that, once you click "Make It," you don't exactly get your design elements laid out quite the way in which you imagined they would be. In some cases, this wonky layout will also mean that those shapes are plotted outside of where your material is on the mat. If you're in this situation, go back to Cricut Design Space, highlight all the images in the design grid, click "Group," then click "Attach." This should bring everything back around to where it should be on the preliminary Make It screen.

Will I need to buy all the Cricut accessories and tools before starting my first project?

No! The tools that you will want to have on hand are:

Weeding Tool – This is a hook with a very fine point that allows you to peel blanks from your cut vinyl. This tool will come in handy for most, if not all the projects you do with your Cricut. It helps you to remove your design from the excess material without having to bend, fold, or fight with your material. This helps to keep the edges of your design crisp, clean, and sharp every time.

Scraper/Burnishing Tool – This simple little tool might seem unassuming, but you will find that this tool will be the most commonly used one in your projects, with the exception of perhaps the weeding tool. You will find that once your designs are lifted from the backing sheet, transferring them to your project surface will require burnishing with even pressure from your scraping tool. Many crafters have found that, in a pinch, this tool can be replaced with other items, but the fine edge, rigid material, and rounded back of this tool are ideal for the job.

Scissors – Any crafter that is worth their salt knows the value of a good pair of scissors. Having a pair of scissors that can make clean and precise cuts is just about the most valuable thing that a crafter can have at their disposal. While the scissors that Cricut offers are exceedingly sharp with fine points and blades, there are other pairs of scissors on the market that will suit your crafting needs and purposes quite well.

Craft Tweezers – The craft tweezers that Cricut offers are reverse-action tweezers that have a strong grip that is exerted at very precise points and can alleviate the cramping that can come from prolonged use. Thanks to the ergonomic grip, it's possible to keep an iron grip on your materials throughout your project so you can keep everything where you need it when you need it there. It's almost like having that extra pair of hands you always wished you had during your crafting projects!

Spatula – Sometimes you might find that you need a little extra control and maneuverability over your project, which might make you call out for an extra pair of hands. This spatula can offer that control and maneuverability that you require, when and where you need it.

You will find that, with the help of the above tools, you will be able to complete your first Cricut project with ease and that you will be able to get a spectacular result every time you work on your crafts.

To find a more comprehensive list of all the supplies you will need before starting your first project.

If I buy an image in Cricut Design Space, am I allowed to use it more than once?

Once you buy an image through Cricut Design Space, you are free to use that image as many times you like while you have an active account with Cricut Design Space! Feel free to buy and reuse as many images as you'd like!

I welded two images by accident. Is there an unweld option?

At this time, there is no dedicated unweld function, so you will need to catch this mistake quickly and use the "Undo" command to revert them back to their pre-welded state. You can also delete the design elements and import them in again if you find that you have come too far since welding the images to undo the process. It is recommended that you frequently keep local copies of your work so you can start from various stages if something should go wrong at one stage or another.

Can I turn off the grid in Cricut Design Space, so I have an open space to work with?

Yes, this is something that you can toggle on and off in Cricut Design Space. On a Windows or on a Mac computer, you can open the "Account" menu.

This is marked by the three horizontal lines in the upper left corner. Once you've clicked on that, you will be able to select "Settings." This will present you with numerous settings for your Cricut Design Space and your account. Among them, you will find a section for Canvas Grid settings. This is where you can select your grid preference. In the settings menu, you will also see a section pertaining to Keyboard Shortcuts. Select that in order to set a Keyboard Shortcut that will allow you to quickly toggle the grid on and off while you work on your projects.

When you're working in the Cricut Design Space iOS app, you will find the toggle for the gridlines in the settings at the bottom of the screen. You may have to swipe left to view all the settings that are available to you.

How do I change my Cricut Design Space to operate on the metric system?

This is something that you can toggle on and off in Cricut Design Space. On a Windows or on a Mac computer, you can open the "Account" menu.

This is marked by the three horizontal lines in the upper left corner. Once you've clicked on that, you will be able to select "Settings." This will present you with numerous settings for your Cricut Design Space and your account. Among them, you will find a section for setting the default measurement to inches or centimeters.

If you're using the Cricut Design Space on your mobile device, your settings menu will be at the bottom of your screen. You may need to scroll or swipe to the left in order to see all the options that are available to you.

Do Windows, macOS, and Android have access to the "despeckle" and "smooth" tools?

As of right now, those tools are exclusively available to users who are on the iOS or mobile Apple platform. There are no indications as to whether these tools will be made available to users who are on the Windows, macOS, or Android platforms for Cricut Design Space.

What is SnapMat?

SnapMat is an iOS-exclusive feature that gives you a virtual mat preview. This enables you to line up your designs in Design Space, so they'll fit perfectly onto what you have laid on your mat. This feature allows you to place images and text over the snapshot of your mat so you can see exactly how your layout should be in the Design Space.

What are the advantages of using SnapMat?

SnapMat gives you clarity and certainty in where your images will be placed when you send your design to cut through your Cricut. It will show you where your images will be marked, cuts will be done, and how text lines up with other elements. With SnapMat, you can tell your Cricut to cut out a specific piece of a pattern you have stuck on your mat, write in specific areas of gift tags, stationery, cards, or envelopes, and you can get the absolute most out of your materials scraps and spare materials that are left from past projects!

Can I snap multiple mats at one time with SnapMat?

SnapMat can only snap one mat at a time. If you'd like to snap multiple mats, you can do so individually. This ensures that each mat is properly in focus and view and that each one is captured and cut with precision.

Does SnapMat allow me to save the photos of my mats?

SnapMat doesn't currently have a "Save" feature for the images captured in it, so if you would like to retain a photo of your mat, simply take a screenshot in the middle of that process. This will save an image of your mat directly to your photo gallery.

If you find yourself referring to the image for where you have items on your mat, it may be a good idea to wait until you're ready to move on to the next phase of your project.

When it comes to where the cut lines will be on my mat, how exact is the SnapMat feature?

The SnapMat feature is very precise and the lines should be accurate to within a tiny fraction of an inch. While it's best to always give yourself extra space or breathing room when you lay your projects on your mat, you will find that the SnapMat feature is quite exact.

How do I make sure that the mat I have will be compatible with SnapMat?

The SnapMat feature is compatible with all of the Cricut mats that are currently on the market. If you have an older mat or a mat from another company, you might find that you have difficulty. Two of the main things that will cause you difficulty with your mat and this app are black gridlines and bold designs on the mat. These things could confuse the program and could throw off its ability to calculate distances between design elements.

Can I upload images to Cricut Design Space using my Android Device?

Yes, you can! Cricut know how important it is for their users to be accessible to its users who are on the go. As such, this feature has been made widely available on all existing platforms that support Cricut Design Space, from MacOS to Android.

What sorts of images am I able to upload through Cricut Design Space iOS and Android apps?

Any images that are of supported file types in your photo gallery or saved to your Apple or Android mobile device may be uploaded to Cricut Design Space through your application. If you have SVG, JPG, or PNG files saved to your device, simply upload them and you will find that you're set to go!

If you are attempting to upload a PDF or a TIFF file, you will find that Cricut Design Space does not currently support those file formats. If you're having trouble uploading your images, ensure they're not one of these two formats before trying again!

If my hands aren't quite steady, can I still use SnapMat?

Yes! Many Cricut users have found that balancing their phones on the edge of the table and placing the mat on the floor beneath it is a great way to get a stable shot!

How do I delete any images that I've uploaded through the mobile app?

Another great feature that Cricut decided to make available to suit the needs of all its users is the ability to delete images from Cricut Design Space using any device that supports the application. Whether you're using macOS, Windows, iOS, or Android, you can complete this action on your device.

Simply select the Upload option in the bottom list of options. You may need to swipe or scroll to find this option. Once you've tapped that option, select the Open Uploaded Images option. Once you've navigated to this point, you can find the image you wish to delete. Tap the Info button, which is the little green circle with the lowercase "i" in it. This will give you the option to delete the image and voila! It's gone!

Can I upload images to Cricut Design Space while I'm offline?

Uploading images is an action that can only be completed with an active and stable internet connection. You will find this to be true of uploading to any platform or application that is web-based or cloud-based. Once an image is uploaded with a stable internet connection, however, it can be accessed and downloaded to other devices for offline use.

What features are available on which apps?

This handy chart will lay out exactly what features are available to you through the Cricut Design Space, as well as the platforms that have enabled support for each feature. Be sure to consult this chart if you're trying to figure out which platform works best for you and the crafting experience that you're looking to have.

Feature	Desktop Computer	iOS App	Android App
3D layer visualization		✔	
Offline		✔	
Photo Canvas		✔	
Smart Guides		✔	✔
SnapMat		✔	
Attach	✔	✔	✔
Bluetooth compatible	✔	✔	✔

Contour	✔	✔	✔
Curve Text	✔		
Cut & write in one step	✔	✔	✔
Flatten to print	✔	✔	✔
Image upload	✔	✔	✔
Knife Blade cutting	✔		
Link Physical Cartridges	✔		
Machine setup	✔	✔	✔
Pattern fills	✔		
Print then cut	✔	✔	
Slice and weld	✔	✔	✔
System fonts	✔	✔	✔
Templates	✔		
Writing style fonts	✔	✔	✔

Conclusion

Cricut machines are awesome gadgets to own because they not only boost creativity and productivity, but they can also be used to create crafts for business. With Design Space, crafters can create almost anything, and even customize their products to bear their imprints.

All over the world, people use these machines to make gift items, t-shirts, interior décor, and many other crafts, to beautify their homes, share with friends and family during holidays, and even sell.

There are two types of Cricut machine: the Cricut Explore and the Cricut Maker. Both machines are highly efficient in their own rights, and experts in the crafting world make use of them to create a plethora of items, either as a hobby or for business.

Both machines are similar in many ways i.e. the Cricut Maker and the Explore Air 2, but the Cricut Maker is somewhat of a more advanced machine because it comes with some advanced features, as compared to the Explore Air 2.

One distinct feature about the Maker that sets it apart from the Explore Air is the fact that it can cut thicker materials. With the Maker, the possibilities are limitless, and crafters can embark on projects that were never possible with Cricut machines before the release of the Make.

Another feature that puts the Cricut Maker machine ahead of the Explore Air 2 is the 'Adaptive Tool System'. With this tool, the Cricut Maker has been empowered in such a way that it will remain relevant for many years to come because it will be compatible with new blades and other accessories that Cricut will release in the foreseeable future.

Although both machines have several dissimilarities, there are also areas where they are completely inseparable. Take for example the designing of projects in Cricut Design Space.

As a crafter, without proper knowledge of Design Space, you're not only going to cut out poor products, but you will also make little or no in-road in your quest to find success.

Understanding Design Space is important because it empowers crafters with enormous tools and materials to create generalized and custom products. It is an extremely powerful tool that just cannot be overlooked by anyone that intends to follow this path.

Thus, the understanding of Design Space is a MUST for people that intend to make a business out of Cricut machines or even utilize it as a hobby. With the software, crafters can create their designs from scratch or use already-made designs on the Cricut platform. Those that have an active subscription on Cricut Access have access to thousands of images, projects, and fonts. They can cut out their products using these images and projects, and they can also edit them to suit their style and taste before cutting.

Cricut Business

101 Little-Know Ways to Start Your Own Cricut Business | Find Here The Way To Move From A Common Employed To A Full-Time Entrepeneur Mom

Introduction

As a craft enthusiast, I know the value of making your own crafty crafts, but also that no self-respecting crafter should be without a Cricut in her crafty arsenal. Sure, oftentimes you can buy craft projects created with a Cricut for cheap at big-box stores, but where is the fun and pride in crafting something you can not only be proud of, but also say "I made that"?!

The Cricut is a personal electronic cutting machine resembling an electric pencil sharpener. It can cut a variety of different materials such as paper, fabric, vinyl, clay, photo album pages and more. Thanks to the Cricut's Cricut Design Space software you can edit and create your own designs (and upload them for free online).

Are you tired of your current job ? Would you like to make your own money and work your own hours? Look no further. The Cricut is a simple way for you to make easy money! Even if you are not a crafter, you can use the Cricut for a variety of house decorating projects that will make your home look designer and professional.

The machine is affordable, costing about $100 or less with sales, coupons or rewards programs. The machine comes with a variety of different cutting cartridges which you can use to make your own designs.

Is the Cricut for you? Do you have some free time in your hands and a few dollars to spare? Think about it. While we cannot guarantee that you will make any money from your Cricut, we do know that you will enjoy the process of creating unique and quality objects that will be treasured or used!!! Find out more about how to start making crafts with the Cricut.

10 Reasons Why Selling Cricut Projects is a MUST

1. You can make your own schedule, work right from your living room and make as much or as little money as you want.

2. No matter how skilled you are, the Cricut will help you become better and create impressive projects.

3. Once you learn the basics of the Cricut, it is easy to create projects with no previous experience required.

4. Be proud of yourself for creating something unique and learn some valuable new skills.

5. By making crafts on your own, you will be able to engage in a creative and productive hobby with minimal costs.

6. All of your projects will become unique and unique gifts for friends and family members.

7. You can use the proceeds from selling crafts to further your education or to take trips.

8. If you are a crafter, you will be inspired by the process of creating something original on your own. If youre a non-crafter, you will learn a new hobby that can come in handy at an event.

9. You can make a lot of money from crafts! We sell over $8,000 dollars worth of crafts each month just by selling the Cricut.com website and related products through Ebay and Amazon. com.

10. If you are a crafter you will be able to share your work with family and friends. Your work will get noticed by the public and used by those professionals who need it most!

Chapter 1: - Cricut Business Plan

Creating your Cricut Business Plan is a bit like trying to put a puzzle together.

Broadly speaking, your plan is made up of a series of manageable components- whether they're tasks, skills or resources- that work together to bring you and your business to new heights.

Well, if you asked me what the "Big Picture" was I would tell you it was making money!

I am going to show you some Cricut Business Plan steps that will help jump start your business today.

My intention is to guide you, the new Cricut Business owner, through the process of developing your own plan.

In creating this bookI hope to give you a fresh and new perspective of BizQuest. It is my pleasure to share what has worked for me and show you some ways in which you can easily incorporate this information into your business.

I'm going to highlight "The 5 Steps to Cricut Business Success."

The 5 Steps are:

1. Setting Your Goal(s)
2. Building Your Team and/or Yourself
3. Learning The Basics of the Cricut Business System
4. Creating A STRATEGY To Reach Those Goals
5. Developing A Plan That Will Initiate Actions

I will outline these steps in detail for you and, I believe, provide a clear and concise road map that will help you move through the process of creating your own Cricut Business Plan. This plan can be created either on paper or electronically.

Before you begin to develop this plan, I recommend that you first establish exactly what it is that you want (or need) from your business. This is a critical step because without a sound base of knowledge you cannot effectively create a plan and structure your business operations in a manner to achieve your goals.

I want you to have success whether it is making money or fulfilling your passion for crafting.

So let's get started so you can start building your Cricut Business!

Step 1: Setting Your Goal(s)

In this step you will be establishing some goals that will help to give focus and direction to your efforts. It is important to have a clear idea of what it is that you want from your business. So the first step is to identify the goals you have for your business. Goals are simply specific objectives or ends toward which effort is directed.

In order to develop a clear definition of your business goals these 4 questions need to be answered in a way that expresses what is most important to you.

- ➢ What are your long term goals?
- ➢ What are your short term goals?
- ➢ How will you measure the success of your business?
- ➢ How will you know when you have attained those goals?

For example:

"I want to establish a profitable Cricut Business in 6 months. My goal is to earn $1,000 per month net profit. In order to achieve this goal I will:

- ➢ Set aside 1 hour on the weekend to work on my Cricut Business.
- ➢ Create a marketing plan that will allow me to effectively reach my target customer base and generate the leads I need to build my business.
- ➢ I will measure the success of my business based on the number of customers I have signed up to receive my information.
- ➢ I know I have achieved my goals when I have 15 Cricut Business Owners enrolled for my weekly newsletter."

Step 2: Building Your Team and/or Yourself

To aid you in reaching your long-term goals you need to be organized, accountable and have a plan in place so that you can reach success. Having this set of "Building Blocks" will help you introduce your business to the right people at the right time.

In order to break down these goals into manageable steps you will want to first identify who will be responsible for each action. This could include internal staff members or those external to your business.

In order to develop a successful model, you will want to develop a team with certain key areas of expertise. For example:

- ➢ Marketing/Sales/Training
- ➢ Operations/Delivery
- ➢ Administration

Identify those that will play a role in your business and create a plan for your team that will have clear actions and deadlines. You should also have clearly outlined roles and responsibilities for each member of the team so that you know who is doing what.

Step 3: Learning The Basics of the Cricut Business System

Next, you need to be well educated on what it is that you are doing. Even if you do not have any experience in the industry, rest assured this step can be accomplished with only a little bit of research.

This can be a daunting task but it is actually fairly straightforward. I have outlined some of the key areas of your business that need to be addressed so that you are prepared to run an effective business.

There are several ways this can be accomplished:

> Contact the Certified Educator in your area (this person has taken training in the Cricut Business System and is able to help you).

> Purchase a Business Kit from Cricut. com and get started.

> Take a class from Cricut University through the Cricut Success Club.

> Search the Internet and find articles related to your business area of interest.

Here is a list of some key areas that you need to be well informed in: Marketing/Sales/Training   Cricut Business Owner Support/Customer Service Operations/Delivery Cricut   System Maintenance (Programming, Machine Maintenance, Etc.   Administrative   Creating A Plan That Will Initiate Actions

Step 4: Creating A STRATEGY To Reach Those Goals

Research has shown that customers are influenced by the message you convey, not what you say. So you need to ask yourself how to get the information (information that is needed to fill your customers needs) and at a price they will want to pay.

Simple, right? In this step you will want to develop a strategy that will allow you to effectively reach your goals.

So how do you do this? You need to come up with a plan that will effectively reach your customers. There are a number of ways this can be accomplished:

> Identify who are the customers and start reaching out to them by using traditional methods like mailings, phone calls and email.   Social Media is another great marketing tool as it allows you to connect directly with a person who is interested in what you have to offer.   Create profiles on Facebook, Twitter and LinkedIn.   Write blog articles and post them on your website.   Join online groups and forums that are related to your interests.

> Use the Cricut Business System to reach your customers. Try setting up an online campaign where you will mail out newsletters and marketing materials directly from the Cricut Business System console. You can schedule campaigns anywhere from once a week to once a month to reach those that want more information on what you have available in your business.   Write ad copy and submit it to local publications.   Use your Events Calendar to have a series of information sessions.   Use the Cricut Business System to create a customer database from those who sign up for your mailing list or email list.

Step 5: Developing A Plan That Will Initiate Actions

Now that we have finalized our goals it is time to develop a plan. This is the accumulation of all of our planned activities over the next few months designed to achieve our goals and make sure we reach success.

Your plan needs to be clear and concise so that you can easily communicate it to others. Your plan can be created electronically but it is just as effective if you work on a written plan.

So don't hesitate to write down your plan for yourself and then present it to others or implement the plan immediately in order to achieve success.

Take this opportunity not only to start developing your Cricut Business Plan but also to improve upon your business skills. It is a way to make sure you are focused and in control of your business.

Chapter 2: - Where to Find Materials for Project Ideas

When you start working on Cricut projects, you will need some important to get started. Here's a rundown of what those basics are if, as an example, you're going to do an adhesive vinyl project.

Your Cricut Machine

Once you choose the model that's best for you, you'll want it to be set up, prepared, and ready, with the fine point blade filled into the accessory clamp B.

Cricut Machine Cutting Mat

This mat is a very basic but integral part of the Cricut cycle of crafting. Cricut has many thin pads, with an elastic grip and a pattern on them. When your material is poured onto this mat and loaded into your Cricut machine, you can be confident that your material is right where it needs to be, to get the perfect cuts and strokes on it. It is one of the products best left to the Cricut brand, due to its special size and grip strength. Looking for another mat with equivalent skills may end up being more expensive, or just less successful. For this particular component, the Cricut brand is really the one to go with.

Your Hand Tools

Some of the resources done in this list can be satisfied with the things you have around the house. Cricut does sell a starter kit that includes all of these devices, however. This kit is very reasonably priced and contains everything you may need to get started. The tools you need to look for before you get started are: Weeding Tool-This is a really fine point hook that helps you to strip blanks from your cut vinyl. For most, if not all, the projects that you do with your Cricut, this device will come in handy. It lets you remove the excess material from your design without having to bend, fold, or battle with your material. This helps keep your template edges smooth, clean, and sharp whenever you like.

Scraper / Burnishing Tool–With the possible exception of the weeding tool, this basic tool would be the most-used Cricut tool. You will find that once you raise your cut designs from the back layer, it will take gentle, steady pressure to burn your projects beautifully to move them to your project board. This tool can be replaced with other things in a pinch, but this tool does the best job.

Scissors–Every artisan knows that scissors are part and parcel of their tool kit. Although the scissors provided by Cricut are exceptionally sharp, with very fine dots on each blade, any pair suitable for your craft will serve you well here.

Craft Tweezers–Despite extended use, these reverse-action tweezers have a good grip, precise points, and relieve cramping. The ergonomic grip helps you to maintain a firm hold on your materials during the whole process, giving you the extra pair of hands, you'd always wish you had when you were made.

Spatula-Often when you're peeling or setting down a job, you feel like you need an extra pair of hands. This tool gives you the extra support and maneuverability you need.

These tools will help you complete your first project with a fantastic outcome once you set out to use them.

Transfer Tape

Transfer tape is a lightweight, mild adhesive tape that comes in sheets. The aim of this material is to take from their back sheet your freshly cut designs, keep them securely in place perfectly, which you can then easily burn to your project. The adhesive is such that it does not harm the design or the material it is intended to start with. Later on, you'll find some tips on how to get the most out of your transfer tape, while you're using it, and on selecting a transfer tape that you can get in the right grip power, consistency, and quantity for your projects. For example, if you're doing a lot of projects on materials that have a really gritty or glittery surface, you'll need a higher grip strength transfer tape to hold it in place when you're working on them.

It is going to tell you right out of the gate that the Cricut brand transfer tape comes in a single sheet that's rolled up, measuring 12"x 48." You can cut the sheet to your taste, in whatever size or shape your project requires, and every piece you cut can be used several times before disposal. For your local sewing store, these Cricut brand sheets currently stand at $8.99 MSRP, while some other brands sell a 6-10' roll of 12 "long transfer tape for a comparable price.

To get the best information on which products are perfect for the types of projects you want to do, YouTube is an amazing tool that has the latest and greatest knowledge from the people who do these types of crafts every day. Although transferring tape is an utter requirement when doing projects with your Cricut machine, the brand doesn't matter as much as getting anything to use. Do some shopping around, find a sample size of the tapes you want to try and start! Like any new craft, you are doing, discovering the materials and items that best match your needs, and which will work better for you in the long run, will wake up a bit of trial and error.

Isopropyl or Rubbing Alcohol

Because the adhesive is a major theme and part of the Cricut method and the method of using the Cricut machine, it is important to ensure that the surfaces you use (the pad, the materials, the object on which your design will be burned) are cleaned as humanly as possible. You'll want to rub the surface with some rubbing alcohol, especially with a slick surface like glass or ceramic, to remove any dirt, dust, debris, or anything that could ruin your design. If you wipe it with alcohol rubbing, pat dry, then let it stand for thirty seconds, your concept is ready to go! Be sure that any paper towels or other items you use for this phase will not leave behind any fibers or debris that could jeopardize your design, particularly those smaller or more delicate ones.

A Blank Stage for Your Design

It is the thing you'll be burning your template to. It is necessary to remember that while the planet is your oyster and with Cricut crafting, there is very little that is unavailable to you, I suggest a flat surface for the first project. Being able to view the entire surface of this object, without constantly worrying about curvature or other obstructions, will make learning how to work with your materials much simpler. Although a travel mug is a wonderful idea for a Cricut project, doing it as your first one may give you more trouble than you would have expected at first. We don't want you to embark on a project that will cause you trouble. Try then placing a custom template or expression on your screen, or on a binder.

A Computer with Internet Access

The Cricut Design Space can only be used with a stable internet connection, so making sure your machine has uninterrupted access over the course of your design is crucial! You may always want to save your job, just in case the link hiccups. In such a case, you wouldn't wish to lose any design development. Self-adhesive vinyl Last but not least, you'll need a piece of self-adhesive vinyl, which is the color and form you want. You will load this onto your Cricut cutting pad, and it will be cut out of your template in no time! All that's got to it! You're ready to tackle your first self-adhesive vinyl concept with all those things.

What Materials Can You Use with your Cricut?

Cricut boasts being able to work with over 100 materials to bring your creations to life like never before. Due to the vast array of media that Cricut will carry to your crafting station, the sky is the limit for what you can do with your Cricut computer, irrespective of the model you want to purchase.

Here are 100 materials which your Cricut can use without any problems.

Fabric

Polyester

Linen

Printable Fabric

Silk

Cotton Fabric

Wool Felt

Canvas

Metallic Leather

Oil Cloth

Felt

Faux Suede

Flannel

Denim

Burlap

Duck Cloth

Leather

Faux Leather

Foam

Glitter Foam

Craft Foam

Foil

Aluminum Foil

Embossable Foil

Aluminum Sheets

Foil Poster Board

Foil Embossed Paper

Adhesive Foil

Foil Iron-On

Foil Acetate

Paper

Poster Board

Contact Paper

Metallic Paper

Glitter Cardstock

Solid Core Cardstock

Flocked Cardstock

Printable Sticker Paper

Notebook Paper

Parchment Paper

Photo Framing Mat

Metallic Vellum

Vellum

Freezer Paper

Metallic Cardstock

Flocked Paper

Metallic Poster Board

Corrugated Paper

Peal Cardstock

Glitter Paper

Paper Board

Tissue Paper

Rice Paper

Cardboard

Shimmer Paper

Pearl Paper

Craft Paper

Photographs

Cardstock

Temporary Tattoo Paper

Copy Paper

Washi Sheets

Scrapbook Paper

Post Its

Construction Paper

Washi Tape

Paper Grocery Bags

Adhesive Cardstock

Wrapping Paper

Plastic

Shrink Plastic

Transparency Film

Duct Tape

Window Cling

Magnet Sheets

Plastic Packaging

Stencil Material

Printable Magnet Sheets

Vinyl

Holographic Iron-On

Removable Adhesive Vinyl

Flocked Iron-On

Neon Iron-On

Matte Vinyl

Metallic Vinyl

Stencil Vinyl

Outdoor Vinyl

Adhesive Vinyl

Printable Vinyl

Printable Iron-On

Glitter Vinyl

Glossy Vinyl

Glossy Iron-On

Chalkboard Vinyl

Matte Iron-On

Glitter Iron-On

Permanent Adhesive Vinyl

Dry Erase Vinyl

Holographic Vinyl

Metallic Iron-On

Paint Chips

Wood

Chipboard

Wood Veneer

Adhesive Wood

Corkboard

Balsa Wood

Birch Wood

Chapter 3: - Where Can I Find Business?

Suppose you can begin getting gainful deals rapidly. At the same time, previous a touch of that additional cash in the first place, the benefit can be piped into development openings like new apparatus, product offerings, or showcasing. The benefit is the top dog. By separating the different gatherings, we can offer to and understanding the spots to discover them for both neighborhood and web-based deals; you can measure where to invest your significant time and energy best. A touch of procedure presently can spare you from sitting around, cash, vinyl, and stamina not far off.

Selling Locally

Neighborhood deals can be separated into two portions, business to business (B2B) and business to client (B2C). If you choose to be a neighborhood dealer, it's ideal to pick between one of these two sections. These two gatherings don't have a lot of cover in the things they buy, or where you can market to them. The reasonable entrepreneur won't burn through their time pursuing leads and tossing showcasing cash at customers they aren't arrangement to help.

<u>Volume Sales</u>

The objective here is to utilize the productivity of delivering in bigger numbers to drive the cost you pay per thing down. The bigger the creation run, the lower your expense for item and time per unit delivered. This is the hardest work to get into for another Cricut or Silhouette based business. The open doors are less, and customer desires are higher.

These standards are equivalent to with business to business mass work, yet you're going to discover your clients in new places and have different contributions. You will sell things that retail clients need to purchase. This incorporates one of a kind shirts, tumblers, espresso cups, or whatever else you can think of. The key is to have expansive intrigue, something you can create various with the desire that they will sell.

Models:

An agreement with the nearby government or school to deliver shirts or signage.

Yearly occasion signage and advertising.

Often, authoritative work can be finished in a solitary meeting. This implies you can buy from merchants in mass, permitting you to arrange lower material expenses. You will likewise have less exchanging between vinyl hues or product offerings, which means you can complete more in less time. This leaves you with more opportunity for different undertakings or promoting endeavors.

Cons

It will be difficult to get one of these agreements. Truly, I haven't attempted. It is sensible to expect that another person is now serving these open doors in your locale. If they aren't, jump at the opportunity.

Custom Work

Custom work for business clients can be an incredible gig with tremendous upside. Organizations are happy to pay as much as possible for quality, solid work. You can work with organizations to help make a brand personality, make mindfulness, and make special advertisements.

Models:

If a business is simply beginning, you can offer a business dispatch starter pack. At least, you ought to incorporate logo structure, signage for a retail front, and establishment.

You can likewise offer organization marked swag like shirts, cups, or mugs as an extra. Every one of these administrations can be independent for new or existing organizations.

Signage, for example, sandwich sheets or yard signs.

You are making associations with developing organizations. After your first fruitful exchange, you become their place of contact for future business marking, decals, mindfulness materials, and even visual communication. This relationship can deliver future profits.

Business customers accompany numerous open doors for upselling. More often than not, it is a success win for both of you.

Cons

It tends to be difficult to track down new, quality leads. For most existing organizations, they as of now have a sign organization they trust. All things considered, they needed to get their unique signs someplace, correct?

Entrepreneurs will, in general, be insightful, with elevated requirements and a solid feeling of what is a suitable cost for your administration. Try not to be amazed or outraged if they get numerous offers and arrange cost before tolerating your offer.

Models:

Leasing a space at an old fashioned shopping center or specialty reasonable. Make sure to evaluate how a lot of room you really need, the cost per square foot, and the commission your landowner is requesting.

Discover Space In Popup Shops

Discover regular occasions in your town that offer modest or free retail space, similar to a rancher's market or occasion reasonable.

Pass out business cards to neighborhood shops where you envision your items may sell well.

Stars

Your imagination will be the driver of your deals. If you concoct a cunning thought with mass or specialty advance, and you are in the correct spot to offer it, you will receive the benefits. Additionally, you get the opportunity to figure out what media and medium you work in. Shirts, mugs, or whatever else, the decision is yours.

Cons

You'll require a retail space to offer your things. The spots with higher pedestrian activity will be increasingly costly; however, pedestrian activity doesn't really rise to deals.

To be effective, you'll be eager to explore different avenues regarding different areas and item contributions.

Selling Online

Concentrating on internet selling requires a higher specialized information base, be that as it may, as I can bear witness to, you don't need to be a software engineer to make it work. You can bring in cash with vinyl online by giving quality custom work, turning into a data center, or giving mass contributions. Once more, it's not prudent to attempt to do every one of the three.

Your time is best spent working in one of the three alternatives to start. In this way, if you choose to give custom work, don't likewise attempt to turn into a data center point simultaneously.

Experts

If you sell on a current stage, the startup costs are exceptionally low. The minute you dispatch, you're contending in the worldwide marketplace. You approach a large number of potential clients.

Also, extraordinary plans will permit you to charge a superior rate. Be that as it may, online custom costs will in general, be lower than a similar work done locally. It's an opportunity to clean up and expand your plan range of abilities too.

Cons

Access to the whole world likewise implies you are going up against anybody with a web association. The expanded rivalry will prompt lower costs for your plans and difficulty finding occupations if you aren't seriously evaluated or offering a one of a kind structure point of view.

Selling on the web implies you additionally need to learn coordination. You're going to need to get entered in with a transportation organization, make sense of pressing material, and consider that cost your valuing.

Professionals

You can begin to fabricate a genuine retail business selling this sort of work. After some time, you will have the option to figure out what the interest for the structures you offer and plan creation ahead as needs be. This will build your productivity and lower the time you need to spend making items.

You'll likewise be making more items. Without a doubt, you will get less cash per deal, however, this will allow you to purchase a vinyl in mass at a diminished cost.

Cons

You're going toward the world here. There's a huge amount of rivalry so that the edges will be lower, and quite possibly somebody can undermine your little edges with phony or fake things anytime.

It takes significant stage information to sell on the entirety of the different commercial centers (eBay, Amazon, Etsy, and so on.).

Data Hub – Have you at any point visited a blog for guidance on the best way to utilize your machine or undertaking motivation?

Models - There are some extraordinary instances of online journals offering specialized skill and task motivation with an art shaper.

What Are You Waiting For?

Beginning by picking a business technique may be unashamedly old school, yet I'm certain you can perceive any reason why it's the establishment for your future achievement. Via cutting a couple of hours to consider where you can you are best situated, you'll in a flash set yourself apart from the vast majority of your rivals. You'll know who your clients are, what sort of things you can sell them, and the traps to maintain a strategic distance from.

Selling art and handcrafts online can fall under four categories:

- Marketplace websites with shops for participating artists and artisans
- Auction services featuring arts and handcrafts
- Sites where customized art and craft products are created on-demand
- Places to build your own website

There are even more ways to sell online, and there is a lot of overlap within these categories. This book does not promise to list everything available, because if there is one thing you can count on with the Internet, it's that things change all the time.

Selling online has become one of the most profitable ways for artists to sell their art. For the year September 2011 to August 2012, 25 percent of polled artists reported that online sales were how they made their best income. In comparison, 22 percent preferred selling from their own studio, 10 percent favored art festivals, and 9 percent found gallery sales most profitable.

Marketplace Sites for Art and Handmade Goods

Marketplace websites allow you to create your own shop or gallery within the site's overall shopping system. They handle the selling transactions, and you will receive all or most of the money you get from sales; you ship your own orders. Buyers come to the marketplace site seeking handmade goods and can discover your products using a variety of search tools. Your shop is also available for customers who are attracted through your own marketing efforts. There are differing fees for participating in marketplace sites, starting with free, which is a nice place to begin for many artists and crafters who don't have much money to invest upfront.

Etsy (www.etsy.com)

One of the largest online sellers, Etsy.com averaged over 8 million unique visitors per month during 2012, with traffic that continues to grow. This level of traffic is far beyond the scale of the other arts-and crafts marketplace sites (millions of monthly visitors compared to thousands). The size is also reflected in the number of sellers on Etsy, with over 500,000 active shops competing for this traffic.

Etsy.com Landing Page

Finding a way to stand out in the crowd is a challenge. Etsy sellers can list handmade items, vintage goods, and arts and crafts supplies. Rest assured that stepping into the Etsy system is not a financial burden, as sellers open a free shop and then list their products for a per-item fee of 20 cents for 4 months. Etsy takes a small percentage of each sale. It's all worth it, though, as Etsy is both a marketplace and a vibrant community, with highly developed tools to help artists and crafters build a successful business.

Many More Marketplace Sites

There are several smaller marketplace websites around, each offering a different philosophy, interface, selling tools, and fee structure. Traffic at these sites is a trickle compared to the gigantic Etsy, but the number of items is likewise much smaller. Simply said, your products have a better chance of standing out in the crowd. Sellers who plan to sell primarily to their own customers (traffic coming from the artist's own website, blog, or gallery) may find the selling tools and community at a smaller venue suits them perfectly.

Chapter 4: - Facebook and Instagram

Facebook Profile Creation

Here is the step-by-step process for creating an amazing fan page. I will assume that you already have a Facebook account, if you haven't registered yet, just go to Facebook.com and sign up for a free account.

NOTE: These steps are updated to the latest Facebook release

Step 1: Create A Page

Step 2: Add page info

Make sure that you put your business name and the correct category for your new page

1. Enter your page name
2. Choose the category (for example "Business")
3. Write a brief description of your business (What do you do? What are your specialties?)

NOTE: You can add images, contact info and other details after you create the Page. In fact, after clicking on "Create Page" these tabs will be added:

Step 3: Profile Picture

For your page's profile picture, make sure that you put your company logo.

Step 4: Cover Photo

The last step for basic fan page creation is to add your cover photo. Do not leave your cover photo blank. It's unprofessional, and it's ugly. Make your cover photo simple and clean. Feature your product if you can.

HOT TIP: You can add special promotion details in your cover photo, a lot of people usually look at the cover once they land on the page.

After inserting the two photos, your page is ready and you will be able to access the management panel:

Instagram

Instagram is a mobile-dominated platform for telling visual stories—98% of Instagram content comes from phones. While Instagram has over a billion users, 59% are under thirty years old. Many Etsy sellers report they get more sales via Instagram than Pinterest or Facebook. Understandable, since over 1,926,000 Instagram users follow Etsy's profile there. Instagram members have a high engagement rate. Over 70% of users have bought something found there using their mobile phone.

Set Up an Instagram Account

- Download the Instagram app and install on your phone. If you plan to use Instagram to promote your handmade items, set up your new account as a business account or convert your existing profile to a business one.

- Like with other social sites, a business account allows you to promote or advertise your posts. You also get access to "Insights" (analytics) about your posts, hashtags, visitors, and engagements.

- Choose the same username (or a close variant if taken) that you use on Etsy and all your social media profiles. Upload the same profile image you use on other social sites.

- Include a link to your Etsy or any other online shop in your profile.

Posting Images

- With the app open, take a photo with your phone, write a cute caption, and push "share." You have the option to add image-editing filters before you share your photos.

- The app automatically sizes your uploaded image to display on mobile devices. Horizontal (portrait) oriented images fit the screen well as most people naturally hold their phones horizontally.

- Sharing images comes with options. You can share to your other social media profiles. You can add hashtags. You can tag other people in the image. And you can add your location, so viewers will know where the image was taken.

- You can also upload images from your computer.

- In your post, you can add a brief caption. Caption text is found through search, so include relevant hashtags.

Videos

- Instagram lets you add and edit videos up to sixty seconds long. Videos can come directly from your phone or from content you have transferred to your phone from another source.

- Sellers can add a call to action at the end of a video. Just add a line of text in the last moments.

Instagram Stories

- Instagram stories, like FB stories, feature your photos and videos at the top of your follower's feeds. They remain there for twenty-four hours.

- Upload your story-behind-the-scenes of your handmade gig. Post stories about how you got started in your craft business, how you make your products, and what inspires you.

- Use the "poll" feature to ask your followers questions. Discover what they think about your stories.

Hashtags

- Hashtags are mashed-up phrases preceded by the # sign. Example: #handmade. The # sign turns the phrase into a clickable link. Hashtags help your posts get found in search.

- Hashtags can help you uncover other sellers with products like yours.

- Multi-worded hashtags help you attract buyers instead of just researchers. If you make and sell home items, broad topic hashtags like #decor won't be as useful to you as more specific hashtags like #handmadefurniture, or #woodtray.

- Use apps to find hashtags related to your niche like keywordtool.io, displaypurposes.com, skedsocial.com, hashtagify.me, or all-hashtag.com. AutoHash is a mobile app that analyzes your images and suggests hashtags.

- You can add up to thirty hashtags when you post or comment, but adding so many looks spammy. The fix is to add a comment and include hashtags in the comment.

- Studies show posts with multiple hashtags get twice the amount of interaction with viewers.

- Mix your choice of hashtags among your posts and comments.

- Use one of your hashtags for your Instagram name.

- Look at the posts on the most popular profiles in your niche. See hashtags you had not thought of?

- After your profile has received likes, comments, and followers over time, use the "Insights" feature in your business account to discover which hashtags brought the most traffic to your Etsy store or website.

- Find keywords by starting to type in the search bar at Instagram and note the auto-complete drop-down list of popular tags. Instagram's auto-complete comes from actual searches.

- Save all your hashtags in a text file or spreadsheet. Separate them by niches, products, people, or other categories. When you need hashtags, just go to your file and copy them.

- Use hashtags used by communities related to your product's niche.

Where to Place Hashtags

- As a sticker on your images and videos

- Your post's description
- Comments you leave
- Comments you get
- Your Instagram stories
- Your profile bio

Tips for Posting

- When someone likes or comments on your image posts, send them a thank you. It's a natural way to start a conversation.
- If your creative muse takes a vacation, post other people's content.
- Study the posts of the most popular Instagram profiles in your niche. Look for content that attracted the most comments. This is a way to get inspired by what you could post.
- Follow the followers of other sellers in your niche. If they appear to be frequent or recent posters, start liking their images. Many of them will follow you back.
- Follow Etsy sellers with complementary product lines to yours. Comment and like their content. Message them and see if they would like to cross-promote each other's lines.
- Post often. Uploading content twice a day has shown to increase followers. Use one of the social media scheduling tools described earlier.
- Instagram is highly social. Tagging others (adding @personsusername) can earn goodwill and increase your post comments.

Instagram Advertising

- Like with most social platforms, you can promote your Instagram posts through paid advertising. For business accounts, the "Insights" function provides clues about which of your posts make good candidates for promoting.
- Start with a small budget and test. Target your ad to reach followers of popular sellers in your niche.
- As with all paid promotions, include a call to action. Make it clear what you want viewers to do: visit your Etsy shop, make a purchase, sign up for your newsletter, or other action.
- Monitor your Etsy shop stats closely when you run an Instagram or other ad campaign. Your Etsy stats will tell you if you are getting traffic from Instagram or other social networks. If ads are working, increase your budget and try new audiences.
- If your ads do not result in profitable sales, stop the campaigns. Change your content, or your offer, or your audience.

Chapter 5: - Etsy

If you are frequently on the Internet, you might have heard of Etsy, even if you have never personally visited it. This online sales website has been around for about a decade, and it has helped many people to buy and sell unique products. Depending on your level of creativity, you may know that this is a marketplace for selling handmade goods. People appreciate handmade goods. Since every handmade piece is unique and different, finding these goods is a real adventure for some. Etsy is person to person selling website that focuses on selling handmade and vintage goods. The range of goods that are sold on this website is diverse and interesting. You can even buy craft supplies on this site! Depending on what you're looking for, Etsy has the edge on all the handmade items.

History of Etsy

A small company by the name of Io Space launched Etsy in 2005. The founders of the company chose its name because they could build a brand from the bottom up and not have it seem similar to other companies. Attention was given to helping new entrepreneurs use tools to enable them to establish a great business. During its growth, the company has learned to become a more globally centered company that sells goods all over the world. By offering a wide range of goods, it has become a go-to website for those who are looking for something unique.

Learn the Basics First

Etsy has been around for quite a while now. It's not as famous as Amazon and eBay because it does not care for all kinds of audience. In my opinion, what really sells on Etsy is **CREATIVITY.** If you spend 30 minutes on Etsy, you'll notice something different in their product pages that's not on Amazon and eBay. Instead of just products, I believe that most customers and even seller considered them as art.

Set-Up and Operation of the Website

When you first go onto the website, you will immediately see a search bar. Simply type in what you're looking for and let the site take you to shop suggestions. On the selling end of the spectrum, Etsy offers an area where you can look at articles on a wide range of topics that will influence your business. Everything from legal aspects to marketing is covered. So, if you want to get some professional insight on how to do something on the website, this is a great area to go!

Etsy is very user friendly. With the search engine built right into the website, you can easily find what you're looking for or similar items. The website is focused on giving the owners of the shop a chance to show their goods rather than being flashy and decorative. So, when you first see it, it seems simple. However, the selection that you will find on it is anything but simple!

How to Open Up a Shop

Like most internet sales sites, anyone who wishes to sell on Etsy can set up shop. You simply go in and fill out a profile and answer the questions that the company poses to you. Again, like the other sales websites, Etsy does charge fees for listing and selling your items. These fees are minimal and usually can be counteracted with the asking price of your items. When you first go to the website, you can go to the bottom where it gives you a link to open your new shop. Simply follow the link and put in the required information. Once you have all of your information entered, you can start listing your items for the public to buy!

Your page is basic as well. It gives a picture of the item along with a description and a price for the item. You must fill in the information and description.

Knowing What Sells

When you first go to the website, you will notice that the top trending items are there for you to look at right away. Take a look through these and see what people are really buying. If you notice that you do a similar handmade item, then you are probably good to sell on Etsy! Investigate the trending shops and see how the items are described and pictured. This might give you some good ideas on how to post your items later on.

Since Etsy is a great up and coming company for the crafty sellers, take some time to get to know the features of the site. In this book, I will cover how to market your goods on the site creatively, but by knowing what sells and what they do to sell it, you will find that you have an edge when creating your own shop.

Now that we have some basic information and background on Etsy let's take a look at how to sell and market your own personal Etsy shop!

How Do I Advertise My Goods?

Have you ever been looking for something unique for your home or wardrobe? If so, you probably have turned to the Internet to find it. The odds are that you probably have come across quite a few Etsy businesses that offer unique products. If you're a crafty person, then you probably have wondered how they have been able to get online and sell their items. Who knows, you might even have tried to set up your own Etsy store and just couldn't think of ways to get the business going!

Having a website like Etsy can make a crafter into an entrepreneur. By taking items that you make and selling them for a profit, you're not only doing what you enjoy doing, but you are also getting paid for it. Wouldn't it be nice if we could get paid for all the things that we enjoy doing? If you have thought about taking the leap and trying your own business or already have one that is suffering, I hope that some of the tips and suggestions that I give in this book will make you excited to get going!

Marketing is a very important element in a successful business. People will not know that your business even exists unless you advertise it. It might be difficult, to begin with, but you must get the word out on your business in order to build a reputation and actually sell what you're offering. The same thing is true when you sell your handcrafted and vintage items on Etsy. Even though you will initially be selling to people who visit the website, you have to have good marketing abilities in order for your shop to gain attention and shoppers.

Gaining this attention can be done through many avenues. From visual elements such as pictures to descriptive elements such as keywords and phrases, finding a way to get yourself out there is incredibly important if you expect to get your business off the ground and for it to succeed. How do you think you can market your creations?

Creative Ways to List Your Goods

Now that you have established what you want to sell and who you want to sell it to, the next step is to figure out how to catch the attention of those shopping online. Etsy shops not only show up on Etsy itself, but they will pop up in search engines when someone puts in the right keywords. Think about how you want others to perceive your Etsy shop as and then take a look at some of the suggestions for listing your goods in order to get the maximum amount of traffic.

Have Great, Eye-catching Pictures

Since your buyer cannot pick up and hold the item in his or her hands before buying it, it is extremely important to have detailed and clear pictures of your products. People want to know what they are getting before they buy an item. Try to give them as much detail as you possibly can. It can make a difference when a shopper is indecisive on whether or not to buy the item.

The next element in your pictures should be eye-catching details. If you can lure someone in by your picture, the odds are that you will have a sale. Try making your backgrounds stand out with colors or designs. Don't overpower your item, but make it pop by using background details. You might also want to use props or models.

Pose Your Products to Look Their Best

When taking the picture, you want to make the item look the best that it can look. Since you will more than likely only have one picture of it, you want it to look good. Try using background elements and props to bring out the details for your item. Show the best side of it. If it has unique detail, make sure that it can be seen within the thumbnail.

Use Colorfully Descriptive Words

When I talk about colorfully descriptive words, I mean use words that will kick your product while still thoroughly describing it. People love it when you add flair to your description. Don't get incredibly wordy, but make sure you're selling your item with a unique and thorough description.

Make Your Background Unique

Plain backgrounds have been done. Sometimes your products will need a simple background. However, you might want to switch it up and make it stand out a little more by have a different type of background than what is normally seen. Again, you don't want the background to take away from what you're selling. You just want to make sure that it compliments your product.

Show Other Customer Reviews on Your Page

When setting up your shop, you will have a section on your personal page that will show customer ratings and reviews. People typically look at the seller reviews before buying from you. Your past customers will leave reviews based on their experiences. Sometimes, the reviews are unfair to you, but others know when the reviewer is out of line. Give your customers what they want, and you will be well on your way to having others who will want to buy from you.

Put Your Shop into Several Categories

If your products have several different functions, put them into different categories. The more exposure you have in different categories, the better the chances are of you being able to sell your item quickly effectively. However, don't throw your shop into a category where it obviously does not belong. This is frustrating to the users of the sight. Think about creative ways to list your items. This can be done through pictures and written descriptions. Use your resources to make your products stand out without making them obnoxious. Make your shop unique and someplace that you would visit if you were a buyer. The best thing you can do is to put yourself into the shoes of the public looking to buy from your shop.

Chapter 5: - Business Ideas You Can Make with Your Cricut

It will be helpful if you can be making a part-time income from what you like doing. You can be having fun with your design and yet be making money from it. There are many people already making money from their designs. You can turn this into a great business that will give you so much money within a month and will take care of all your family expenses. So, if you have Cricut at home and you are not maximizing the use, and you have time, then this section should be of great help to you.

50+ Business Ideas You Can Make with Your Cricut and Sell

- Wall art canvas
- Leather bracelet
- Frosty wreath
- Iron-on T-shirt
- Customized tools
- Customized cutting board
- Customized kitchen towels
- Customized lanyards
- Doormats
- Rustic signs
- Coffee mugs
- Holiday bucket
- Customized plates
- Pillows case
- Bedsheets
- Paper succulent
- Planner stickers
- Sports cuff
- Key chains
- Wooden signs

- Monogrammed ornament
- Blankets
- Laptop cases
- Monogrammed pillows
- Car stickers
- Home decals
- Christmas greeting cards
- Interior designs
- Pet tags
- Cake tops
- Scrapbook pages
- Gift boxes
- Addressed envelopes
- Felt coasters
- Customized tote bags
- Flower bouquets
- Monogrammed water bottle
- Model decals
- Paper pennants
- Metallic tags
- Paper peonies
- Santa sacks
- Christmas advent calendar
- Paper heart box
- Paper tulips
- Magnolia blossom
- Gift card holder
- Paper flower lanterns
- Paper purse
- Paper poppers

- Halloween buddies
- Paper fiery house and more

How to Turn Your Designs into Money

So many people have asked the question, "How do I make money using my Cricut?" or "Should I buy a Cricut, is the market too full? Can I still make money? How do I start?" Sometimes it is hard to give a satisfactory answer to all these questions because some of the people using Cricut do not want to tell you how to make money from this craft. They do not want to share their secrets. But this book is here to give you all the inside information you need to know if you want to make money with Cricut.

When a lot of people are starting out, and they are venturing into a craft. Maybe they have a Cricut or another vinyl cutting machine, or perhaps they do not have one, and they want to get one. They have all these questions about how to get started, and it is overwhelming at first. It can be confusing and complicated and then sometimes you will reach out to those that have one, and they do not want to share their secrets, they are afraid that you might become their competitor. But the truth is that everyone can succeed if you will build each other up there is room for us all to succeed. So, let us start with the first question.

Let us now see how we can make money from all the knowledge we have gotten. Someone rightly says, if you cannot make money from the knowledge you have gotten or if you have the knowledge and it is not useful to you in any way, then the knowledge is useless to you and society. In order not for this knowledge to be useless to you, I will show you how to make money from it. This is not to say if you are not making money from your design, the knowledge is useless if you use it only for your family and friends. If you use this only for your family and friends, the knowledge is still useful.

Several of us are on Facebook, we go to marketplaces, you may have visited Etsy, and you've seen so many shops selling signs, selling shirts, selling one thing or the other, you're like, can I still make money with craft? The simple answer to the question, Yes, you can, and it is not that hard. With everyone specializing in the area he or she knows how to do better, the market can never be saturated. Take, for instance, someone might major only in the making of T-shirts, while another on making cups, other on woodwork design, and many more. The truth is that you will not find many people that are good in one particular area. So, the market can never get filled.

Now you are ready, and you have gotten your Cricut, and you are wondering, "Where do I start?" The easiest place to start is literally by making things for your friends and family. There are so many things that you can make for your friends that they will appreciate and pay you for. Examples of some of them are stickers, design their name on their T-shirts, writing the motivational word on their T-shirts. You can brainstorm on some things you think your friends would like and start designing it for them. You can also make a design for your children and your spouse. When you are done with those designs, paste them on Facebook; you might get people that would want you to do the same design for them. This is the easiest way to start without investing so much money, and no one is buying it from you.

Selling the Craft You Have Made with Cricut

There are a lot of things we have pointed out already that you can start doing and selling to your friends and neighbors. You don't have to convince your friends to buy many of those things because I know they will like it if you make personal designs for them. So, what you have to do is to find out what your friends like and make such a design for them. For example, if you have a friend that likes football and has a team, you can design the logo of the team as a sticker for such a friend and write something good about the team for him or her too. You might also have a friend that sees clothes and likes what he or she does. You can make a lovely design with his business name for him or her. Also, you can make a sticker of his logo for him or her to put on every dress he makes.

Another way you can make money with your design is to look for people that would want you to iron-on their clothes for them. There are a lot of people out there looking for someone that would design their clothes for them. Look for the people that sell in boutiques and sell your designs to them. This is how this is done. You can offer to do a free design for someone that sells plenty of plane T-shirts for him or her to see what you do. If he or she likes what you have done for him, you can then charge the person how much you would like to receive for designing each piece of clothing for such a person. So, look for local sellers around you that you think might need your design.

Another very easy way you can make money with this is through selling to groups. You can walk up to a group of people that wear a uniform and have a group name and ask to do a design for their group. This is easy to get because each person in the group would like to be identified as a member of the group and would like to pay you for your work. Examples of some of these groups are clubs, choirs, associations of friends, etc. The best way to go about this is to offer to do a free design for the leader of the group first. The idea behind this is that, if you can convince the leader of the group with your design, you can easily sell your work to every member of the group. Secondly, the group members will be seeing the design of the leader and would be asking where he did the design. Some will even suggest to him that why 'don't the group do the design for everyone. Then he will be forced to ask you to do the design for every member of the team. Get the leader interested, and you will penetrate the group easily.

Another great way you can sell your design is online. You can create a website and sell whatever you design through the website, or you can sell through an e-commerce site like Amazon. Almost everyone is online these days, so, you won't find it challenging to sell your designs if they are excellent and attractive.

How to Save Money While Using Your Cricut Explore Machine for Business

For beginners, this is the part that gives them the most headaches, especially when your pocket is not friendly to accommodate your supplies for project and craft. So, I want to help you suggest ways you can make the most use of your Cricut Explore machine for business and get your supplies at the cheapest prices. You do not have to be fleeced of your hard-earned money any longer.

The first thing is to read the instructions on how to use your Cricut Explore machine properly. It is not for fun that manufacturers place instruction guides for their products. It is meant to help you get the most out of your machine. Follow the instructions carefully and you will save yourself some extra cash that would have been used for repairs and new purchases outrightly.

You will replace your cutting mat, depending on the usage, from time to time. Try to make use of the 12" x 24" mat because the long mats save you a lot of money. You can turn to the other side when the adhesive strength of the first side begins to diminish. Instead of buying another one, just flip it over and continue with your next project.

The blades can drain your pocket when you do not make the most use of it. I do not need to tell you about the importance of a sharp blade when cutting. If you must save money, take proper care of your blades, organize them, and never misuse the blade to cut inappropriate materials. Anything contrary to that means you will be replacing your blade often which is money draining from your pocket.

For your vinyl products, I suggest you use Expressions Vinyl which is cheaper than the other vinyl materials and even gives the same feel to your project.

Best Piece of Vinyl to Use for Your Projects: Business and Personal

There are different vinyl manufacturers churning out different products for craft, different colors, textures, and options. Be careful what piece of vinyl material you use for your project so that you do not ruin your project. Know the different types if you must work with the vinyl material or use the recommended one for your project.

Adhesive Vinyl

This is the most common vinyl material on the market. You will come across it regularly sometimes in your starter kit with your machine. It comes attached to a carrier sheet coated with silicone and you can easily pull the vinyl off. Use transfer tape to transfer it to its final place on your project, that is, after it has been cut and weeded.

There are two types of adhesive vinyl materials: removable and permanent. Removable adhesive vinyl is the regular Cricut vinyl material mostly used for indoors, temporal outdoor events, or placed on any surface that will not touch regularly or in need of a wash (wall decal). If I will suggest, I will go for Oracal 631. On the other hand, permanent adhesive vinyl is waterproof and lasts longer than temporal adhesive vinyl. They are usually rated to last six years or more. Its application is in DIY projects that need washing regularly like tumblers, shot glasses, exterior walls, car decals, and more.

Heat Transfer Vinyl

This is the type used for fabrics. It is designed to bond to the fabric when heat and pressure are applied to it. There are a number of features that can help you determine the best quality of heat transfer vinyl material: color, finish, ease of weeding, price, durability, and cut reliability. Unlike adhesive vinyl, heat transfer vinyl does not require transfer tape. I will suggest Siser EasyWeed Heat Transfer Vinyl as the best of the rest.

Cling Vinyl

This is a type of vinyl material with no adhesive attached to it but uses static electricity to attach to smooth surfaces like windowpanes and removable decorations on mirrors. It can be removed and reused again on dry and clean surfaces. I will suggest Grafix Cling Vinyl Film to you.

Chapter 6:- Cricut Project with Vinyl

Giant Vinyl Stencils

Vinyl stencils are a good thing to create, too, but they can be hard. Big vinyl stencils make for an excellent Cricut project, and you can use them in various places, including bedrooms for kids.

You only need the explore Air 2, the vinyl that works for it, a pallet, sander, and of course, paint and brushes. The first step is preparing the pallet for painting, or whatever surface you plan on using this for.

From here, you create the mermaid tail (or any other large image) in Design Space. You will now learn immediately that big pieces are hard to cut and impossible to do all at once in Design Space.

What you do is the section of each design accordingly and remove any middle pieces. Next, you can add square shapes to the image, slicing it into pieces so that it can be cut on a cutting mat that fits.

At this point, you cut out the design by pressing *'Make It,'* choosing your material and working in sections.

From here, you put it on the surface that you are using, piecing this together with each line. You should have one image after piecing it all together. Then, draw out the line on vinyl and then paint the initial design. For the second set of stencils, you can simply trace the first one and then paint the inside of them. At this point, you should have the design finished. When done, remove it very carefully.

And there you have it! Bigger stencils can be a bit of a project since it involves trying to use multiple designs all at once; but with the right care and the right designs, you will be able to create whatever it is you need to in Design Space, so you can get the results you are looking for.

Cricut Quilts

Quilts are a bit hard to do for many people, but did you know that you can use Cricut to make it easier? Here, you will learn an awesome project that will help you do this. To begin, you start with the Cricut Design Space. Here, you can add different designs that work for your project. For example, if you are making a baby blanket or quilt with animals on it, you can add tiny fonts with the animals' names or different pictures of them. From here, you want to make sure you choose the option to reverse the design. That way, you will have it printed correctly. At this point, make your quilt. Do various designs and sew the quilt as you want to.

From here, you should cut it on the iron-on heat transfer vinyl. You can choose that, and then press *'Cut.'* The image will then cut into the piece.

At this point, it will cut itself out, and you can proceed to transfer this with some parchment paper. Use an EasyPress for the best results and push it down. There you go, an easy addition that will enhance the way your blankets look.

Cricut Unicorn Backpack

If you are making a present for a child, why not give them some cool unicorns? Here is a lovely unicorn backpack you can try to make. To make this, you need ¾ yards of a woven fabric, which is strong since it will stabilize the backpack. You will also need half a yard of quilting cotton for the lining. The coordinating fabric should be around about an eighth of a yard. You will need a yard of fusible interfacing, some strap adjuster rings, a zipper that is about 14 inches and does not separate, and some stuffing for the horn.

1. To start, you will want to cut the main fabric; you should use straps, the loops, a handle, some gussets for a zipper, and the bottom and side gussets.

2. The lining should be done too, and you should make sure you have the interfacing. You can use fusible flex foam to help make it a little bit bulkier.

3. From here, cut everything and then apply the interfacing to the backside. The flex-foam should be adjusted to achieve the bulkiness you are looking for. You can trim this, too. The interfacing should be on the backside, then add the flex foam to the main fabric. The adhesive side of this will be on the right-hand side of the interfacing.

4. Fold the strap pieces in half and push one down on each backside. Halve it, and then press it again; stitch these closer to every edge, and also along the short-pressed edge, as well.

5. From here, do the same thing with the other side, add the ring for adjustment, and stitch the bottom of these to the back piece's main part.

6. Then add them both to the bottom.

7. At this point, you have the earpieces that should have the backside facing out. Stitch, then flip out and add the pieces.

8. Add these inner pieces to the outer ear, and then stitch these together.

9. At this point, you make the unicorn face in the Design Space. You will immediately notice that everything will be black when you use this program, but you can change this by adjusting the desired layers to each color. You can also just use a template that fits, but you should always mirror this before cutting it.

10. Choose vinyl, and then insert the material onto the cutting mat. From there, cut it and remove the iron-on slowly.

You will need to do this in pieces, which is fine because it allows you to use different colors. Remember to insert the right color for each cut. At this point, add the zipper, and there you go!

Custom Back to School Supplies

This tutorial will show you how to use your iPad to create and convert designs for your Cricut machine to cut!

Materials needed:

- Vinyl
- Standard Grip Mat
- White Paper
- Markers (including black)
- Pencil Case
- 3 Ring Binder
- iPad Pro (optional)
- Apple Pencil
- Cricut Design Space App
- Drawing app (e.g., ProCreate)
- ProCreate Brushes

Instructions:

1. The first thing to do is convert your kid's drawing into an SVG file that the Cricut Design Space recognizes. This will be done by tracing it in the ProCreate app.

2. Get your child's design – it should not be too complex to minimize weeding.

3. Open the Procreate app on your iPad.

4. Create a new canvas on ProCreate. Click on the *'Wrench'* icon and select *'Image.'*

5. Next, click *'Take a Photo.'* Take a picture of the design. When you are satisfied with the image, click *'Use It.'*

6. On the Layer Panel (the two squares icon), add a new layer by clicking the *'plus'* sign.

7. In the layers panel, select the layer containing the picture and click the *'N.'* Also, reduce the layer's opacity so that you can easily see your draw lines.

8. From your imported brushes, select the *'Marker'* brush. To avoid the need to import a brush, choose the inking brush. You can resize the brush in the brush settings under the *'General'* option.

9. On the new layer, trace over the drawing.

    a. Click on the *'Wrench'* icon, click *'Share,'* then *'PNG.'*

    b. Next, *'Save'* the image to your device.

c. Alternatively, use your black marker, trace the drawing on a blank piece of paper, and then take a picture of it using your iPad or phone.

d. The next stage is to cut the design out in Cricut Design Space

e. Open up the Cricut Design Space app on your iPad.

f. Create a 'New Project.'

g. Select *'Upload'* (located at the screen's bottom). Select *'Select from Camera Roll'* and select the PNG image you created in ProCreate or the image you traced out.

h. Follow the next steps.

i. Save the design as a cut file and insert it into the canvas. Here, you can resize the design or add other designs.

j. Next, click *'Make It'* to send it to your Cricut.

k. Choose *'Vinyl'* as the material.

l. Place the vinyl on the mat and use the Cricut to cut it.

10. Now, you can place the vinyl cutouts on the back to make your child stand out!

Gift Tags

Materials needed:

- Cricut machine
- Variety of cardstock and a vinyl
- A ready-made Design Space project, for tags that say 'I love you.'
- Glitter pen of your choice
- Account for Design Space

Instructions:

1. Follow the prompts to draw, and then cut each layer as the project needs.

2. Glue two paper layers together. *'Align'* the heart-shaped hole at the top of the tag.

3. Add your vinyl, and then burnish it to make sure it will adhere properly and thoroughly.

4. Add ribbon or twine to the hole for the tag.

Paper Pinwheels

Materials needed:

- Cricut Maker or Cricut Explore
- Standard Grip mat
- Patterned cardstock in desired colors

- Embellishments
- Paper straws
- Hot glue

Instructions:

1. Log into the *'Design Space'* application and click on the *'New Project'* button on the screen's top right corner to view a blank canvas.

2. Let us use an already existing project from the Cricut library and customize it. So, click on the *'Projects'* icon and type in *'Paper Pinwheel'* in the search bar.

3. Click on *'Customize'* to edit the project to your preference further, or simply click on the *'Make It'* button and load the cardstock to your Cricut machine, and follow the instructions on the screen to cut your project.

4. Using hot glue, adhere the pinwheels together to the paper straws and the embellishments, as shown in the picture above.

Rugrats T-Shirt

The materials that you will need for this project are:

- The Explore Air, or the Maker
- An iron
- A small piece of fabric or linen cloth
- T-shirts
- A Rugrats file (SVG file)
- Supplies from the Cricut company which are:
- Access membership
- The standard cutting mat
- Weeder
- Scissors
- An iron-on lite (vinyl)
- An iron-on glitter

The instructions that you need to make this design are listed here:

1. Open your design in the Design Space.

2. Choose a color scheme you want to use.

3. Attach your images to cut.

4. Place your vinyl onto the cutting mat, and be sure that the shiny side is down.

5. Load your mat into the machine.

6. Click the *'Go'* button to start the cutting process. Make sure that your image is mirrored. You will have to check the box that says *'Mirror Image.'*

7. Weed your cut design.

8. Repeat the process with the different pieces of your images using different vinyl pieces to add color.

9. Place the image on the shirt how you want it to look.

Iron. Be careful.

Focus on the corners of your design.

It should peel easily.

These shirts are a really great way for you to get creative and have fun. Does your child like unicorns or superheroes? You can do this too! With the Cricut machine, you are only limited by your own creativity. There are thousands of designs that you can use for T-shirts: from movies, cartoons, anime, your favorite childhood characters, and anything else you can imagine, including favorite animals and quotes.

Chapter 7: - Other Cricut Project

Night Sky Pillow

Supplies Needed:

- Black, dark blue, or dark purple fabric
- Heat transfer vinyl in gold or silver
- Cutting mat
- Polyester batting
- Weeding tool or pick
- Cricut EasyPress

Instructions:

1. Decide the shape you want for your pillow, and cut two matching shapes out of the fabric.
2. Open Cricut Design Space and create a *'New Project.'*
3. Select the *'Image'* button in the lower left-hand corner and search *'Stars.'*
4. Select the stars of your choice and click *'Insert.'*
5. Place the iron-on material on the mat.
6. Send the design to the Cricut.
7. Use the weeding tool, or pick to remove excess material.
8. Remove the material from the mat.
9. Place the iron-on material on the fabric.
10. Use the EasyPress to adhere it to the iron-on material.
11. Sew the two fabric pieces together, leaving allowance for a seam and a small space open.
12. Fill the pillow with polyester batting through the small open space.
13. Sew the pillow shut.
14. Cuddle up to your starry pillow!

Clutch Purse

Supplies Needed:

- Two fabrics, one for the exterior and one for the interior
- Fusible fleece
- Fabric cutting mat

- D-ring

- Sew-on snap

- Lace

- Zipper

- Sewing machine

- Fabric scissors

- Keychain or charm of your choice

Instructions:

1. Open Cricut Design Space and create a *'New Project.'*

2. Select the *'Image'* button in the lower left-hand corner and search for *'Essential Wallet.'*

3. Select the basic wallet template, and click *'Insert.'*

4. Place the fabric on the mat.

5. Send the design to the Cricut.

6. Remove the fabric from the mat.

7. Attach the fusible fleecing to the wrong side of the exterior fabric.

8. Attach lace to the edges of the exterior fabric.

9. Assemble the D-ring strap.

10. Place the D-ring onto the strap and sew it into place.

11. Fold the pocket pieces wrong side out over the top of the zipper, and sew it into place.

12. Fold the pocket's wrong side in and sew the sides.

13. Sew the snap onto the pocket.

14. Lay the pocket on the right side of the main fabric lining so that the corners of the pocket's bottom are behind the curved edges of the lining fabric. Sew the lining piece to the zipper tape.

15. Fold the lining behind the pocket and iron in place.

16. Sew on the other side of the snap.

17. Trim the zipper so that it is not overhanging the edge.

18. Sew the two pocket layers to the exterior fabric across the bottom.

19. Sew around all of the layers.

20. Trim the edges with fabric scissors.

21. Turn the clutch almost completely inside out and sew the opening to close it.

22. Turn the clutch all the way inside out and press the corners into place.

23. Attach your charm or keychain to the zipper.

24. Carry your new clutch wherever you need it!

Personalized Water Bottle

Supplies Needed:

- A water bottle with a smooth surface (these are very easy to find in superstores)
- Transfer tape
- A brayer or a scraper
- Outdoor vinyl

Instructions:

1. Your first step is to open the design app. Let us say for this example that we are going to be making the name *'Adam.'*

2. Choose a font that you like, and then use the eyeball icon in the layers panel.

3. Create a second text box, and you can make the initial letter bigger.

4. You will need to attach the two layers together so that the *'Name'* and the *'Initial'* are cut out together.

5. Resize and make it fit your water bottle.

6. To make sure that this will adhere to your bottle, you will need to use transfer tape. The brayer can help here because you can help press the transfer tape down.

7. Start in the center of the letter and work out when adhering to the bottle. Be sure to smooth all bubbles.

8. Peel off the tape very carefully, and when you are finished.

Fabric Coaster

Supplies Needed:

- The Maker
- Rotary cut and mat, or a pair of scissors
- A sewing machine
- An iron
- Cotton fabric and a coordinating thread
- Fusible fleece

Instructions:

1. Cut your fabric to the inches you need to fit on your cutting mat.

2. Open Design Space and hit the button that says *'New Project.'*

3. Click on *'Shapes'* and then insert a heart shape. You will do this from the pop-up window.

4. Resize your heart to 5.5 inches. Click *'Make It.'*

5. Change the project copies to four (left corner at the top). Then, click *'Apply.'*

6. Click *'Continue'* (bottom right).

7. Set your material to medium fabrics like cotton.

8. Load your mat with the fabric attached; Cut.

9. Repeat all steps, but this time, you will place the fusible fleece on the cutting mat.

10. Change the heart shape to 5.7."

11. When you select the material, click *'View More'* and then type in *'Fusible Fleece.'*

12. Cut out two fleece hearts.

13. Attach a fleece heart to the back of a fabric heart. You will use a hot iron to do this (be careful not to burn yourself).

14. Repeat with the second heart.

15. With the right sides together, sew two heart shapes together. Make sure the fleece is attached. Leave a gap in the stitches for turning.

16. Clip the curves.

17. Turn the heart's right side out, then press with the iron.

18. Fold in the edges of the opening and then press once more.

19. Stitch around the heart a quarter inch from the edge.

Glitter Tumbler

Supplies Needed:

- Painters tape
- Mod podge and paintbrush
- Epoxy
- Glitter
- Stainless steel tumbler
- Spray paint
- Vinyl

- Sandpaper Wet/dry
- Gloves
- Plastic cup
- Measuring cup
- Rubbing alcohol

Instructions:

1. Tape off the top and bottom of the tumbler.
2. Make sure to seal them well enough that paint will not get on either.
3. Spray paint twelve inches away from your tumbler in an area that is well ventilated.
4. Make sure that the items you used are approved and will not make you sick.
5. Once your tumbler is dry from the paint you have used, you can add the glitter.
6. This will make a mess, so have something under it to catch the glitter.
7. Put the mod podge in a small container.
8. Use a flat paintbrush to put it on.
9. Take the lid off and rotate the cup, adding glitter.
10. Make sure it is completely covered.
11. Make sure that an excess glitter will come off before removing the tape and letting it dry.
12. When dry, take a clean flat brush and stroke down the glitter to get any additional pieces not glued down.
13. Add a piece of tape above the glitter line.
14. Do the same to the bottom.
15. Get a plastic cup and gloves.
16. Use the epoxy and measure equal parts of solution A and B into measuring cups. If it is a small mug, you only need about 5 ml each. Larger ones need 0 ml.
17. Pour them both in a cup and scrape down the sides using a wooden stick.
18. Stir for three minutes and pop all bubbles.
19. Your gloves should be on but if not, put them on now.
20. Add the glitter to the epoxy and stir.
21. Add the mixture to the tumbler and turn it often while you are doing this. Having a roller or something to turn it on will help make sure it is in the air, so nothing is touching it.
22. When the drugs are not coming as fast, you can slow the turning down, but while it is, the turning is constant.

449

23. Take the tape off after forty-five minutes.

24. Spin the tumbler for five hours, and it should be dry. If not, leave it on a foam roller overnight.

25. Sand the tumbler gently with wet sandpaper.

26. When it is all smooth from sanding, clean it with rubbing alcohol

27. Then open the Cricut design space and cut out your glitter vinyl.

28. Weed the design.

29. Add strong grip transfer tape.

30. Transfer the decal to the tumbler.

This is a very hard project that takes a lot of time, and you need to make sure that children are nowhere near these products, as it will be fatal to them if they swallow them. Another thing to remember is spinning and making sure it is dry. By following these instructions, you should have a great glitter tumbler that you can take anywhere and rock a stylish look. This is a great idea for business owners as well because decorated tumblers are a hot commodity right now, and everyone loves them.

Personalized Mermaid Bottle

Supplies Needed:

- You will need a water bottle with a smooth surface (these are very easy to find in dollar stores, superstores, specialty stores, or really any store you would like to go to)

- Transfer tape

- A brayer or a scraper

- Outdoor vinyl

Instructions:

1. Your first step is to open the design app. Let us say, for this example, we are going to be making a mermaid.

2. Choose a font that you like, and then use the eyeball icon in the layers panel. If you do not want to make it yourself, simply go into the design space and choose one of their ready to do projects.

3. Create a second text box, and you can make the picture bigger.

4. Now you will need to attach the two layers together to cut together the picture and the initials.

5. Resize and make it fit your water bottle.

6. To make sure that this will adhere to your bottle, you will need to use transfer tape. The brayer can help here because you can help press the transfer tape down.

7. Start in the center of the letter and work out when adhering to the bottle. Be sure to smooth all bubbles.

8. Peel off the tape very carefully, and when you are finished

9. To make the shark, follow the same instructions.

By utilizing the tips in this book, you will be able to do some great projects and really get used to your machine and its inner workings, as well as unleash your own creativity and learn. The Cricut machines have made crafting so much easier and a lot more fun. The fact that Cricut also works with companies for you to be able to use their designs if you want to utilize them makes this perfect for fans of pop culture.

Enjoy taking your crafting skills to the next level and learning great new projects with the Cricut machines!

Leather Cuff Bracelet

Add a little charm to your wrist this year with a custom leather cuff bracelet or make a few to give out as presents for birthdays and other special occasions. They are stylish and comfortable, a winning combination!

Supplies Needed:

- Hot glue gun
- Faux leather in pebbled texture and rich brown color
- Measuring tape
- Scissors

Instructions

1. Measure around your wrist and write down the measurement.

2. In Design Space, create a new workspace and create a rectangle about 1 ½ inches wide and the length of your wrist plus two inches long. For example, if your wrist is seven inches around, you would add two inches to that measurement, and design your rectangle nine inches long.

3. Add a shape, such as a triangle, to your rectangle shape in the center. Create three shapes if you want to create the example above. Attach all three together and then align them in the center horizontally and vertically by clicking on "Attach" and then "Align."

4. Create two smaller rectangles about two inches by ¼ inch. When all the pieces are created, send the file to cut. Play your material on your mat and follow the prompts.

5. Remove your pieces from the mat, including removing the inside little triangles, and use a dab of glue to turn the two small rectangles into loops that go around the larger rectangle. Glue the loops to the large bracelet rectangle towards the end of one side. Trim the other side at an angle. This helps the end slide in and out easier.

Leather Earrings

Kind of like the leather feather necklace, this project uses a metallic accent over the leather to add a little drama to the jewelry, but this time instead of paint, the project calls for iron-on adhesive! This is a great project to try your hand at the iron-on with the faux leather and then you will know which process you prefer to get a similar look.

Supplies Needed:

- Iron-on vinyl in rose gold
- Faux leather in cream pebbled texture
- Earring kit and materials
- Sharp needle
- Adhesive to attach your earrings front and back pieces, such as Fabric Fusion.

Instructions

1. In Design Space, begin laying out your pieces. Create four exact teardrops—two pieces will be glued together back-to-back so the felt side does not show.

2. Decide how you want the vinyl to be added to your project and create those images now. You can use the "Slice and Weld" option to help you get good angles and precise pieces.

3. When your project is laid out, send the files to cut. Load your leather material with the texture side facing down and the felt side facing up. Follow the prompts on when to add your vinyl.

4. Remove all your pieces. Glue the front and back of the earrings together. Position your vinyl over your earring pieces and place a soft, clean cloth over the top. Lay your iron over the top and press until the vinyl adheres to the leather. Do not set your iron to the "cotton" setting, but maybe just a few notches lower. Press for about 30 seconds. Remove the backing after the project cools a bit.

5. Use your needle to puncture holes in the top of the earring pieces and then insert the earring hardware through the holes to make your earrings.

Conclusion

If you are a craft blogger, then this machine was built with people like you in mind. Purchasing the Cricut depends entirely on your needs and how often you make crafts. If you love to craft, do personalized projects, you do plenty of scrapbooking—then this machine will save time and money for you in the long run.

How often you use the Cricut will also determine whether this machine is worth the price. Would you use it once every three months? Would you only use it when Christmas is around the corner and you want to make personalized gifts? Would you use it every week? Do you want to make labels and stickers for your business? Do you want to have a machine that helps you create signage for your events or catering business?

All of the answers to these questions will determine if the Cricut is indeed worth its money. One of the ways to use the machine as many times as possible is to consider turning your crafting hobby into a side income.

Focusing on online selling requires a higher technical knowledge base, yet, as I can confirm, you don't need to be a programmer to make it work. You can generate income with vinyl online by offering top quality personalized jobs, ending up being a details Centre or supplying bulk offerings. Again, it's not advisable to try to do all it.

Your time is ideal invested working in among the three alternatives to begin. So, if you decide to give a custom job, don't attempt to come to be an info hub simultaneously. After developing your initial footing and obtaining profitable sales, you can intend on how to use that cash for turning into the other classifications.

Personalized Job-- This is just how I obtained my beginning. I truly believe this is a fantastic means to kick off your Silhouette or Cricut vinyl business for the best individual.

Progressively, individuals are resorting to a Google search to find a custom-made job. With existing markets or your website, you can end up being the one they rely on.

Examples:

Existing web sites that permit you to offer custom-made design solutions.

- Etsy
- Amazon Personalized
- Amazon Handmade is the most widely known. Various other options consist of
- Artfire
- DaWanda
- Gold Mine

- Depop, and

- Tictail.

One more option is to release your very own website. A fantastic instance of this can be seen with A Wonderful Impression. They released an inspirational wall decal website, along with a custom-made layout solution. You can get any kind of sticker; in any type of dimension you desire from them.

If you sell on an existing system, the startup costs are very reduced. The minute you launch, you're competing in the worldwide marketplace. You have access to countless prospective clients.

Additionally, distinct designs will certainly permit you to bill a premium price. However, on the internet, custom costs tend to be lower than the very same work done locally. It's a chance to polish up and increase your design capability as well.